环球卓越
www.geedu.com

谭松柏 /
李兰荣 /

MW01706847

4周攻克 雅思阅读周计划

英语周计划系列丛书
ENGLISH WEEKLY PLAN SERIES

机械工业出版社
CHINA MACHINE PRESS

“英语周计划系列丛书”是针对我国读者的英语学习特点开发的、以“周”为谋篇布局单位、以“日”为具体实施单元的极具特色的英语辅导用书，具有思维创新、规划科学、目标明确、讲练结合、直击实战等特点。《4 周攻克雅思阅读周计划》是本系列针对 IELTS 的一个分册。

编者从雅思阅读部分的题型特点和设题规律出发，针对考生复习中经常遇到的问题，为考生提供了一个完整的 IELTS 阅读 4 周复习方案，每周安排 7 天（星期一至星期日），合计 28 天。第一周为您提供雅思阅读考试最核心的策略；第二周和第三周针对各种题型进行专项训练；第四周设置了 7 套模拟试题，检验复习成果。4 周的安排，目标明确，科学合理，帮助考生理清复习思路，最终成功通过考试。

图书在版编目（CIP）数据

4 周攻克雅思阅读周计划/李兰荣主编. —北京：机械工业出版社，2011.1（2011.10 重印）
（英语周计划系列丛书/谭松柏主编）
ISBN 978-7-111-33005-9

Ⅰ. ①4… Ⅱ. ①李… Ⅲ. ①英语—阅读教学—高等教育—自学参考资料
Ⅳ. ①H319.4

中国版本图书馆 CIP 数据核字（2010）第 264477 号

机械工业出版社（北京市百万庄大街 22 号 邮政编码 100037）
责任编辑：孙铁军
责任印制：杨 曦

保定市中画美凯印刷有限公司印刷

2011 年 10 月第 1 版第 2 次印刷
184mm×260mm · 18 印张 · 420 千字
6 001－10 000 册
标准书号：ISBN 978-7-111-33005-9
定价：39.80 元

凡购本书，如有缺页、倒页、脱页，由本社发行部调换

电话服务
社服务中心：(010)88361066
销 售 一 部：(010)68326294
销 售 二 部：(010)88379649
读者购书热线：(010)88379203

网络服务
门户网：http://www.cmpbook.com
教材网：http://www.cmpedu.com

丛书序

现如今的中国人，上学不再满足于清华北大，工作也不仅放眼于国企。而是走向一个更为宽广的世界——出国深造和就业。这是中国政治、经济、文化发展的结果，是好事，利国利民，利己利人。然而并非每个有出国梦想的人都能如愿以偿，很多人都被雅思这个拦路虎拦在了国门以内。

由于雅思考核学生听说读写的综合运用能力，这与中国传统的英语教学完全不接轨。尽管近年来中国的外语教学有了很大的改进和发展，但苦于没有语言环境，教学和学习效果依然不理想。加之教育改革周期长，效果缓慢，很多中国考生依然是传统应试教育的产物或二代产物。仔细想来，题做了不少，词汇记了无数，语法也学了很多，但一旦落实到应用，尤其是听说和写作，就最多只能是中式英语，这不符合雅思的考核标准。因此，很多中国考生都万事俱备，只欠雅思，但这雅思一分难求，所以，很多考生只能望洋兴叹。虽心有不甘，但也只能脚踏实地走进英语课堂，走遍各个培训学校，听遍所有名师课堂，虽感觉老师们说的很有道理，感觉找到了救命稻草，但是，回到家中，冷静下来，却发现自己依然不会说英语，也听不懂，单词记不住，好不容易记住的那些，可能又忘了。

殊不知，语言学习是技能学习，和学开车、学游泳是一个道理。那就是，要想学好外语，必须增加练习，光听“教练”讲道理是不够的。考生在听完名师讲解雅思考试规律和复习技巧外，还要坐下来，安静地看看书，从中获取养分，夯实英语基本功才是硬道理。不能抱着侥幸心理，想着混过雅思。考生更应该借雅思这个东风，真正把英语水平提高，毕竟，走出国门后，就得靠英语生存、学习和工作了，那时多少分不再是硬道理。

英语的学习必须是听说读写词汇并进，很多考生屡考不过是因为缺乏严密的计划。而且，三天打鱼两天晒网，语言的学习在没有形成能力之前，往往一日不练十日空。因此，要想学好外语，还要作好科学的规划，并按这个规划去执行。很多考生要么完全不知道怎么学习，要么是盲从别人的方法，或是众说纷纭，不知所从。

“英语周计划系列丛书”是在分析考生的现状和种种困难的基础上形成的一整套完善的雅思复习计划。本系列书以提高考生英语应试水平、迅速提高雅思分数为目的，一举两得。雅思周计划共 5 本书，囊括了听、说、读、写四大雅思考试板块，并涵盖学习英语的基本功：词汇。这 5 本书依次是：**《4 周攻克雅思听力周计划》、《4 周攻克雅思口语周计划》、《4 周攻克雅思阅读周计划》、《4 周攻克雅思写作周计划》、《4 周攻克雅思词汇周计划》。**

之所以叫周计划，是因为每本书都是以周为单位进行学习。其实，攻克雅思并非有多难，难就难在没有掌握技巧和方法，而本套书通过 4 周完整缜密的规划，将听、说、读、写并进，再辅以词汇，引领考生攻克雅思考试大关！

本系列丛书特点如下：

- **系统全面，涵盖雅思考试听说读写四大板块。**让雅思考试备考一气呵成，自成体系。
- **计划科学、完整、缜密，可操作性强。**每本书按 4 周进行，每周 7 天，每天任务具体、清晰、充实。考生无须再去苦恼该干什么，不该干什么。

● **科学的应试备考过程，从易到难，循序渐进**。每本书的第一周是“引进门”，并对雅思考试技能迅速了解；第二周是“打基础”，让考生基本功得到迅速夯实；第三周则是“技巧强化”，迅速提升语言水平，为考试作好充足的准备；而第四周则是“模拟考场”，让考生每天如战马驰骋，实战沙场，以达到考前最佳状态。

● **一书在手，众生皆宜**。这是本套丛书的又一大特色。无论是从未涉足雅思考试的新手，还是久经沙场的“烤鸭”，本套丛书均能满足需求，尤其是对于那些急于攻克雅思考试并渴求获取雅思高分的考生，本套丛书更是书海中的首选！

每每在讲课之余，我都能碰到心急如焚的考生；每当看到他们那种求助的眼神，我都暗下决心要为他们做点什么。我也曾是一名外语学习者，也有过和他们一样的困惑和迷茫，但如今，我已是一名从事外语教学多年的老师，这种责任和使命感促使我必须要拿出切实的行动。在全国著名的培训机构——**环球卓越**的大力组织下，一批和我一样热心于雅思教学的师资团队走到了一起，用我们多年的教学成果，共同铸就了我们这套丛书——雅思周计划系列！

路，总是在延伸，一望无尽；但是，路，却有畅通无阻，也有曲折迂回。真心希望，这套周计划能让众多雅思考生少点犹豫，少点徘徊，少点弯路，尽量把大好的青春年华用在有用的事情上。更希望众多的雅思考生，能够成为一名有志的中国学子，早日走出去，在实现自己梦想的同时，也为祖国富强添砖加瓦。我这区区外语教师，也算是不枉十年寒窗了。

谭松柏
2011年元旦于北京

前　言

雅思是一种对应试者的英语能力进行全面考核的水平考试，阅读部分则考核了考生的英语阅读能力。而对于大多数考生来说，阅读部分最常见的问题是时间紧、题量大、文章长，一个小时下来感觉难以应付。究其根本原因，通常有如下几个：

第一，语言基础知识薄弱，词汇量小，语法基础知识贫乏，导致文章看不懂，甚至连题目都读不懂；

第二，有一定的语言积累，但平常对学术类的文章体裁接触甚少，因而阅读通篇都是正式的学术词汇和较复杂的语言结构时感觉困难；

第三，知识面狭窄，文章涉及的相应的背景知识比较匮乏；

第四，阅读速度缓慢，且不适应雅思阅读中的多种题型和大题量。

那么该如何解决这些问题呢？

我们首先从雅思阅读考试的目的谈起。雅思阅读考查的是考生的英语阅读能力，包括理解文章中的一般信息和具体信息的能力，以及带着目的寻找细节的能力。完成雅思阅读题目通常需要三种阅读技巧：略读、查读和细读。因此如果想攻克雅思阅读，我们还是应该从它要考查的具体阅读能力和技能入手。理解书面信息是建立在一定的词汇量和语法基础知识的基础之上的，因此建议词汇量严重不足的考生务必重视积累词汇。但文章中不可避免地会出现一些我们从未见过的生词，针对这种情况，本书教给大家一些有效处理生词的策略。

针对雅思阅读文章的语言特点，本书在第一章教给大家如何读懂文章中的长、难句。另外，雅思阅读实际上考查了考生带着目的去文中快速获取信息的能力，因此我们在做阅读题目时根本没有必要逐字逐句地精读，而是要学会如何略读、查读、并迅速辨别转述的技巧。对于阅读部分考查的这些核心阅读能力和技能，本书在第一章中都进行了专门的介绍和训练。**对雅思阅读中的核心技能进行针对性地训练是本书最大的特点**。

本书的第二章和第三章是对雅思阅读中的每一种题型的专项训练，目的是为了让考生熟悉并掌握每种题型的特点，抓住解题规律。并在每一章的最后安排两套综合模拟试题进行巩固。

本书最后一章是 7 套针对雅思阅读部分的专项模拟试题，在文章的难度、体裁、编排方面，按照雅思阅读部分的试题要求严格、精心设计，建议读者在做完相应练习后，再精读每一篇文章，从而达到扩大知识面并积累词汇的效果。

最后感谢为此书付出辛勤劳动的编辑们，愿此书能助考生们一臂之力，并祝愿考生们在雅思考试取得好成绩！

李兰荣

2010 年 12 月

目　　录

4周攻克

雅思阅读周计划

第一周　掌握有效的阅读策略

星期一 透视雅思阅读

一 雅思阅读概况

雅思阅读包括学术类（A 类）和移民类（G 类）两种形式，前者适合欲留学到以英语为本族语的国家的考生，后者适合准备移民到这些国家的考生。

雅思 A 类阅读考试一共有三篇文章，词数为 2000～2705，单篇文章最长词数在 1000 左右。每篇文章后有 13 到 14 道题目，共计 40 道，每题 1 分，题目出现在文章之前或之后。考试时间为 1 小时，考生需要把答案写在答题纸上。所选文章均改编自欧美各大报刊、杂志、书籍等。文章选材广泛，内容涉及经济、教育、科技、生物、心理、认知、环境等多个领域。题材有说明文、议论文等，三篇文章中至少有一篇是议论文。

雅思 G 类阅读的题量、考试时间跟 A 类一样，分为三部分。第一部分通常包含 2 到 3 篇短文或者若干段文字（如广告等），第二部分通常有 2 篇文章，第三部分则为一段较长的文章。文章的内容和文体各有不同，难度最大的是第三部分的内容。所选文章形式灵活、多样，多取自广告、通知、传单、说明书、大众报刊、杂志等。

二 雅思阅读评分

雅思阅读评分为 0～9 分，下面是一个答对的题数与分数之间的转换表。

Number of correct Reading answers 答对题数	IELTS band score 分数	Number of correct Reading answers 答对题数	IELTS band score 分数
39-40	9.0	13-15	4.5
37-38	8.5	10-12	4.0
35-36	8.0	6-9	3.5
33-34	7.5	4-5	3.0
30-32	7.0	3	2.5
27-29	6.5	2	2.0
23-26	6.0	1	1.0
20-22	5.5	absent 缺考	0.0
16-19	5.0		

三 雅思阅读10大题型

雅思阅读考试的题型主要有10种，某些题型在具体考试可能会出现形式上的一些细微变化。

题型1：选择题（Multiple Choice）

题型2：简答题（Short-answer Questions）

题型3：完成句子（Sentence Completion）

题型4：完成笔记、摘要或表格/流程图（Notes, Summary or Table/Flow-chart Completion）

题型5：标示示意图（Labelling a Diagram）

题型6：为文章的段落或部分选标题（Choosing Headings for Paragraphs or Sections of a Text）

题型7：信息定位（Locating Information）

题型8：判断题，辨别作者的观点/主张和文章信息（Identification of Writer's Views/Claims or of Information in a Text）

题型9：分类题（Classification）

题型10：匹配题（Matching）

四 考试目的

雅思A类阅读考查考生从文章中获取信息的能力，具体来讲，主要考查以下阅读能力：

1. 辨别作者的写作目的、读者群等
2. 辨别和理解作者的中心观点
3. 识别观点、态度和事实
4. 寻找具体信息
5. 阅读具体信息
6. 提取相关信息
7. 区分大意与细节
8. 识别摘要的要点
9. 根据既定标准对文中相应信息进行分类
10. 选取文中的相关信息并用示意图来表示
11. 推理
12. 正确拼写并正确使用语法的能力

为了保证全面客观地考查考生的英语阅读能力，雅思阅读题型灵活、多样。例如雅思A类阅读每篇文章有2～3种题型，完成任何一种题型都需要综合运用以上几种能力。

五 高分策略

通过以上对雅思阅读部分的介绍，我们可以看出这部分测试有如下特点：文章长，题目多，题型活，时间紧。它重点考查的是考生根据既定目的去文中获取相关信息的能力。因此，如果想在这部分考取理想的分数，应该从以下几个方面入手：

第一，夯实语言基础，提高一般的英语阅读能力。阅读尽管是一种技能，但如果没有一定的词汇、语法等基础语言知识，技能的提高也无从谈起。此外，雅思属于水平考试，考生的一般英语阅读能力对雅思阅读有直接影响。因此，建议考生除了进行专门的雅思阅读题目的练习，平时也应该多进行其他的英文阅读练习。

第二，掌握多种阅读策略。雅思阅读考试的目的和特点决定了我们不能像阅读教科书一样逐字逐句地精读，而是要综合运用查读、略读、跳读、速读等多种阅读策略来提取文章信息。我们要做的不是理解文章的每一部分，而是保证在规定的时间内尽可能地做对最多的题目。同时对于雅思考查的一些核心阅读能力，我们应该进行有针对性地训练和提高。

第三，熟悉题型，掌握必要的应试技巧。很多考生之所以感觉阅读这部分比较难，主要原因是不熟悉题型，没有掌握必要的做题技巧。不但要熟悉每个题型，当面对 2～3 种题型时，我们需要掌握一定策略，有效地利用时间，提高做题的效率。

在以后的章节里，我们将逐步从以上几个方面展开，帮助考生掌握一些有效的阅读策略和各种题型的解题技巧，提高核心阅读能力，从根本上提高考生的雅思阅读成绩。

六 Test Yourself

下面我们先做一套雅思阅读题，体验一下雅思阅读的题型、难度，并检查你现有的阅读水平。

READING PASSAGE 1

*You should spend about 20 minutes on **Questions 1-13**, which are based on Reading Passage 1 below.*

The people of ancient Egypt emerged as one of the first Western civilisations. Sustained by the River Nile and protected by vast deserts, the Egyptians lived in comparative security, prosperity and peace far thousands of years. When such conditions exist, the civilisation and its arts usually flourish. To this day, many of the Egyptian artistic creations display the wealth, splendour and talent of this great civilisation.

Ancient Egypt has been called a land of temples and tombs, and for centuries people have been filled with wonder at the ingenuity of the Egyptians, whose impressive works have withstood the ravages of time so well. Had it not been for the long-lasting nature of their monuments and carved inscriptions in the form of hieroglyphics, much evidence of their activities would have vanished from all historical records. In about 3000 BC, Upper and Lower Egypt were united under the first pharaoh, and generally from that time until the invasion by Alexander the Great in 332 BC, Egypt prospered as a nation of skillful craftsmen and artists.

The Egyptians were an industrious, highly civilised and deeply religious people, who obediently accepted the supreme authority of their pharaohs. The people were content to serve and work for the state in return for a secure livelihood. They considered this earthly life to be a segment in a great cycle, at the end of which everything would be returned to its original form. The richer and more important the person, the more careful and elaborate would be his or her burial, and the stronger and safer the tomb in which they would be buried.

The burial of the dead in the ground was not considered sufficiently safe for kings, queens and court officials, so sunken, sealed tombs were ingeniously constructed to protect personal treasures, food and instructions for the safe conduct of the soul after death. The design of these tombs developed into the stepped pyramid, and finally into the square pyramid that we know today.

There are about 80 ancient pyramids in Egypt. The Great Pyramid at Gizeh, which King Cheops built as his tomb 5,000 years ago, holds most interest. It stands with two other pyramids on a slight rise overlooking the River Nile. At the centre of the pyramid is the King's Chamber and leading down from there is a long narrow area known as the Grand Gallery. The pyramid covers 13 acres and contains 2,300,000 blocks of limestone, each weighing an average of 1.5 tons. Its pyramidal form has a perfectly square base with sides of 756 feet and a height of 481 feet. Situated directly below the King's Chamber is the Queen's Chamber and there are two air channels leading upwards from the centre of the pyramid to the outside.

Originally the exterior was covered in highly polished limestone slabs, all of which have been stolen over the years. It is estimated that a total of 100,000 men laboured for 20 years to build this gigantic structure, and although architecturally unimportant in design, it has aroused the curiosity of millions of people because of the uncanny accuracy of its measurements and proportions. It reveals the remarkable ingenuity and the great organising ability of the ancient Egyptians.

Near these pyramids stands the Great Sphinx, the origin and purpose of which constitute one of the world's most famous puzzles. Shaped from an outcrop of stone in the form of a human-headed lion, the face is possibly a portrait of King Khafra, the son of Cheops, who was buried in the second largest pyramid. The Sphinx is one of the biggest statues ever made.

The Egyptian people showed reverence towards natural objects such as the lotus flower, the scarab beetle, the falcon, the lion, the sun and the River Nile. All these subjects and many more were used symbolically and conventionally as motifs in low-relief carving and painting. It was the custom of the Egyptians to depict the various parts of the human figure, usually in the most characteristic positions. The head was shown in profile except for the eye, which was represented from the front, the shoulders and a portion of the arms were portrayed from the front, while the hips and legs were side views. Wall decoration showed little or no attempt to indicate depth or perspective, except by placing distant objects above near things. It was essentially two-dimensional, and relative size indicated the status of the person, so the pharaoh was the largest figure in the composition.

Egyptian art is characterised by a passion for permanence, a desire to impress by size, and a determination to make each item serve its function without much regard for the whole. It is obvious that art among these people reached a very high level and the strong influence of Egyptian art can be seen in the work of nearby civilisations.

The fortunate discovery and subsequent deciphering in 1822 of the Rosetta Stone, which showed the same laws inscribed both in Egyptian hieroglyphics and the Egyptian demotic, or popular version of their language, as well as the Greek language, eventually gave the key to the meaning of Egyptian inscriptions, and therefore the significance of much Egyptian art.

Questions 1–3

Complete the sentences below.

Choose ***NO MORE THAN THREE WORDS*** *from the passage for each answer.*

Write your answers in boxes 1–3 on your answer sheet.

1. Security and peace are two ______ that are necessary for a civilisation to be successful.
2. Ancient Egyptians worked as both ______.
3. Ordinary Egyptians expected to receive ______ for their hard work.

Questions 4–7

Label the diagram below.

Choose ***NO MORE THAN THREE WORDS AND/OR NUMBERS*** *from the passage for each answer.*

Write your answers in boxes 4–7 on your answer sheet.

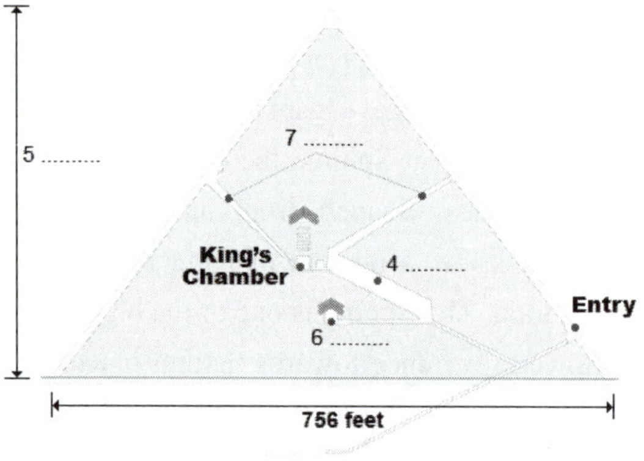

4 ____________ 5 ____________ 6 ____________ 7 ____________

Questions 8–12

Do the following statements agree with the information given in Reading Passage 1?

In boxes 8–12 on your answer sheet, write

TRUE	*if the statement agrees with the information*
FALSE	*if the statement contradicts the information*
NOT GIVEN	*if there is no information on this*

8. The surface of the Great Pyramid is covered in polished limestone slabs.
9. King Khafra died before King Cheops.
10. Egyptian carvings were often based on things found in nature.

11. Important characters in Egyptian carvings were bigger than less important characters.

12. Egyptian art was greatly influenced by the art of neighbouring cultures.

Question 13

*Choose the correct letter **A**, **B**, **C** or **D**.*

Write the correct letter in box 13 on your answer sheet.

The writer's aim in this passage is to ______.

A. describe the construction methods of the pyramids

B. explain the beliefs of the ancient Egyptians

C. offer an interpretation of Egyptian art and sculpture

D. provide an overview of early Egyptian society

READING PASSAGE 2

*You should spend about 20 minutes on **Questions 14–26**, which are based on Reading Passage 2 on the following pages.*

Questions 14–20

Reading Passage 2 has seven paragraphs, **A–H**.

*Choose the correct heading for paragraphs **A** to **G** from the list of headings below.*

*Write the correct number, **i–xi**, in boxes 14–20 on your answer sheet.*

List of Headings

i	Research into earphones inserted in the ear canal
ii	Listening through earphones for too long
iii	The maximum noise level of the "Walkman"
iv	The benefit of silence and the prevalence of noise
v	An environment of constant noise
vi	Three problems caused by inserted earphones
vii	The maximum safe noise dosage
viii	The curse of silence (Example)
ix	A cure for "tinnitus"
x	Alarming statistical evidence
xi	The seriousness of hearing impairment
xii	The danger of falling asleep

14 Paragraph **A**

15 Paragraph **B**

16 Paragraph **C**

17 Paragraph **D**

18 Paragraph **E**

19 Paragraph **F**

20 Paragraph **G**

Example	*Answer*
Paragraph **H**	**viii**

Hearing Problems

A The old adage extols the virtue of silence by claiming it is golden, yet experience tells us that silence is as hard to come by as the precious metal itself. The benefit of silence to the human ear is scientifically demonstrable. Less superfluous noise; less impairment to the hearing. Yet this precious commodity is no longer valued. Noise is ever present in modern life and is an accumulative experience. The ill effects of noise pollution are of two kinds: acute—exposure to an individual instance of a very loud noise, such as a gunshot or explosion; and chronic—the experience of too much noise over an extended period of time.

B City and urban dwellers exist in an increasingly noise-ridden environment, and it is now almost impossible to escape exposure to high noise levels. Even if we exclude the more obvious sources of noise pollution such as jet plane engines, road works, power tools, loud music at dance parties and so on, it is clear that noise is a constant and often unwelcome companion. We have only to walk through a suburban shopping mall or department store, or catch a bus or train to be subjected to noise levels that a few decades ago would have been considered beyond human endurance. The popular practice of "layering" sound, by adding a louder source of noise to that which already exists in order to mask it, merely compounds the problem. Because of the accumulative nature of noise abuse, constant noise is worse than noisy periods interspersed with silence.

C Our noise level acceptance threshold is rising in step with the number of persons developing hearing problems. Data available from a recent survey conducted by the Australian Bureau of Statistics show that 7.4% of people over 14years of age have some discernible hearing problem. According to the survey, 24.6% of the 7.4% of persons with affected hearing have problems caused by subjection to a constant barrage of noise, either at work, in the everyday living environment, or as the result of a particular choice of leisure activity. The problem is most severe for males aged between 25 and 64 years of age, 9.1% of whom have a hearing disability, and for which the cause is constant noise in 44.4% of cases.

D Of current concern to acoustical engineers and psychologists at the National Acoustics Laboratories in Sydney, Australia, is the potential for damage to the eardrum caused by the transmission of loud sound through earphones placed directly into the ear canal. An almost universal fad among young people, the pocket-sized radio-cassette player (commonly known by the brand name "Walkman") may be exposing its owner to greater than the maximum safe dosage of noise recommended for industrial workers — 90 decibels* over a period of 8 hours. This dosage, called Dose 1, can be achieved much sooner by exposing the ear to only slightly more than 90 decibels. Increases to the decibel level logarithmically shorten the exposure time required to reach a given dose. For instance, to achieve Dose 1 in 4 hours, it is necessary to raise the decibel exposure level by a mere 3decibels.

E One danger posed to young ears is that the peak sound level from these radio-cassette players is often far too great; at high volume it is all too easy to receive Dose 1 in a short period of time. Any further noise heard above 90 decibels that day and the recipient is causing measurable damage to his or her ears. Another danger is the likelihood of a change in the pain threshold of noise resulting in users compensating by increasing the volume to levels way above what is considered safe. Finally, insertable earphones block the ear canal, thereby further increasing the noise level absorbed.

F But perhaps the most alarming potential for danger caused by insertable earphones is the ease with which the listener can exceed the safe time length of exposure to noise. The small earphones can be comfortably worn for extended periods of time. What is more, there is the danger of falling asleep with the earphones inserted, leading to an accumulation of excess noise while unconscious.

G Noise abuse soon leads to varying degrees of hearing loss. What may begin as an acute temporary condition, in time becomes a chronic and irreversible disability. A common complaint is "tinnitus", or a "ringing in the ears" which fails to subside after the ears are subjected to a short but extreme dose of noise. It is an exhausting condition that can seriously threaten the composure of the sufferer who can be driven to near madness. It is believed the composer Beethoven was particularly aggravated by this malady. At present, there is little that can be done in the majority of cases, although the victim might be able to obtain some temporary relief by using a masking device which blocks out the offending frequencies of sound with other, less annoying frequencies.

H Inevitably, though, years of excessive noise accumulation take their toll and partial or complete deafness results. If silence is the cure for ailing ears (or, at least, the best way to prevent further deterioration of one's hearing), it is sobering to realize that it is also the unfortunate and permanent curse of a lifetime of noise abuse caused by ignoring the warnings.

* *decibel*: standard unit of sound measurement

Questions 21–26

Do the following statements agree with information given in Reading Passage 2?

In boxes 21–26 on your answer sheet, write

YES	*if the statement agrees with the writer*
NO	*if the statement contradicts the writer*
NOT GIVEN	*if there is no information about this in the passage.*

21. Silence is no longer a precious commodity.
22. "Layering" sound reduces the overall amount of sound by masking it.
23. More and more people are having hearing problems.
24. To achieve dose 1, the ear only needs to be exposed to 93 decibels for 4 hours.
25. Insertable earphones cause more damage to the ear than other sound sources. NG.
26. Beethoven's ability to compose music was threatened by his "tinnitus".

READING PASSAGE 3

*You should spend about 20 minutes on **Questions 27-40**, which are based on Reading Passage 3 below.*

Lessons from the Titanic

From the comfort of our modern lives we tend to look back at the turn of the twentieth century as a dangerous time for sea travelers. With limited communication facilities, and shipping technology still in its infancy in the early nineteen hundreds, we consider ocean travel to have been a risky business. But to the people of the time it was one of the safest forms of transport. At the time of the Titanic's maiden voyage in 1912, there had only been four lives lost in the previous forty years on passenger ships on the North Atlantic crossing. And the Titanic was confidently proclaimed to be unsinkable. She represented the pinnacle of technological advance at the time. Her builders, crew and passengers had no doubt that she was the finest ship ever built. But still she did sink on April 14, 1912, taking1, 517 of her passengers and crew with her.

RMS Titanic left Southampton for New York on April 10, 1912.On board were some of the richest and most famous people of the time who had paid large sums of money to sail on the first voyage of the most luxurious ship in the world. Imagine her place on her end: she was larger at 269 meters than many of the tallest buildings of the day. The Titanic carried 329 first class, 285 second class and 710 third class passengers with 899 crew members, under the care of the very experienced Captain Edward J.Smith.

RMS Titanic was believed to be unsinkable because the hull was divided into sixteen watertight compartments. Even if two of these compartments flooded, the ship could still float. The ship's owners could not imagine that, in the case of an accident, the Titanic would not be able to float until she was rescued. It was largely as a result of this confidence in the ship and in the safety of ocean travel that the disaster could claim such a great loss of life.

In the ten hours prior to the Titanic's fatal collision with an iceberg at 11:40p.m., six warnings of icebergs in her path were received by the Titanic's wireless operators. Only one of these messages was formally posted on the bridge; the others were in various locations across the ship. If the combined information in these messages of iceberg positions had been plotted, the ice field which lay across the Titanic's path would have been apparent. Instead, the lack of formal procedures for dealing with information from a relatively new piece of technology, the wireless, meant that the danger was not known until too late. This was not the fault of the Titanic crew.

Procedures for dealing with warnings received through the wireless had not been formalized across the shipping industry at the time.

Captain Smith's seemingly casual attitude in increasing the speed on this day to a dangerous 22 knots or 41 kilometers per hour, can then be partly explained by his ignorance of what lay ahead. But this only partly accounts for his actions, since the spring weather in Greenland was known to cause huge chunks of ice to break off from the glaciers. Captain Smith knew that these icebergs would float southward and had already acknowledged this danger by taking a more southerly route than at other times of the year. So why was the Titanic traveling at high speed when he knew, if not of the specific risk, at least of the general risk of icebergs in her path? As with the lack of coordination of the wireless messages, it was simply standard operating procedure at the time. Captain Smith was following the practices accepted on the North Atlantic, practices which had coincided with forty years of safe travel. He believed, wrongly as we now know, that the ship could turn or stop in time if an iceberg was sighted by the lookouts.

There were around two and a half hours between the time the Titanic rammed into the iceberg and its final submersion. In this time 705 people were loaded into the twenty lifeboats. There were 473 empty seats available on lifeboats while over 1,500 people drowned. These figures raise two important issues. Firstly, why there were not enough lifeboats to seat every passenger and crew member on board. And secondly, why the lifeboats were not full.

The Titanic had sixteen lifeboats and four collapsible boats which could carry just over half the number of people on board her maiden voyage and only a third of the Titanic's total capacity. Regulations for the number of lifeboats required were based on outdated British Board of Trade regulations written in 1894 for ships a quarter of the Titanic's size, and had never been revised. Under these requirements, the Titanic was only obliged to carry enough lifeboats to seat 962 people.

The belief that the Titanic was unsinkable was so strong that passengers and crew alike clung to the belief even as she was actually sinking. This attitude was not helped by Captain Smith, who had not acquainted his senior officers with the full situation. For the first hour after the collision, the majority of people aboard the Titanic, including senior crew, were not aware that she would sink, that there were insufficient lifeboats or that the nearest ship responding to the Titanic's distress calls would arrive two hours after she was on the bottom of the ocean. As a result, the officers in charge of loading the boats received a very halfhearted response to their early calls for women and children to board the lifeboats. Not realizing the magnitude of the impending disaster themselves, the officers allowed several boats to be lowered only half full.

As the Titanic sank, another ship, believed to have been the Californian, was seen motionless less than twenty miles away. The ship failed to respond to the Titanic's eight distress rockets. Although the officers of the Californian tried to signal the Titanic with their flashing Morse lamp, they did not wake up their radio operator to listen for a distress call. At this time, communication at sea through wireless was new and the benefits not well appreciated, so the wireless on ships was often not operated around the clock. In the case of the Californian, the wireless operator slept unaware while 1,500 Titanic passengers and crew drowned only a few miles away.

Questions 27–34

*Complete the summary using the list of words, **A–T**, below.*
*Write the correct letter, **A–T**, in boxes 27–34 on your answer sheet.*

The Finest Ship Ever Built

The North Atlantic Ocean crossing of the Titanic was expected to set a new standard for __27__ travel in terms of comfort and __28__. The shipping industry had an excellent safety __29__ on the North Atlantic Crossing over the previous forty years and the Titanic was the finest and safest liner ever built. The Titanic combined the greatest __30__ of the day with sheer __31__, luxury and new safety features. The Titanic's owners were __32__ that even if the Titanic were letting in __33__ she would float indefinitely until __34__ arrived.

A. passengers	B. dangers	C. fast	D. help
E. happy	F. ocean	G. ship	H. orders
I. advanced	J. worried	K. water	L. size
M. orders	N. enormous	O. record	P. sink
Q. confident	R. technology	S. fast	T. safety

Questions 35–37

*Choose the correct letter, **A**, **B**, **C** or **D**.*
Write the correct letter in boxes 35–37 on your answer sheet.

35. Which is most at fault for the magnitude of the Titanic disaster?
    A. The ship.
    B. The Titanic's owners and builders.
    C. Standard operating procedure.
    D. The captain and crew.
36. The number of lifeboats on the Titanic ____.
    A. would have been sufficient if all boats had been filled to capacity
    B. met the regulations for much smaller ships but not the Titanic
    C. had been designed in 1894 by the British Board of Trade
    D. could carry more people than required under the regulations
37. The Titanic was ____.
    A. higher than the tallest buildings of her day
    B. divided into 16 watertight compartments
    C. unsinkable
    D. the most technologically advanced liner of her time

Questions 38–40

The writer mentions a number of factors related to poor communication which contributed to the disaster. Which 3 of the following factors are mentioned? Write your answers (A–H) in boxes

38–40 on your answer sheet.

A. The Titanic was travelling too fast.

B. Ships were not required to operate their wireless continually.

C. There were insufficient lifeboats on the ship.

D. The Titanic's wireless was not operating around the clock.

E. Ice warnings were not dealt with systematically.

F. The Californian's wireless had broken down.

G. The Titanic's wireless had broken down.

H. Captain Smith did not give his officers enough information.

Keys:

Passage 1: 1. conditions　2. craftsmen and artists　3. a secure livelihood
4. Grand Gallery　5. 481 feet　6. Queen's Chamber
7. air channels　8. F　9. NG
10. T　11. T　12. F　13. D

Passage 2: 14. iv　15. v　16. x　17. i　18. vi　19. ii　20. xi
21. NO　22. NO　23. YES　24. YES　25. NOT EIVEN　26. YES

Passage 3: 27. F　28. T　29. O　30. R　31. L　32. Q　33. K
34. D　35. B　36. B　37. D　38. B　39. E　40. H

如果你答对 0～19 道题	如果你答对 20～27 道题	如果你答对 28～40 道题
如果你想获得 5.5 分以上的分数，你可能需要在一段时间的准备，建议你在英语基础知识方面如词汇、语法上多下点儿工夫，并先从难度上稍微简单的阅读材料入手，每天进行一定量的精读和泛读练习，循序渐进，最后过渡到雅思阅读的训练。	你现在需要对雅思阅读考查的核心阅读能力和策略进行更多的训练，每天进行一定量的与雅思阅读考试难度相当的阅读训练，同时注意进行雅思阅读词汇方面的积累，可望在1～2 个月内取得理想的成绩。	你目前的水平可能已经达到多数大学、教学机构对英语阅读水平的要求，但每次考试的具体情况各异，如果你想拿到更高的分数，你需要分析自己在雅思阅读的弱势所在，并展开针对性的训练，同时你需要熟悉雅思阅读题型并掌握必要的答题技巧。

答案详解

Passage 1

Questions 1–3：完成句子题，属于细节信息题，考查了略读、查读，以及识别转述的能力。

题　号	原　文	分　析
1	…, the Egyptians lived in comparative **security**, prosperity and **peace** far thousands of years. When such conditions exist, the **civilisation** and its arts usually **flourish**.	原文中出现了题目中的 security 和 peace，同时接下来的一个句子中出现了 civilisation，题目中问“安全和和平是两个____，它们对一个文明的繁荣非常重要”，successful 和 flourish 是近义表达，因此答案是 conditions。
2	…, Egypt prospered as a nation of skillful craftsmen and artists.	题目中很明显是问古代埃及人的职业的。我们在文章第二段的最后一句话中可以发现两个表示职业的名词：craftsmen 和 artists，因此答案是 craftsmen and artists。

（续）

题　号	原　文	分　析
3	The people were content to serve and **work** for the state **in return for** a secure livelihood.	文中这句话的意思是："（埃及）人民很满足为他们的国家服务和工作，以此换来一种有保障的生活。"文中与题目中照应的词有 work，expected to receive 是 in return for 的转述，因此答案是 a secure livelihood。

Questions 4–7：标示示意图，属于细节信息题，重点考查了查读和识别转述的能力。

题　号	原　文	分　析
4	At the centre of the pyramid is the **King's Chamber** and leading down from there is **a long narrow area** known as the Grand Gallery.	第 4 题要求填写连接 King's Chamber 的一个较为宽敞的倾斜的通道的名称。我们可以先回到原文中寻找 King's Chamber，然后再细读周围的文字，找出线索。文中含有 King's Chamber 的这句话的意思是"金字塔的中心是国王的寝室，而从那通往一条狭长的区域，这个区域被称为大走廊"，故答案是 Grand Gallery。
5	Its pyramidal form has a perfectly square base with sides of 756 feet and a **height** of 481 feet.	第 5 题要求填入金字塔的高度，塔底的宽度已经给出，我们可以直接把 756 feet 作为定位词，据此寻找答案在文中的大致位置。很明显，答案是 481 feet。
6	Situated directly below the King's Chamber is the Queen's Chamber…	第 6 题要求填入位于国王密室下方一个较小的房间的名字。文中这句话的意思是"位于国王寝室下方的是王后的寝室"，因此答案是 Queen's Chamber。
7	…and there are two air channels leading upwards from the centre of the pyramid to the outside.	第 7 题要求填入连接国王房间且通向金字塔外面的两个狭长通道的名字。文中这句话的意思是"从金字塔的中心有两条通向外界的通风管道"，因此答案为 air channels。

Questions 8–12：判断题，综合考查了查读以及对原文信息进行分析、综合、概括、推理等能力。

题　号	原　文	分　析
8	Originally the **exterior** was covered in highly **polished limestone slabs**, all of which have been stolen over the years.	文中的 exterior 照应了题目中的 surface，同时题目中的 polished limestone slabs 也出现在原文中。由于文中说"最早的金字塔表面使用的是磨光的石灰岩板材，但是后来都被偷光了，"意思也就是现在金字塔表面已经没有什么石灰岩板材了，因此题目应为 False。
9	Shaped from an outcrop of stone in the form of a human-headed lion, the face is possibly a portrait of King Khafra, the son of Cheops, who was buried in the second largest pyramid.	文中虽然都提到了题中的两个人名：King Khafra 和 King Cheops，并且说 King Khafra 是 Cheops 的儿子，但文中并没有说明谁先死，谁后死，因此这道题目为 Not Given。
10	The Egyptian people showed reverence towards **natural objects** such as the lotus flower, the scarab beetle, the falcon, the lion, the sun and the River Nile. All these subjects and many more were used symbolically and conventionally as motifs in low-relief **carving** and painting.	文中说"埃及人对自然界的事物，荷花、圣甲虫、猎鹰、狮子、太阳和尼罗河，都充满了敬意。所有这些事物以及更多的事物都成为带有浅浮雕的雕刻和绘画的传统的具有象征意义的主题"。题目中说埃及的雕刻是建立在自然界可以发现的事物之上的，实际上是对原文的一种总结和概括，因此是 True。
11	…and relative size indicated the status of the person, so the pharaoh was the largest figure in the composition.	文中说"（人物的）相对大小显示了这个人的身份，因此法老是组图中最大的人物"。题目中说在埃及的雕刻中重要的人物比不太重要的人物要大，这实际上是基于原文信息的一种正确推理，因此是 True。
12	It is obvious that art among these people reached a very high level and the strong **influence** of Egyptian art can be seen in the work of nearby civilisations.	文中说"很明显这些（埃及）人达到了一种非常高的水平，而且埃及艺术的这种影响在与它毗邻的文明中随处可见。这说明埃及的艺术对邻国产生了很大影响"。但题目却说埃及艺术受到邻国的艺术的极大影响，与原文正好相反，因此为 False。

Question 13： 单项选择题，大意题，考查考生在综合把握文中内容的基础上理解作者写作意图的能力，完成本题需要考生具备略读和区分主旨和细节的能力。

分析： 题目问作者写这篇文章的目的是：A. 描述了金字塔的建造方法；B. 解释了古埃及人的信仰；C. 对埃及的艺术和雕塑提供了一种解释；D. 对早期的埃及社会提供了一个综览。A、B、C 在文中的各个段落均有涉及，但它们只是文章的部分内容，并不是作者的写作目的，只有 D 选项才比较全面地反映了文章的整体内容和作者的写作意图，因此答案为 D。

Passage 2

Questions 14–20: 找标题，考查了考生把握文章段落中心大意的能力，重点考查了略读和区分主题、主旨和细节的能力。

14 题：A 段首先说沉默非常宝贵，但是这种“沉默”越来越难以得到了。接着说宁静对于耳朵的好处早已被科学证明了，多余的噪声越少，对耳朵的损伤越少。然而人们不再重视这种宝贵的商品了。噪声在现代生活中随时存在，而且不断累积。接着提到噪声污染的两种不良影响：剧烈性和长期性。可以看出，这段是围绕宁静的好处和现代社会中到处存在的噪声展开的，因此应该选 iv。

15 题：B 段的主题句是第一句，承接第一段，进一步说明城市居民面临的噪声无处不在的环境，接下来通过举例来说明现在噪声的来源和严重程度。因此应选 v。

16 题：C 段首先说随着有听力问题的人的数量的增加，我们对噪声水平的忍受界限也在提高。随后给出大量数据，表明环境中持续的噪声给人们带来的听力问题，本段应选 x。

17 题：D 段第一句说悉尼国家声学实验室的声学工程师和心理学家们的目前担心，插在耳孔处的耳机传出的很大的声音对耳膜可能会造成损伤。借来下具体解释为什么这种方式可能对耳朵造成损伤，因此第一句还是主题句，故此段的小标题应选 i。

18 题：E 段具体阐述了耳孔插入式耳机对耳朵造成的三种危害，连接词分别是 one danger，another danger，finally。因此本段应选 vi。

19 题：F 段说也许插入式耳机造成的最为让人担忧的危害是听者很容易就超过了接受噪声的安全时限。然后说这样的原因，并举出一个具体例子，说明人们入睡后还带着耳机的严重性。整段的主题句是第一句，说明带太长时间插入式耳机的危害性，因此应选 ii。

20 题：G 段第一句说过多的噪声会导致不同程度听觉丧失。接着说刚开始可能是暂时的急性病，但随着时间的推移就可能演变成慢性且不可逆转的残疾。接着举出一个常见的病症“tinnitus”，然后说这种病的症状以及对病人的危害。最后，段落提到对于大多数的病例都无有效治疗方法，尽管病人可以使用一种屏蔽装置得到暂时的缓解。争端都是围绕噪声导致的听力问题的严重性展开的，因此应选 xi。

Questions 21–26

题　号	原　文	分　析
21	The benefit of silence to the human ear is scientifically demonstrable. Less superfluous noise; less impairment to the hearing. Yet this precious commodity is no longer valued.	21 题：安静不再是一种珍贵的商品了。但原文第一段说安静对人耳的好处已经被科学证明了。多余的噪音越少，对听觉的损伤越少，只是这种珍贵的商品不再被人们珍视了。这种珍贵的商品就是安静，因此该题为 NO。

（续）

题　号	原　文	分　析
22	The popular practice of 'layering' sound, by adding a louder source of noise to that which already exists in order to mask it, merely compounds the problem.	题目说屏蔽“laying”声音能够通过掩盖声音来降低总音量。但原文B段中最后两句说“layering”声音的做法是通过增加音量，以更大的声音来掩盖原来的声音，而这只能使问题更严重。因此，可以看出，这种做法实际上增大了总音量，因此应为NO。
23	Our noise level acceptance threshold is rising in step with the number of persons developing hearing problems.	23题说越来越多的人有听力问题。答案在原文第三段第一句。这句话的意思是，随着有听力问题的人的数量的增加，我们对噪音水平的忍受界限也在提高。因此这题是正确的，应选YES。
24	90 decibels* over a period of 8 hours. This dosage, called Dose 1, can be achieved much sooner by exposing the ear to only slightly more than 90 decibels. Increases to the decibel level logarithmically shorten the exposure time required to reach a given dose. For instance, to achieve Dose 1 in 4 hours, it is necessary to raise the decibel exposure level by a mere 3decibels.	题目说，为了达到剂量1，耳朵只需要在接受4个小时的93分贝的声音即可，答案在原文D段最后两句话。文中先说安全噪音剂量1是连续8个小时90分贝的音量，而使耳朵接受超过90分贝可以很快达到这个安全剂量。因为分贝水平的增加可以以对数水平缩短接受声音的时间。例如，为了在4个小时内达到剂量1，只需要把分贝提高3分贝即可。也就是说连续4个小时让耳朵接受93分贝的音量可以很快达到安全剂量1，因此本题是YES。
25	Finally, insertable earphones block the ear canal, thereby further increasing the noise level absorbed.	题目说插入式耳机比其他声源对耳朵造成的危害更大，文中E段最后一句提到插入式耳机，但只是说插入式耳机堵住了耳孔，因此增加了吸收的噪音水平，但并没有把插入式耳机对耳朵造成的危害与其他声源进行比较，因此是NOT GIVEN。
26	A common complaint is "tinnitus", or a "ringing in the ears" which fails to subside after the ears are subjected to a short but extreme dose of noise. It is an exhausting condition that can seriously threaten the composure of the sufferer who can be driven to near madness. It is believed the composer Beethoven was particularly aggravated by this malady.	题目说贝多芬谱曲的能力受到过“tinnitus”的危胁。原文G段第三句话提到了“tinnitus”，说是一种在耳朵接受短暂但是高剂量的噪音后还不消失的耳鸣现象。这是一种让人疲倦的病情，它可以严重影响患者内心的稳定，并可能把病人逼疯。人们认为作曲家贝多芬就曾遭受过这种病的折磨。因此本题应选YES。

Passage 3

Questions 27–34：选择式完成摘要题，考查了考生区分主旨和细节，以及识别转述的能力。

题　号	原　文	分　析
27	With limited communication facilities, and shipping technology still in its infancy in the early nineteen hundreds, we consider **ocean travel** to have been a risky business.	27题的句子说“人们期待泰坦尼克号的北大西洋之行在舒适____和____方面为____航行设立一个新标准”。而文中一开始就提到了ocean travel，因此，应该是ocean，选F。

（续）

题　　号	原　　文	分　　析
28	And the Titanic was confidently proclaimed to be unsinkable.	文中这句话说“泰坦尼克号被自信地称为是不会沉没的船”，说明人们相信它很安全，因此该空应填入的单词是 safety，选 T。
29	At the time of the Titanic's maiden voyage in 1912, there had only been four lives lost in the previous forty years on passenger ships on the North Atlantic crossing.	文中说“在泰坦尼克号开始它 1912 年的首次航行之前，横跨北大西洋的船只在过去的 40 年中，只有 4 个人丧生”。29 题的句子说航运业在过去的 40 年里，在横跨北大西洋的航行中有一个非常好的安全 ______。很明显，应该是 record（记录），选 O。
30	She represented the pinnacle of technological advance at the time.	题目说“泰坦尼克号结合了当时最伟大的____和____”。文中说“泰坦尼克号代表了那个时代技术进步的顶峰”，因此该空应为 technology（技术），选 R。
31	Imagine her place on her end: she was larger at 269 meters than many of the tallest buildings of the day.	由于奢华（luxury）和安全性（safety features）都已经提到，我们应该找泰坦尼克号的其他特征。文中这句话都是在描述该船是多么大，因此应该填 size（大小），选 L。
32	RMS Titanic was **believed** to be unsinkable because ….. It was largely as a result of this **confidence** in the ship and in the safety of ocean travel that the disaster could claim such a great loss of life.	题目中说“泰坦尼克号的拥有者非常____认为……”文中出现的 believed 和 confidence 揭示了答案应该为自信，选 Q。
33	Even if two of these compartments flooded, the ship could still float.	题目中说“即使泰坦尼克号进了____，她也能浮在水面上”。而文中说“即使它其中的两个舱进水了，船也能浮着”。因此该空应该是 water，选 K。
34	The ship's owners could not imagine that, in the case of an accident, the Titanic would not be able to float **until she was rescued**.	文中说“泰坦尼克号的拥有者不会想到万一发生了事故，泰坦尼克号是不会浮在水面上的，只能等着被救援”，而 34 题前面的单词也是 until，但后面的 arrived 说明该空应填入一个名词。根据文章，我们知道应该是填入 rescue，但由于词库中没有 rescue，我们只能选它的近义词 help，选 D。

Questions 35-37：单项选择题，考查的能力因具体题目而不同，既可以考大意题，也可以考细节题。

35 题：题目问哪项因素最大程度地造成了泰坦尼克号的灾难？A 选项说是船，B 选项说是泰坦尼克号的拥有者和建造者，C 选项说是标准的操作程序，D 选项说是船长和船员，但通读全文后可以发现 A、C、D 都是表面和片面因素，不是造成灾难的根本原因，只有 B 选项才是作者强调的重点，并在文章中多处提到，因此应该选 B。

36 题：题目说泰坦尼克号上的救生船 ______。文中有两处提到船上的救生船：“In this time 705 people were loaded into the twenty lifeboats. There were 473 empty seats available on lifeboats while over 1,500 people drowned. ” “The Titanic had sixteen lifeboats and four collapsible boats which could carry just over half the number of people on board her maiden voyage and only a third of the Titanic's total capacity. ” 这两处说明当时泰坦尼克号上的乘客约有 2000 人，它上面的 20 条救生船即使都载满也只能坐约 1 000 人，这 1 千人仅仅是泰坦尼克号乘客可承载量的三分之一。A 选项说如果所有的救生船都装满，救生船的数量就够了，与文中所给信息矛盾。B 选项说可以满足比泰坦尼克号小得多的船的规定，但泰坦尼克号不行，根据课文信息这个结论是正确的。C 选项说是 1894 年由英国贸易部规定的。但文中说英国贸易部只是规定了相当于泰坦尼克号四分之一大小的客轮的救生船数量，对于像泰坦尼克号这么大的船，英国贸易部一直没有修改过时的条例，所以还没有出台相应的规定，而造船者们却死板地遵守了当时的规定，从以上可以看出，文中并没有说泰坦尼克号上的救生船数量是由英国贸易部规定的。D 选项说根据规定本可以承载更多的人，这个选项很具有迷惑性，因为根据文章救生船确实可以承载更多的人的，但由于题目的主语是救生船的数量，与 D 项无法组成一个句意通顺的句子，因此 D 也须排除。正确选项是 B。

37 题：题目说泰坦尼克号是：A 比当时最高的建筑物都高。但文中只是说 she was larger at 269 meters than many of the tallest buildings of the day（她比那个时代很多高的建筑物都高），但并没有说她比当时最高的建筑物都高，因此不能选 A。B 说被分为 16 个防水的舱，这个选项也很具有迷惑性，但文中说船身被分为 16 个舱（the hull was divided into sixteen watertight compartments），而不是整只船，因此排除该项。C 选项说是不会沉没的，明显是错误的。D 选项说是她那个时代科技最为先进的邮轮，与文中 She represented the pinnacle of technological advance at the time. 这句话相照应，因此 D 是正确选项。

Questions 38-40：多项选择题，细节题，考查考生略读、查读和对相关信息分析、综合的能力。

分析：题目说作者提到了一些导致灾难的与不良的沟通相关的因素，让从 8 个备选项中选出 3 个作者提到的选项。

A 项说因为泰坦尼克号行驶太快了，这是船遇难的直接因素。

B 项说因为船上没有要求一直都开着无线电，**这个因素在倒数第二段中提到**，正是由于当时还没有要求 24 小时都开着无线电，才导致在泰坦尼克号刚刚撞上冰山时发出的求救信号没有被离她最近的船及时接收到，船上的人也未能及时去营救遇难的乘客，因此 B **选项是正确选项**。

C 选项说船上的救生船数量不够，这是导致灾难的一个因素，但跟沟通无关，因此不能选该项。

D 选项说泰坦尼克号上的无线电没有 24 小时都开着，这个是事实，但这个因素与灾难无关。

E 选项说关于冰山的警告没有系统的处理，这是作者**在第四段中罗列出**的第一个造成灾难的因素，且这个因素确实是跟沟通有关，正是由于没有系统处理冰山警告信号，没能画出和确定冰山的位置和数量，才导致船长没意识到前方的危险而加快船速，最终导致灾难的发生。

F 选项说加里福尼号上的无线电系统出现故障，而文中根本没有提及。G 选项说泰坦尼克号上的无线电出现故障，文中也未提及。

H 选项说史密斯船长没有给他船上的官员提供足够的信息，这个也正确。在文中的**第八自然段**，提到人们不愿意到救生船上去，因为还坚信泰坦尼克号是不会沉没的，而史密斯船长对人们持有这种态度无动于衷，他并没有把真实的情况告诉他的高级官员们。由于很多人都不愿意上到救生船上去，所以很多的人都丧生了。因此正确选项是 B、E、H。

七 学习提示

从以上的这套模拟试题我们可以看出，雅思阅读题型灵活多样，这是为了保证能全面客观地考查考生的英语阅读水平，但从总体来讲，雅思阅读考查了几项核心阅读能力：**略读、查读、识别转述、区分主题、大意和细节**等。读者可以根据自己这次模拟雅思阅读测试的成绩来分析自己的优势和弱势，在接下来的章节中我们首先进行核心阅读策略和阅读能力的训练。

星期二

词汇的5项处理策略

可以毫不夸张地说，词汇是阅读的命脉。如果词汇量太少，阅读就会举步维艰，相反，如果词汇量丰富，阅读起来就会轻松快捷。然而，词汇量的提高需要日积月累，很多考生由于词汇学习方法不正确，总是事倍功半，甚至望词汇书兴叹，直到放弃背诵词汇。其实，词汇学习并不是那么难，如果方法得当，可以变得很轻松，很有趣。如果你已经掌握了3000左右的单词，通过恰当的方法，让你的词汇量翻一番是很容易的事。

很多考生背诵了大量的词汇，但是在雅思阅读考试时，还会遇到很多生词。也因此变得焦虑，徘徊纠结于那些生词，浪费了大量的考试时间，这样的考试策略是不科学的。其实，在阅读的时候，我们不需要认识所有的文章词汇。有百分之十的生词都不会干扰你做题。所以，考生要练习对阅读中的生词的容忍度和处理生词的技巧，否则，临场时你会因焦虑影响做题速度和准度，这样必然考不出自己的最好水平。下面就是一些最为常见的处理阅读中出现的生词的策略。

一 策略点拨

1. 利用文章后面的生词表（glossary）

雅思阅读测试中，一些比较难的关键词会在文章下面给出。因此当你读到难的词汇时，你可以先看一下后面的词汇表，看是否有自己需要理解的单词。

2. 利用语境提供的线索

文章后的词汇表中列出的词毕竟是有限的。对于词汇表中没有出现的生词，我们首先可以利用语境提供的线索来猜测意思。语境是生词所在的句子、段落。一个单词的意思总是跟它所在的句子及前后的句子紧密相关。当遇到生词时，我们可以先看一下单词所在的句子或段落中是否有相关的解释、定义、例子，或能帮助我们解释生词意思的熟悉的近义词、反义词等，来帮助我们理解该词的意义。常见的语境线索有以下几种。

近义词	例：My opponent's argument is fallacious, *misleading* —*plain wrong*. 假设 fallacious 在这里是个生词，我们可以通过后面的熟悉的单词：misleading, plain wrong 这两个词是并列的同义词，意思都是“错误的”，由此我们可以推理出 fallacious 也是“错误”的意思。
反义词	例：Although some men are loquacious, *others hardly talk at all*. 通过 although 这个连接词，我们知道 loquacious 和后面的 hardly talk at all 的意思正好相反，这样我们就可以推理出 loquacious 的意思可能是“特别爱说话的”。其他的表示相反意义的标志词还有：but, in contrast, however, instead of, unlike, yet 等。

（续）

定义或解释	例：Sedentary individuals, *people who are not very active*, often have diminished health. sedentary 后面的同位短语，为 sedentary 提供了解释，即“不好动的，总是坐着的”。其他的表示定义或解释的标志词还有：is defined as, means 等。
举例	例：Celestial bodies, *such as the sun, moon, and stars,* are governed by predictable laws. 上面句子中的 sun, moon, and stars 为 celestial bodies 提供了解释，即“天体”。其他的标志词还有：for example, for instance, like 等。

有时，我们仅需要根据常识和逻辑来推理出单词的大致意思即可。看下面的例句，请为句中黑体的单词选择合适的意义。

The snake ***slithered*** through the grass. It was hunting.

A．stopped moving

B．slept in the grass

C．ate something

D．moved or traveled

正确的选项是 D。原因在于：

A 不对，因为上面的句子说“through the grass”。through 就意味着 slither 这个词应该是一个动作词。

B 不对，因为后面的一句“It was hunting”。蛇在捕猎的时候是不可能睡觉的。

C 不对，因为蛇捕猎的时候是不吃东西的。

D 是最符合逻辑的一个答案。move 或 travel 都包含了一定的动作在内，所以这个是最接近 slither 原义的单词。

在阅读中，通过语境猜测单词是一种非常有效的策略。但有时我们会发现上下文提供的线索非常少，很难猜出单词的意思。而且如果一篇文章的生词量太多，已经达到严重妨碍我们对文章理解的程度，那么这个策略就不太奏效了。在不能借助词典的情况下，我们可以尝试根据构词法来试着猜出单词的意思。

3．根据构词法

通过构词法，也就是利用词根（root）、词缀（affix）的知识来猜测生词的意思。这对于想扩大词汇量的考生来说也是一种比较有效的途径。在雅思阅读中，考生可能会遇到很多比较长的单词，但我们如果知道单词的词根和词缀的含义，那么把单词各部分的含义组合起来，就不难推断出单词的大致意思。比如如果已经知道 comprehend 这个词，那么当看到 incomprehensible 时，就可以根据我们熟悉的单词部分的意思推断出它的意思。in-经常用来表示否定的前缀，如 incorrect，inaccurate，而-ible 是表示形容词的后缀，因而 incomprehensible 的意思是“不能理解的”。再比如，若我们知道“anti-”作为前缀是表示“opposite”的意思，而“-pathy”作为词根表示“feeling”的意思，那么这两部分合起来 antipathy 就是“against the feeling”的意思。这时我们就不难推断出 antipathy 的意思是“反感”。同理，单词 sympathy 可以分为两个部分“sym-”和“-pathy”，“sym-”是“together”的意思，与“-pathy”合起来就是“feeling together”的意思，即“同情心”的意思。

4. 特殊字体词处理策略

如果你遇到了在一起出现的几个首字母大写的单词，如 Sergio Pellis of Lethbridge University，那么它就是个专有名词，在这里你不需要知道 Sergio，Pellis 或 Lethbridge 是什么意思，只需要知道它是某个大学的名称就行了。遇到这样的专有名词，你可以把它们当成一个整体来读，只需要粗略地了解知道它们表示的是机构名、地名，还是某个团体的名称即可。如果是斜体的单词，那么它可能是某本书、杂志、电影的名称或某个专业术语，你也不用了解它们的意思，只需要知道它们代表什么事物即可。

5. 判断重要与否

当雅思阅读考试遇到生词而上述策略都无法运用时，你也不用着急。因为考试本身并没有要求你能理解文章中的每一句话，每个单词。在考试时间有限的情况下，如果你遇到的生词跟文后的题目无关，或者那个生词并不影响你回答某个题目的话，你可以跳过不管。因为，在绝大多数情况下，生僻词汇不是考点，也就不是答案所在的地方，所以考生大可忽略不计。

以上情况都是在考场上应对雅思阅读测试的有效策略。考生在准备考试的时候，要反复练习这些策略，达到炉火纯青的状态，在考试的时候就会非常自然地使用这些策略，也就上升为一种生词处理能力了，只有这样才能真正节省考试时间。当然，这些策略的使用，是基于考生识别大部分词汇的基础之上的，所以，考生在考前应该尽可能多地扩充词汇量，减少考试碰到生词的可能性，唯有这样才是最为安全的。而且，雅思考试只是出国的第一步，考生在通过考试出国后，面临着生存和学习的压力，需要更多的词汇来应对，因此，考生应该借雅思考试这个东风，真正提高自己的语言水平，为出国后的学习生活打下坚实的基础。

二 专题演练

练习 1：请为黑体的单词选择合适的释义。

1. The tiger's **roar** could be heard in villages far away.
   A. food a tiger eats
   B. a tiger's dream
   C. a tiger's ear
   D. a sound a tiger makes
2. The thought of eating a rat is **abhorrent** to most people.
   A. fun, lively
   B. horrible, repugnant
   C. delicious, tasty
   D. sweet, sugary
3. My **absent-minded** teacher loses his keys, his book and his chalk almost every day!
   A. be hateful
   B. not pay attention
   C. be intelligent
   D. not like someone

4. You can trust the salesmen at that store because they always conduct business in an **aboveboard** manner.
   A. honestly, openly
   B. sneaky, dishonest
   C. horrible, repugnant
   D. strange, unusual
5. Petra has so many friends because she is a **gregarious** person.
   A. introverted, self-contained
   B. shy, quiet
   C. friendly, outgoing
   D. rude, hostile
6. The lovely **egret** is in danger of extinction because clothing manufacturers use their long, beautiful tail feathers to make ladies' hats. What is an egret?
   A. a small child
   B. a type of food
   C. a sound a tiger makes
   D. a type of bird
7. I can't believe it! Right in the middle of our conversation, Peter turned around **abruptly** and walked out of the room!
   A. formally
   B. slowly, in no hurry
   C. suddenly, without notice
   D. quietly, in an unusual manner
8. After the harvest, we had an **abundant** amount of apples. We made apple pie, apple sauce, and apple juice because we had so many apples!
   A. a shortage
   B. not enough
   C. very red
   D. plentiful
9. When Sara was sick, her voice was almost **inaudible**. We couldn't hear what she was trying to say clearly.
   A. very loud, easy to hear
   B. very soft, hard to hear
   C. very strange, uncommon
   D. very shy, introverted
10. The hill was too **arduous** for us to climb. We had to walk our bicycles up the hill.
   A. tall, sharp
   B. fun, exciting

C. easy, not challenging

D. difficult, steep

练习 2：根据语境猜测黑体单词的意思，并说明语境提供的是哪一种类型的线索。.

1. The girl who used to be very **vociferous** doesn't talk much anymore.
2. **Pedagogical** institutions, including high schools, kindergartens, and colleges, require community support to function efficiently.
3. He was so **parsimonious** that he refused to give his own sons the few pennies they needed to buy pencils for school. It truly hurt him to part with his money.
4. His **pertinacity**, or stubbornness, is the cause of most of his trouble.
5. Rather than involved in **clandestine** meetings, they did everything quite openly.
6. **Ecclesiastics**, such as priests, ministers, and pastors, should set models of behavior for their congregants.
7. The girl was **churlish**—rude, sullen and absolutely ill-mannered.
8. Because the **conflagration** was aided by wind, it was so destructive that every building in the area was completely burned to the ground.

练习 3：请用已给出的词根、词缀把下面的单词补充完整。

corp = body	cred = belief	dis = without, apart
re = again, back	temp = time	viv, vit = life

1. She was openly in ______ ulous at her sister's stories about UFOs and alien abductions.
2. A supporter of animal rights, the supermodel ______ avowed her connection to the designer who decorated his fall creations with fur.
3. The hope is that the new arena will ______ alize the community.
4. High-calorie, high-fat fast foods are being blamed for the sharp increase in the number of Americans who are ______ ulent.
5. Hip-hugger jeans were popular in the 1960s, but they have once again become a con ______ orary fashion.
6. People who are outgoing and ______ acious are usually popular party guests.
7. He did not approve of ______ oral punishment, so he never spanked his son.
8. Our neighbors are con ______ ial people who socialize with their friends every chance they get.
9. Among his con ______ oraries, the writer was widely respected, but the generations that followed did not share the same enthusiasm for his work.
10. A ______ ible website will always provide the author's name and the sources of the information given.

三 专题答案

练习 1：1～5：DBBAC　6～10：DCDBD

练习 2：

1. type of context clue—antonym
   definition of vociferous—talkative; outspoken
2. type of context clue—example
   definition of pedagogical—having to do with teaching
3. type of context clue—explanation
   definition of parsimonious—stingy; tightfisted
4. type of context clue—synonym
   definition of pertinacity—mulish; stubborn
5. type of context clue—antonym
   definition of clandestine—secret; hidden
6. type of context clue—example
   definition of ecclesiastics—member of the clergy
7. type of context clue—synonym
   definition of sullen—rude
8. type of context clue—explanation
   definition of conflagration—fire

练习 3：1. cred　2. dis　3. vit　4. corp　5. temp
6. viv　7. corp　8. viv　9. temp　10. cred

星期三

难句的处理策略

雅思阅读文章的特点之一是长句多且句子结构复杂，也是雅思阅读的难点之一。英语长句的特点是修饰成分比较多，若抓不住主干、理不清句子各成分之间的关系便无法理解句子的意思。另外由于英汉两种语言在表达上的差异，英语中某些特殊结构的句子也容易造成理解上的困难。下面为大家把在雅思阅读中经常遇到的这些长、难句的类型作一下总结和分析，帮助考生排除这些阅读理解的障碍。

一 策略点拨

在分析雅思阅读难句之前，我们先来回顾一下英语中的基本句型。首先来看下面 5 个英语短句：

1）She left.

2）He opened the door.

3）John is a teacher.

4）I gave Mary a book.

5）Who made you cry?

以上是**英语简单句的 5 种最基本的类型**。每个简单句可以分为两个大部分，即主语（位于句子开头的名词或代词）和谓语（句子除主语外的其他部分）。其中谓语中最为重要的是谓语动词。谓语动词的特征是有时态、人称等方面的限制，所以又被称为限定动词。理解英语句子的关键就是要找到主语和相应的谓语动词。以上的句子之所以成为简单句，并不是因为它们简短，而是因为它们只包含了一套主谓。一个简单句也可能变得很长，主要是因为主语和谓语又添加了其他的修饰成分，比如，我们来看下面的句子：

例句：Lying exposed without its blanket of snow, the **ice** on the river **melts** quickly under the warm March sun.

我们把上面句子中的修饰成分都去掉，则变成 ice melts，成为一个只有主语和谓语的简单句。而这个句子中逗号前面的部分和 on the river 都是来修饰 the ice，quickly under the warm March sun 则是来修饰 melts 的。

我们再来看下面两个简单句：

1）I tried to speak Spanish.

2）My friend tried to speak English.

把这两个句子合并即成为 I speak Spanish, and my friend speaks English. 像这样连接并列

的两个分句的句子，叫**并列句（compound sentence）**，and 被称为**并列连词**。连接并列句的连词还有 but，or 等。去掉了中间的连词，并列句中的任何一个分句都可以独立成句。从上面的分析可以看出理解并列句，只要找到中间的连词，然后分别找并列的分句的主干即可。

我们再接着看下面两个简单句：

例句：Abraham Lincoln was born in the house. The house is still standing.

如果把这两个句合起来就是：The house which Abraham Lincoln was born in is still standing。这个句子中的 which Abraham Lincoln was born in 是来修饰主语 the house 的，它的作用相当于一个形容词，不能独立成句，因而是一个附属从句。而像这样包含两套（及以上）主谓关系的句子被称为**复合句（complex sentence）**。由于复合句中附属从句的某个成分还可以再有别的从句来修饰，而且与汉语表达习惯不同，作修饰成分的从句都是后置，所以容易造成理解上的困难。理解这类句子的要点在于，先抓住主句的主干，当句内出现 **which, that, who, whom, when, why, what , where** 之类的从属连接词时，往往标志着附属从句的出现，这时候**把出现的限定动词和它们相应的主语相匹配然后分层理出它们的关系即可**。我们来看下面一个典型的比较长的复合句：

例句：Behaviorists suggest /that the child / <u>who</u> **is raised** in an environment / <u>where</u> there **are** many stimuli / <u>which</u> **develop** his or her capability for appropriate response / will **experience** greater intellectual development.

这个句子包含 30 个单词，且修饰成分众多。因此第一步就是先找成套出现的主语和谓语动词（用黑体来表示）。最先出现的主句中的 Behaviorists suggest，that 表明后面是一个附属从句。The child 后面是 who，说明又有一个修饰 child 的从句出现，依次看下去，直到看完 which 引导的从句后，我们才看到一个限定动词 will experience。由于之前出现的从句都有自己的主语和谓语动词，因此我们可以确定 will experience 是 the child 的谓语动词。以上这个长句子包含以下几套主谓：

1）behaviorists suggest

2）child will experience greater intellectual development

3）the child is raised in an environment

4）there are many stimuli in the environment

5）the stimuli develop the child's capability for appropriate response

其中，5）来修饰 4）中的 stimuli，4）又是来修饰 3）中的 environment，3）又是来修饰 2）中的 the child，而 2）又是 1）中的 suggest 的内容。由此我们可以看出，像这样的复合句之所以理解起来难度较大是英语的表达习惯造成的，即做修饰成分的从句后置，从句又可以由别的从句来修饰，且中间往往使用从属连接词连接起来，这跟汉语中顺序用短句表达修饰成分的习惯正好相反。因此，**理解这样的句子的根本在于能够辨别清楚主句、从句以及它们之间的修饰关系**。而辨别主从句的出发点在于找到它们各自的谓语动词，并清楚从句的起始点。

在雅思阅读中，较为常见的则是并列复合句，由连词 and，but，or 连接的两个及以上的并列句，其中至少有一个是复合句，如：The package arrived in the morning, but the courier left before I could check the contents。这个句子的 but 前的分句是一个只包含一套主谓的简单句，而 but 后面的分句是包含两套主谓的复合句，因此这个句子是一个并列复合句。理解这类的句子我们应该以连词为分界点，其他部分的分析方法跟理解复合句类似。

下面对在剑桥雅思阅读中出现的一些典型的带从句的结构比较复杂的句子进行分析。在下面的分析中，黑体表示出现的谓语动词，下划线表示从属连词。

1. 带从句的句子

①Children / <u>who</u> **work** on the streets / **are** generally involved in unskilled, labour-intensive tasks / <u>which</u> **require** long hours/, such as shining shoes, carrying goods, guarding or washing cars, and informal trading.

步骤：Step1：找出引导从句的标志词（句中下划横线的词）；

Step2：找出动词（句中以黑体表示）；

Step3：找出各个动词的相应的主语（顺序原则）；

Step4：确定从句与主句的关系。

分析：例句①后面的 who 表明是修饰 children 的一个从句，从句中的谓语动词是 work，对应了主语 who，而后面的动词 are 由此可以判断是 children 的谓语动词。在 task 后面又出现了一个 which 引导的从句，其相应的谓语动词是 require。由此看出，这句话包含以下 3 个简单句：

1）Children work on the streets.

2）Children are involved in tasks.

3）The tasks require long hours.

其中 1）和 3）分别是修饰 children 和 tasks 的从句，它们的作用相当于形容词，因此又被称为形容词性从句。

有的形容词性从句前会省略引导词，特别是当这个从句所修饰词在句中做动词的宾语时，如下句：

②People **worry** / <u>that</u> the endless rise in the amount of stuff/ everyone **throws away/** will **cause** the world to run out of places to dispose of waste.

分析：主句中的谓语动词 worry 后的连接词 that 表明后面引导的是 worry 的宾语从句。宾语从句中的主语中心词是 rise，接着可以发现限定动词 throws away，但把它断定为 rise 的谓语动词的话则不合逻辑，因为 throws away 说明它的主语应该是一个有生命的物体。按照英语的表达顺序，我们可以看到距离 throws away 最近的代词 everyone，由此可以判断，everyone 是 throws away 的主语，由此得出从句 everyone throws away，而这个从句正是 stuff 的定语从句。rise 的谓语动词则是后面的 will cause。这句话包含 3 个简单句：

1）People worry.

2）The rise in the amount of stuff will cause the world to run out of places to dispose of waste.

3）Everyone throws away stuff.

其中 3）是 1）的宾语，而 2）是 3）中 stuff 的修饰语。

③IQ could **help** to bridge the gap and resolve the tremendous uncertainty about how much of what we **are** seeing **is** natural capriciousness and how much **is** the consequence of human activity.

分析：主句的谓语动词是 help。句子后半部分由 and 连接的并列的两个 how much 表明了从句的出现，同时我们还注意到在第一个 how much 后出现了 what，这说明第一个从句内部又出现了一个从句。这之后的限定动词分别是 are，seeing 之后的 is，和第二个 how much 之后的 is。第二个 is 的主语很好确定，就是前面的 how much。那么如何确定 are 和 is 的主语呢？这时，我们还是依照就近原则，即当顺序出现了限定动词后，通常第一个限定动词的主语是它左边离它最近的那个名词或代词，因此 are 的主语是 what。而第一个 is 的主语还是 how much 的从句 what we are seeing，翻译成汉语即为“我们所看到的”，它的作用相当于一个名词，因此又被称为名词性从句。

④One form of pollution—the release of greenhouse gases that **causes** global warming – **does appear** to be a phenomenon that **is going to extend** well into our future, but its total impact **is** unlikely to pose a devastating problem.

上句是一个并列复合句，因为我们可以发现连接并列分句的 but 和 but 前的句子中的两个从属连接词 that。四个限定动词分别是 causes，does appear，is going to 和 is，说明这个句子包含四套主谓。根据就近原则，两个 that 前的名词分别是从句的逻辑主语，这两个从句也分别来修饰 that 前的名词。而 does appear 的主语则正是主句中的 one form of pollution。这样一来，整句话的内部关系就很明朗。

2. 带非谓语动词短语的句子

非谓语动词，顾名思义，即不能做句子的谓语动词。非谓语动词有三种形式，即 to + 动词原形、动词的-ing 形式和动词的-ed 形式，这三种也就是常说的动词不定式、动名词和分词（包括现在分词和过去分词）。它们不能做句子的谓语，但可以做谓语之外的其他句子成分，而且可以像谓语动词一样有自己的宾语并由其他成分修饰。由于不能做谓语，它们不像句子的谓语动词带有自己的主语，但它们绝大多数都有自己的逻辑主语。非谓语动词的使用可以使句子表达简洁的同时承载更多的信息，但非谓语动词的使用在某些情况下会干扰我们辨别句子的谓语动词，因而容易造成理解上的困难。下面是对几个例句的分析。在下面的分析中，依然统一用黑体表示谓语动词，用方框表示容易引起理解困难的非谓语动词。

① The efforts [to improve] the efficiency of the existing transport services **were not** very successful because the motorized vehicles in the district **broke down** and there **were** no resources to repair them.

分析：例句①的主语 efforts 后没有马上出现它的谓语动词，而是一个比较长的动词不定式短语（用方框来表示），而且这个动词不定式短语比较长，主要原因是因为它的宾语 efficiency 同时又被一个 of 的介词短语来修饰。这个动词不定式短语是 efforts 的后置修饰语，它的作用相当于一个省略了 which is 的定语从句。主语的谓语动词 were not 位于不定式短语的后面。主句的后面又有一个表示原因的并列从句，它们分别有自己的谓语动词。

策略：当主语有后置的动词不定式短语修饰时，为了理解上的方便，可以先跳过不管，直接找到主语的谓语动词，然后再回过头来读这个修饰语。当然，随着阅读量的加大，考生应该慢慢学会顺序阅读这种名词短语，并能迅速找到谓语动词。

② A representative sample of language, compiled for the purpose of linguistic analysis, **is** known as a corpus.

分析：例句②是个简单句，原因是只有一个谓语动词，方框中是一个过去分词短语，我们也可以把它看成是省略了 which is 的定语从句，而 compiled 的逻辑宾语则是它前面的名词短语的中心词 sample。整句话的意思是：为了语法分析而编撰的具有代表性的语言样本被称为语料库。做修饰语的分词短语由于被逗号隔开，所以不易与句子中的谓语动词相混淆，但在某些情况下我们则需要仔细辨别，特别是当主语的谓语动词也是-ed 形式时，如例句③。

③ A number of techniques developed since the 1950s have placed the study of these subjects on a sounder and more objective footing.

分析：单独来看，例句③中的第一个动词 developed 和第二个动词 have placed 都可以做限定动词，但它们当中只能有一个是主动词。在没有从属连接词又没有其他名词的情况下，我们一般把主语后的第一个动词看成是修饰主语的过去分词，第二个动词看成是主语的谓语动词。

④ Often, when studying their mother tongue, linguists **act** as their own informants, judging the ambiguity, acceptability, or other properties or utterances against their own intuitions.

分析：例句④有两个现在分词短语，它们的逻辑主语都是 linguists，并且它们都可以用从句或分句来表示。第一个现在分词短语相当于一个时间状语从句，when studying = when they study；而第二个现在分词短语则相当于一个并列的分句，即 judging = and they judge。

⑤ Inuit families going off on snowmobiles to prepare their summer hunting camps **have found** themselves cut off from home by a sea of mud, following early thaws.

分析：例句⑤中出现了 3 组非谓语动词。第一个现在分词短语 going off 相当于 who went off，后面的 to prepare 表示行为的目的。cut off 是过去分词，标志是后面有一个表示被动的 by。在这里 cut off 不再是一个省略了 who was 的定语从句，而是对 themselves 的补充。

3. 带插入语的句子

在雅思阅读中，很多句子中间会插入其他词、短语或从句，表示一些附加解释、说明或总结或表示说话者的态度和看法，或仅仅是承上启下，使句子与前面的语句衔接的更紧密一些。这些被称为插入语。多数插入语位于主语和谓语动词之间，因而对考生的理解造成一定的干扰，特别是比较长的插入语。

① It's no surprise that Edward Wilson, *in his essay, "In the company of ants"*, advises readers who ask what to do with the ants in their kitchen to: "Watch where you step. Be careful of little lives."

分析：例句①中的插入成分用斜体已经表示出来，说明后面那句话的出处。

② An important principle is that all corpora, *whatever their size*, are inevitably limited in their coverage, and always need to be supplemented by data derived from the intuitions of native speakers of the language, through either introspection or experimentation.

分析： 例句②中的插入成分是 whatever their size，是一个状语从句，表示作者的评论。

从以上的例句可以看出，尽管句中有的插入语比较长，但通常被逗号、破折号或句子的其他部分隔开，而且由于和句子其他成分没有直接的关系，建议考生先跳过去不管，等理解整句话之后再回过头来看该插入语。

4. 带复杂名词结构的句子

英语中长句中的名词修饰语众多，这些修饰语可能有些是前置的，有些是后置的，但往往是后置的修饰语容易造成理解上的困难。除了上面所分析的定语从句和过去分词做名词的后置修饰语，还有介词短语等。

① Recent work on the problem of <u>when</u> people first **entered** the America **is** an example of the value of these new techniques.

分析： 首先找出句中出现的从属连接词 when，然后找出限定动词，分别是 entered 和 is。其中 entered 是从句 when 引导的句子的谓语动词，is 是主句的谓语动词。而谓语动词前面是主句的主语，我们可以看出这个名词短语非常长，不仅如此，is 后的名词短语也比较长。遇到这样的例子就可以先把名词短语的修饰成分去掉，找出它的中心词。如例句①，去掉名词前后的修饰语之后，就变成 work is an example，成为一个非常简洁的句子，也很好理解。但这只是一种策略，我们理清句子的主干后，还是要理解名词短语的意思。像本句中的 recent work on the problem of when people first entered the America 按照汉语的表达习惯则是"对于人们何时进入美国的问题的最近的一项研究"，即和英语的表达习惯正好相反，而 an example of the value of these new techniques 则是"这些体现新技巧的价值的一个例子"。

② For example, one graphic illustration to <u>which</u> children might readily **relate is** the estimate <u>that</u> rainforests **are** being destroyed at *a rate equivalent to one thousand football fields every forty minutes*—about the duration of a normal classroom period.

分析： 句中斜体部分是一个以 rate 为中心的名词短语，rate 后面的 equivalent to one thousand football fields every forty minutes 是一个后置的以 equivalent 为中心的形容词短语，为了理解上的方便，我们也可以把它看成是一个省略了 which is 的定语从句。整个句子有两个从句信号词：which 和 that，三个谓语动词 relate，is 和 are。主句的结构是 one graphic illustration is the estimate。第一个从句 to which children might readily relate 是 illustration 的定语从句，that 后的从句是对 estimate 的解释，因而是一个同位语从句，且最后为了进一步解释又用破折号连接了一个同位语从句 about the duration of a normal classroom period。

5. 比较句

在比较句中，为了避免重复，常用代词指代之前或之后的成分。但如果指代词和所指的成分相隔较远，则会造成理解上的障碍。

① Bekoff studied coyote pups at play and found that the kind of behaviour involved was markedly more variable and unpredictable than **that** of adults.

分析：句尾出现了 that of adults。that 指代的是 found 的宾语从句里的主语 the kind of behaviour。但这种行为又是指哪种行为呢？句子开头就写明了 coyote pups at play，因此在这里是 coyote pups' behaviour at play 和成年的 coyote 的行为作比较。

② While the global economy has been expanding at a bit over 3% a year, the volume of trade has been rising at a compound annual rate of about twice **that**.

分析：that 很明显是指前面提到的 global economy 的增长速度 3%。

③ Yet no **such** effect had been detected in any of the ingenious and delicate experiments that physicists had devised: the velocity of light did not vary.

分析：such effect 指代后面的 the velocity of light did not vary。但因为指代词 such 和它后面所指代的内容相隔较远，因而容易造成理解上的困难。

④ To kill weed which may sprawl rampantly among crops in the first several years, effective weedicide is needed to play the same role as ploughing fields **does** to eliminate weed.

分析：the same 指的是 to eliminate weed。

二 专题演练

练习 1：判断下列句子是属于简单句、并列句、复合句，还是并列复合句，并为每个句子选择合适的选项。

1. Pauline and Bruno have a big argument every summer over where they should spend their summer vacation.
   A. Simple Sentence
   B. Compound Sentence
   C. Complex Sentence
   D. Compound-Complex Sentence
2. Pauline loves to go to the beach and spend her days sunbathing.
   A. Simple Sentence
   B. Compound Sentence
   C. Complex Sentence
   D. Compound-Complex Sentence
3. Bruno, on the other hand, likes the view that he gets from the log cabin up in the mountains, and he enjoys hiking in the forest.
   A. Simple Sentence
   B. Compound Sentence
   C. Complex Sentence
   D. Compound-Complex Sentence
4. Pauline says there is nothing relaxing about chopping wood, swatting mosquitoes, and cooking over a woodstove.
   A. Simple Sentence

B. Compound Sentence
C. Complex Sentence
D. Compound-Complex Sentence

5. Bruno dislikes sitting on the beach; he always gets a nasty sunburn.
   A. Simple Sentence
   B. Compound Sentence
   C. Complex Sentence
   D. Compound-Complex Sentence
6. Bruno tends to get bored sitting on the beach, watching the waves, getting sand in his swimsuit, and reading detective novels for a week.
   A. Simple Sentence
   B. Compound Sentence
   C. Complex Sentence
   D. Compound-Complex Sentence
7. This year, after a lengthy, noisy debate, they decided to take separate vacations.
   A. Simple Sentence
   B. Compound Sentence
   C. Complex Sentence
   D. Compound-Complex Sentence
8. Bruno went to the White Mountains of New Hampshire, and Pauline went to Cape Cod.
   A. Simple Sentence
   B. Compound Sentence
   C. Complex Sentence
   D. Compound-Complex Sentence
9. Although they are 250 miles apart, they keep in constant contact on the internet.
   A. Simple Sentence
   B. Compound Sentence
   C. Complex Sentence
   D. Compound-Complex Sentence
10. Bruno took the desktop computer that he uses at work, and Pauline sits on the beach with her laptop computer, which she connects to the internet with a cellular phone.
   A. Simple Sentence
   B. Compound Sentence
   C. Complex Sentence
   D. Compound-Complex Sentence

练习 2：找出下列句子中主句的主语、谓语和宾语（如果有的话）的中心词，并用横线表示。

1. On 2nd August 1999, a particularly hot day in the town of Cirencester in the UK, a large pane of toughened glass in the roof of a shopping centre at Bishops Walk shattered without warning and

fell from its frame.

2. Countries all across the world are actively promoting their 'wilderness' regions – such as mountains, Arctic lands, deserts, small islands and wetlands – to high-spending tourists.
3. The role definitions of, say, a film star or bank manager, are also fairly clearly defined in cultural terms, too clearly perhaps.
4. Looking at role ambiguity from the other side, from the point of view of the members of the role set, lack of clarity in the role of the focal person can cause insecurity, lack of confidence, irritation and even anger among members of his role set.
5. However, the average number of people in a car on the freeway in Los Angeles, which is 1.3, has been falling steadily.

练习 3：把下列复合句改写成若干简单句。

1. The shallowest tunnels belong to a much smaller Spanish species that buries dung in chambers that hang like fruit from the branches of a pear tree.
2. He has the focal role and can be regarded as sitting in the middle of a group of people, with whom he interacts in some way in that situation.
3. Ecologists have assumed that tropical ecosystems were shaped entirely by natural forces and they have focused their research on habitats they believe have escaped human influence.
4. Again, a series of acquisitions might represent a decade's fieldwork documenting social experience as expressed in the varieties of clothing and jewellery styles, tents and camel trappings from various Middle Eastern countries, or in the developing preferences in personal adornment and dress from Papua New Guinea.
5. In Britain, for example, the dull weather of winter drastically cuts down the amount of sunlight that is experienced which strongly affects some people.
6. Psychologists have conducted studies showing that people become less skeptical and more optimistic when the weather is sunny.
7. It seems that time cues provided by the changing lengths of day and night trigger changes in animals' behavior – changes that are needed to cope with cycle of the seasons.
8. However, the belief that rain and murky weather make people more unhappy is borne out by a study in Belgium, which showed that a telephone counseling service gets more telephone calls from people with suicidal feelings when it rains.

三 专题答案

练习 1：1～5：CADCB　6～10：AABCD

练习 2：找出下列句子中主句的主语、谓语和宾语（如果有的话）的中心词，并用横线表示。

1. On 2nd August 1999, a particularly hot day in the town of Cirencester in the UK, a large pane of toughened <u>glass</u> in the roof of a shopping centre at Bishops Walk <u>shattered</u> without warning and

fell from its frame.

2. Countries all across the world are actively promoting their "wilderness" regions – such as mountains, Arctic lands, deserts, small islands and wetlands – to high-spending tourists.
3. The role definitions of, say, a film star or bank manager, are also fairly clearly defined in cultural terms, too clearly perhaps.
4. Looking at role ambiguity from the other side, from the point of view of the members of the role set, lack of clarity in the role of the focal person can cause insecurity, lack of confidence, irritation and even anger among members of his role set.
5. However, the average number of people in a car on the freeway in Los Angeles, which is 1.3, has been falling steadily.

练习 3：把下列复合句改写成若干简单句。

1. The shallowest tunnels belong to a much smaller Spanish species. The Spanish species buries dung in chambers. The chambers hang like fruit from the branches of a pear tree.
2. He has the focal role. He can be regarded as sitting in the middle of a group of people. He interacts with the group of people in some way in that situation.
3. Ecologists have assumed. Tropical ecosystems were shaped entirely by natural forces. Ecologists believe. Some habitats have escaped human influence. They have focused their research on these habitats.
4. Again, a series of acquisitions might represent a decade's fieldwork. The one decade's fieldwork documented social experience. The experience was expressed in the varieties of clothing and jewellery styles, tents and camel trappings from various Middle Eastern Countries. Or it was expressed in the developing preferences in personal adornment and dress from Papua New Guinea.
5. In Britain, for example, the dull weather of winter drastically cuts down the amount of sunlight. The sunlight is experienced. This thing strongly affects some people.
6. Psychologists have conducted studies. The studies showed. People become less skeptical and more optimistic when the weather is sunny.
7. It seems. Some time cues provided by the changing lengths of day and night. These time cues trigger changes in animals' behavior. These changes are needed to cope with cycle of the seasons.
8. Rain and murky weather make people more unhappy. This is a belief. This belief is borne out by a study in Belgium. The study showed. Some people have suicidal feelings when it rains. a telephone counseling service gets more telephone calls from these people.

星期四 学会区分主题、大意和细节

主题（topic）是文章或段落讨论的话题，往往以名词或名词短语的形式出现。而大意（the main idea）是整篇文章或文中某个段落的中心思想，往往以表达一个命题的句子的形式出现。细节（the supporting details）则是对大意起说明、阐释、举例等支撑性作用的段落中的其他部分。主题、大意和细节之间的关系就如一棵树的名字、它的树干和枝叶一样。

一 策略点拨

阅读一篇文章或其中的某个段落，首先需要知道这篇文章或某个段落是围绕什么而展开的，进而了解作者所要表达的主要意思，这也往往是作者想要表达的最重要的信息，细节则可以帮助考生更清楚、全面、深入地理解作者的主旨和意图。区分大意和细节是雅思阅读重点考察的阅读技能之一，某些题型如找标题（list of headings）和完成摘要题就着重考察考生的这个能力。

那么该如何确定文章或段落的主题，区分大意与细节呢？例如：

I have many hobbies, such as playing tennis, collecting stamps, reading novels, and so on.

在上面这一句话中，可以很快看出讨论的核心是作者的 hobbies，这也是该句的主题。而这个句子的前半句提到作者有很多 hobbies，但具体是什么呢？后半句给出了这些 hobbies 的具体内容，因而 hobbies 和后面提到的 playing tennis, collecting stamps, reading novels 等是概括和具体的关系，这也是在单个句子的范围内大意与细节的体现。理解了主题、大意和细节的基本关系，考生还需要进一步能够在阅读文章时找出段落的主题、区分大意和细节，这不但有助于从宏观上把握作者观点的发展和全文的整体脉络，还可以帮助我们极大地提高阅读的效率，因为在有限的阅读时间内可以学会有选择地阅读，对于不太重要的细节可以跳读，而对于包含文章大意的句子则要精读、细读。

1. 确定主题

段落的主题就好比车轮的车轴，因而若要确定主题，你可以试着问自己这样一个问题“这个段落是关于什么的？”，或者寻找段落中反复提到的事物是什么。

为了让考生更好地理解主题、大意和细节的关系，我们先来看一个简单的段落：

The Statue of Liberty is visited by thousands of people every year. The Statue of Liberty is a 151-foot statue of a woman holding a book and a torch. It is located on an island in New York Harbor. It was a gift of friendship from the people of France. It has become a universal symbol of freedom.

很显然，本段的主题是“the Statue of Liberty”，因为其他句子都是围绕它展开的，而且这个字眼在段落中出现的频率也很高。

2. 辨别大意

段落大意往往是以主题为核心的一个陈述，它传达了段落中最主要也是最重要的信息。很多情况下，包含文章主题的那句话也传达了文章的大意或主旨（main idea），而这句话也被称为“主题句”（topic sentence）。主题句相比段落中的其他属于支撑性细节的句子更加概括，在议论性的文章当中，它往往表达了作者对某样事物的观点或印象。

例如：

There are several events that can change the Earth's surface very quickly. Volcanoes can erupt and spread lava, rock and ash for several miles. Earthquakes can leave large cracks in the Earth's surface.

第一句出现“several events”就比较概括，因为单读这一句我们不知道都是哪些具体的“events”，后面的修饰成分“that can change the Earth's surface very quickly”，我们也不知道是如何“change the Earth's surface”以及如何地“very quickly”。而后面两句则是对前面提到这些问题的回答。

练一练： 试着找出下面段落的主题句：

Consumers concerned about the hazards or noise can reduce noise pollution in many ways. They can purchase noisy products such as garbage disposals and lawn mowers with reduced noise levels. They can also use sound-absorbing materials in their home. Carpeting can be installed instead of hard flooring, and cork and fabric can be used in rooms that tend to be noisy. Also, people can become less noisy themselves. They can learn to avoid shouting, to close doors without slamming them, and to play radios, TV sets, and stereos at moderate levels.

我们可以看到上段第一句后面的句子都是对“many ways”的具体说明和阐释。第一句最为概括，它统领、总结了段落中其他部分的信息，因而这句话就是文章的主题句也是文章的大意。许多段落的主题句都位于段首，但也并不总是这样，段落的主题句有时会出现在段中或段尾，或在段首和段尾都出现。

如果主题句出现在段落中间，则其之前的部分则可能是一些背景性的导入，或作者为了引起读者的兴趣而故意先抑后扬，也或者是与上一段的大意有关的起承上启下作用的一句话。出现在段中或段尾的主题句，往往会由一些转折性或结论性的词汇引入，如 **however, but, yet, hence, thus, therefore** 等。我们再看下面一个段落：

The physical complaints of neurotics – people who are overly anxious, pessimistic, hostile, or tense – were once largely ignored by physician. Many doctors believed that the frequent complaint of neurotic were exaggerations. However, new research shows that neurotics are more likely to have physical problems. Specifically, researchers found neurotics stand a grater chance of having five particular ailments: arthritis, asthma, ulcers, headaches, and heart disease. In addition, there is evidence that people who are pessimistic in their teens and twenties are more likely to become ill or die in their forties.

主题句是第三句。前两句是对neurotics以及过去医生们对这种问题的态度的背景性介绍，后面则是对新的研究发现的进一步介绍。

上面的段落的大意都比较明显，直接就包含在主题句之中，但有时段落的大意比较暗隐，这种情况下就需要把所有的细节结合起来进行推理和概括，我们在以后的章节再专门讨论这个问题。

3. 认识细节

支撑性细节帮助我们全面、深入理解段落的一些事实、数据、例子等，它们是对段落大意的阐释、说明、解释、描写、延伸和例证等。简单地说，支撑性细节就是回答与文章大意有关的 who，what，when，where，why 和 how。根据功能来分，支撑性细节通常有以下几种：

（1）举例

例：Setting unrealistic goals. **For example**, you just bought a computer and you want to learn a program by tomorrow.

（2）比较

例：Skilled college students are **like** the unskilled students in their desire for a diploma.

（3）对比

例：**In contrast**, his successor Lyndon Baines Johnson is often remembered as something of a buffoon.

（4）数据

例：**75 percent of** the students who do not attend class regularly receive grades of C or worse.

（5）图表

例：**Figure 9-1** is one type of graph.

（6）引言

例：Professor Smith admits, **“I tell students they don’t need to attend my class if they don’t want to. I know, however, that if they don’t come, they won’t pass.”**

（7）描写

例：The students took the exam from the professor’s hand, quickly looked at the grade, gave a sigh or relief and began to smile.

根据与大意之间的关系，支撑性细节可以分为主要细节（major details）和次要细节（minor details）。主要细节直接来支撑段落的大意，而次要细节是主要细节的延伸、解释和说明，它们比主要细节更为具体，用来间接地支撑段落的大意。我们来看下面的一个段落：

①Neighborhood watch programs are good for everyone. ②One reason for this is that neighborhood watches unite neighbors in a common goal. ③Neighbors work together to protect each other. ④One family’s security becomes everyone’s concern. ⑤Another reason is that neighborhood watches reduce crime in a couple of ways. ⑥Posted signs act as deterrents to criminals. ⑦Neighbors in these areas are more likely to report any suspicious persons or activities. ⑧And finally, watch programs keep neighbors alert. ⑨Because neighbors meet regularly, everyone is more aware of events, rules, or changes in the community.

以上的段落中的句子①是主题句，也是本段的大意。接着主要细节分别是：句子②、句子⑤和句子⑧，它们从不同角度为主题句中的观点“good for everyone”来提供原因。而次要细节则是分别位于句子②、⑤、⑧后面的部分，它们的作用是为主要细节提供进一步的支持和阐释。比如第一个主要细节中提到“unite neighbors in a common goal”，我们单看到这一句还是不知道这里所谓的“common goal”究竟指的是什么。而后面的“Neighbors work together to protect each other. One family's security becomes everyone's concern.”则提供了进一步的阐释。

从上面的段落中我们也可以发现，支撑性细节前面常出现一些连接性词汇，它们把细节联结成一个支撑段落大意的整体。类似的词汇还有：for example, for instance, in addition, another, furthermore, moreover, therefore, as a result, consequently, first, second, third, next, then, last, finally 等。

二 专题演练

练习 1：为下面文章的各部分选择合适的主题。

i The word Kangaroo was adopted into Standard English where it has come to mean any member of the family of kangaroos and wallabies. The belief that it means “I don't understand” or “I don't know” is a popular myth that is also applied to many other Aboriginal-sounding Australian words. Male kangaroos are called bucks, boomers or jacks; females are does, flyers, or jills and the young ones are joeys. The collective noun for kangaroos is a mob, troop, or court.

ii Kangaroos have long been regarded as strange animals. Early explorers described them as creatures that had heads like deer (without antlers), stood upright like men, and hopped like frogs. Combined with the two-headed appearance of a mother kangaroo, this lead many back home to dismiss them as travellers' tales for quite some time.

Kangaroos have large, powerful hind legs, large feet adapted for leaping, a long muscular tail for balance, and a small head. Like all marsupials, kangaroos have a pouch called a marsupium in which their young complete their development after birth.

iii Kangaroos are large herbivores, feeding on grass and roots, and they chew cud. All species are nocturnal and crepuscular, usually spending the days idling quietly and the cool evenings, nights and mornings moving about and feeding, typically in mobs.

iv Along with dingoes and other canids, introduced species like foxes and feral cats also pose a threat to kangaroo populations, as they do most populations of native animals. Kangaroos and wallabies are apt swimmers, and often flee into waterways if presented with the option. If pursued into the water, a large kangaroo may use its forepaws to hold the predator underwater to drown it. Another defensive tactic described by witnesses is catching the attacking dog with the forepaws and disembowelling it with the hind legs.

v A mob may have ten or more males and females. The dominant male (called a boomer) is based on his size and age. A boomer has temporary exclusive access to females in a mob for mating.

A boomer may find himself wandering in and out of a mob — checking out the females and intimidating the other males who try to mate with the females within the mob.

vi Kangaroos have developed in a number of ways to survive in a dry, infertile continent and a highly variable climate. As with all marsupials, the young are born at a very early stage of development after a gestation of 31-36 days. At this stage, only the forelimbs are somewhat developed, to allow the newborn to climb to the pouch and attach to a teat. In comparison, a human embryo at a similar stage of development would be about 7 weeks old, and premature babies born at less than 23 weeks are usually not mature enough to survive. The joey will usually stay in the pouch for about 9 months or (for the Western Grey) 180 to 320 days, before starting to leave the pouch for small periods of time. It is usually fed by its mother until the age of 18 months.

vii Before white settlement, the kangaroo was a very important animal for Australian Aborigines, both for its meat, its hide, its bones and its sinews. In addition, there were important Dreaming stories and ceremonies involving the kangaroo. Aherrenge is a current kangaroo dreaming site in the Northern Territory. The game of Marn grook was played using a ball made from kangaroo by the Kurnai people.

Heading choices

__i__ Terminology
_____ Kangaroos and humans
_____ Adaptations
_____ Diet
_____ Predators
_____ Courtship
_____ Physical description

练习 2：阅读下面的段落，为段落选择合适大意。

1．Financial genius James "Big Jim" Fisk (1834-1872) died of gunshot wound when he was only thirty-seven years old. During his brief lifetime, Fisk earned and lost huge sums of money, much of it through bribery and theft. During the Civil War, he smuggled cotton from the South to the North. He also printed and sold phony bonds to gain control of the wildly profitable Erie Railroad. Then he bankrupted the railroad while gaining a personal fortune for himself. In 1869, Fisk's attempts to take over the gold market led to financial panic and the collapse of the stock market. Oddly enough, Fisk seemed rather proud of his wicked ways, saying "Some people are born to be good; other people to be bad. I was born to be bad. " A lover of the ladies, Fisk was killed in a fight with a rival over the affections of actress Josie Mansfield.

Main Idea:

a．Big Jim Fisk liked pretty women a little too much for his own good.

b. In his pursuit of wealth, James Fisk never let law or morality stand in his way.

c. James Fisk did not have a long life, but that did not stop him from making a great deal of money.

2. For the ancient Romans, taking a bath was a very special occasion. Because they considered bathing a social opportunity, they constructed huge public baths that put our modern-day indoor pools and spas to shame. Not only were the baths themselves lavishly decorated, they were also surrounded by shops, libraries, and lounges so that a person could shop, read or chat after bathing. The famed Baths of Caracalla, for example, offered Roman citizens massages and saunas in addition to a gymnasium and gardens for after-bath walks in lovely surroundings. Art lovers that they were, the Romans also frequently built art galleries into their bathing facilities. There were also kitchens, where food was prepared to serve hungry bathers. Although initially men and women bathed separately, mixed baths became the fashion until 500 A.D., when the coming of Christianity brought the public baths to an end. (Source of information: Charles Panati, Extraordinary Origins of Everyday Things, p. 200)

Main Idea:

a. The ancient Romans were the first to lead a life of pure luxury.

b. If the Romans had spent more time governing and less time bathing, the Roman Empire would still exist today.

c. The ancient Romans made luxury and socializing a part of bathing.

3. Birds have long played a central role in superstitions. However, the role birds have played varies greatly. While crows were thought to be in league with the devil, blue birds were usually considered signs of good fortune. Blue jays, in contrast, were seldom assigned a positive role in superstition and legend. Most of the time, they were considered companions to the devil. According to one ancient superstition, blue jays were never seen on Fridays. Friday was their day to meet with the devil and pass on any useful gossip about souls who might be ready to go astray. Owls, in contrast, have played a number of different roles, some good, some bad. In several superstitions they are portrayed as wise counselors; in others they are a sign that death is near.

Main Idea:

a. Hardly a superstition exists that doesn't have a bird in it.

b. Birds turn up frequently in superstitions as signs of both good and evil.

c. Despite having the same color, blue jays and blue birds have played very different roles in superstitions.

4. French and American cookbooks obviously share the same subject: They both deal with the preparation of food. But that's where the similarity ends. American recipes are very exact, while French recipes are open to personal variation. In American cookbooks, the teaspoon of sugar, for instance, is described as rounded or flat. French cookbooks are inclined to be less precise. The French cookbook writer thinks nothing of listing a "sprinkling of pepper" or a

"pinch of salt" . French cookbooks are also likely to tell the reader to "season according to taste" . American cookbooks, in contrast, don't seem to have as much faith in their readers' ability to get the recipe right from taste. They tell readers exactly how much seasoning to use.

Main Idea:

a. Despite a common topic, French and American cookbooks differ in the way they give directions.

b. Because they are better cooks, the French write cookbooks that trust their readers' judgment.

c. American cookbooks don't have much faith in the cook's ability to determine the right taste.

5. Not surprisingly, the crime victims are often called upon to identify the person who robbed or attacked them. For a jury, the victim's testimony is often proof positive that the accused is guilty. After all, who can better identify the wrongdoer than the person harmed. This is just common sense. Yet as is so often the case, common sense can be misleading. As it turns out, crime victims don't necessarily make reliable witnesses. Overcome with fear, they often close their eyes or focus fixedly on the weapon being used to threaten them. As a result, they don't get a good look at the thief or attacker. While it's not true that crime victim testimony is always inaccurate, it's also true that one can't assume a victim's identification is automatic proof of guilt.

Main Idea:

a. Crime victims do not always correctly identify those who have harmed them.

b. Crime victim testimony is almost always inaccurate because during the crime, the victim was overcome with terror.

c. The testimony of crime victims has put far too many people in jail.

练习 3：阅读下面的段落，找出该段的主题句、主要细节和次要细节，分别在各自底下标圆点（主题句）、划横线（主要细节）和划曲线（次要细节）表示，并在段落后面写出该段的主题。

1. Studies reveal that people's first names can have an influence on them. Some names reflect on people in a positive way. For example, one survey showed that American men consider the name Susan to be very sexy. And participants in a British study thought Tony to be the name of someone very friendly. However, other names can have a negative impact. In one study, for instance, teachers gave lower grades to essay supposedly written by boys named Hubert and Elmer than to the very same essay when they credited tomboys with more popular names. Another study found girls with unpopular names did worse on IQ and achievement tests than girls with more appealing names.

Topic: ____

2. Which vegetables are most nutritionally sound, frozen or fresh? Many people would answer that

fresh vegetables are the best. The fact is frozen vegetables can be superior for several reasons. Time plays a significant factor in nutritional value. For this reason, fresh or canned vegetables often lose valuable nutrients while being shipped from the farm to the market or cannery. Frozen vegetables are frozen immediately after being picked and thus retain their nutrients. Frozen vegetables lend themselves well to steam preparation. This type of cooking retains important nutrients within the vegetables. Finally, frozen vegetables are clearly labeled with nutritional information. Fresh vegetables on the other hand carry no type of labeling.

Topic:____

3. The oil crisis of the 1970s made American realize the need for alterative fuel sources. While many alternatives have been proposed, Carroll Buckner has developed an alternative which has several advantages. Mr. Buckner's corn burning stove is economical. Anyone could grow their own fuel simply by planting a corn crop. Even if the corn must be purchased from a supplier, it is usually inexpensive. Second, the emissions from the burning corn are nonpolluting. Finally, the growth in the corn industry brought about by an increased demand would add jobs to the struggling agricultural economy.

Topic:____

4. Reactions of people to death vary greatly. However, all people go through specific stages in dealing with grief after the dearth of a loved one. The first stage is disbelief. Often the person is so severely shocked that he or she is unable to believe that the loved one is no longer alive. This disbelief then turns into a second stage called denial. A person in denial will often swear that the person lying in the coffin is breathing. A period of anger usually follows in the next stage. The person is angry at the person for dying and leaving him or her, angry at the medical community for not doing a competent job, and angry at himself or herself for past failures against the loved one. It is during this stage that many people hit rock bottom and must find some way of dealing with their grief. Finally, the person enters a period of acceptance. While the time necessary for entering this stage of grief varies from person to person, most people are able to get to this stage after a few months. During this stage of acceptance, many people turn to spiritual guidance and meditation to achieve inner peace.

Topic:____

5. What causes reading disabilities, or dyslexia? Studies have been conducted for generations in an attempt to find answers to this difficult question. Rather than a single answer, however, several factors have emerged which seem to contribute to the disability. One factor points to a genetic link from one generation to the next. In particular, males are more likely to be affected if a father, grandfather, or uncle had dyslexia. Early difficulty in discriminating sounds appears to be another factor. Children who cannot hear the subtle differences within and among words will also have difficulty in reading those sounds. Finally, visual-perceptual problems, a

difficulty in clearly seeing the written words, also contribute to dyslexia. If the words do not appear clearly, seem to move, or create distortions, the reader will not be able to read fluidly and comprehension will suffer.

Topic:____

三 专题答案

练习 1：vii, vi, iii, iv, v, ii

练习 2：1. b 2. c 3. b 4. a 5. a

练习 3：

1. Studies reveal that people's first names can have an influence on them. Some names reflect on people in a positive way. For example, one survey showed that American men consider the name Susan to be very sexy. And participants in a British study thought Tony to be the name of someone very friendly. However, other names can have a negative impact. In one study, for instance, teachers gave lower grades to essay supposedly written by boys named Hubert and Elmer than to the very same essay when they credited tomboys with more popular names. Another study found girls with unpopular names did worse on IQ and achievement tests than girls with more appealing names.

   Topic: the influence of people's first name on them

2. Which vegetables are most nutritionally sound, frozen or fresh? Many people would answer that fresh vegetables are the best. The fact is frozen vegetables can be superior for several reasons. Time plays a significant factor in nutritional value. For this reason, fresh or canned vegetables often lose valuable nutrients while being shipped from the farm to the market or cannery. Frozen vegetables are frozen immediately after being picked and thus retain their nutrients. Frozen vegetables lend themselves well to steam preparation. This type of cooking retains important nutrients within the vegetables. Finally, frozen vegetables are clearly labeled with nutritional information. Fresh vegetables on the other hand carry no type of labeling.

   Topic: good things about frozen vegetables/why frozen vegetables are better

3. The oil crisis of the 1970s made American realize the need for alterative fuel sources. While many alternatives have been proposed, Carroll Buckner has developed an alternative which has several advantages. Mr. Buckner's corn burning stove is economical. Anyone could grow their own fuel simply by planting a corn crop. Even if the corn must be purchased from a supplier, it is usually inexpensive. Second, the emissions from the burning corn are nonpolluting. Finally, the growth in the corn industry brought about by an increased demand would add jobs to the

struggling agricultural economy.

Topic: ______________________________

4. Reactions of people to death vary greatly. However, all people go through specific stages in dealing with grief after the death of a loved one. The first stage is disbelief. Often the person is so severely shocked that he or she is unable to believe that the loved one is no longer alive. This disbelief then turns into a second stage called denial. A person in denial will often swear that the person lying in the coffin is breathing. A period of anger usually follows in the next stage. The person is angry at the person for dying and leaving him or her, angry at the medical community for not doing a competent job, and angry at himself or herself for past failures against the loved one. It is during this stage that many people hit rock bottom and must find some way of dealing with their grief. Finally, the person enters a period of acceptance. While the time necessary for entering this stage of grief varies from person to person, most people are able to get to this stage after a few months. During this stage of acceptance, many people turn to spiritual guidance and meditation to achieve inner peace.

Topic: Specific stages dealing with grief after the death of a loved one

5. What causes reading disabilities, or dyslexia? Studies have been conducted for generations in an attempt to find answers to this difficult question. Rather than a single answer, however, several factors have emerged which seem to contribute to the disability. One factor points to a genetic link from one generation to the next. In particular, males are more likely to be affected if a father, grandfather, or uncle had dyslexia. Early difficulty in discriminating sounds appears to be another factor. Children who cannot hear the subtle differences within and among words will also have difficulty in reading those sounds. Finally, visual-perceptual problems, a difficulty in clearly seeing the written words, also contribute to dyslexia. If the words do not appear clearly, seem to move, or create distortions, the reader will not be able to read fluidly and comprehension will suffer.

Topic: Factors contributing to dyslexia

星期五

认识10大段落组织结构

文章及其中的段落并不是一些段落和句子的随意组合，而是围绕中心话题和主旨按照一定的结构组织在一起的。认识文章和段落的组织结构，有助于我们更加清晰地把握文章的脉络，理解作者的观点在文章中是如何提出、展开的，同时还可以帮助我们理解和记忆文章的主要信息。

一 知识点拨

常见的组织结构有以下几种：

1. 阐释型

这种结构在议论文中比较常见。一般在段落开头提出一种观点、假说、趋势或印象。然后通过举例来阐释、提供证据等。常见的标志词有：for example, for instance, to illustrate 等。

例：Many modern people are turning themselves into social victims. ***One example*** is a Tennessee woman who is suing McDonald's because she was badly burned on the chin by a hot pickle in her hamburger. A Canadian woman is ***another example***. She wants to ban the South Park television show because her son Kenny is victimized by the show's Kenny character, who is killed in each episode. ***A third example*** is a group of European and Australian women who want to ban urinals in men's restrooms because they require men to stand in a way that suggests violence toward women. ***Another*** group argues that single people are victimized because society ignores them.

2. 时间顺序型

段落提到的事件按照发生的时间先后顺序排列，一般在事件前会有比较明显的年代或日期出现。这种结构类型广泛运用在人类学、历史和政治学等领域中。

例：The famous Leaning Tower of Pisa has been tilting for over 800 years, and recent improvements should allow it to continue tilting for another 300 more. ***On August 9, 1173***, construction began on this well known Italian bell tower. ***Almost immediately***, it began leaning because it was being erected on the soft silt of a buried riverbed. ***Between 1178 and 1360,*** work stopped and started two more times as workers tried to continue the project and figure out how to compensate for the tilt. ***Over the next six centuries***, the tower's lean continued to increase, although tourists were still allowed to visit. ***Then, in 1990***, Italy's prime minister feared the tower would collapse and closed it to the public. ***From 1999 to 2001***, engineers excavated soil from beneath the tower. ***Now***, the tower still leans out about 15 feet beyond its base, but it should remain stable for several more centuries.

3. 因果型

讨论某个或某些事件或行为的后果、影响或起因，也就是提到的事件或行为互为因果关系。常见的**标志词**有：because, for this reason, due to, cause, on account of, if this, then this…as a result, since, consequently, therefore, thus, in effect, resulting, the outcome is...等。

例：Smoking is the single most preventable risk factor for fatal illnesses in the United States. Indeed, cigarette smoking ***accounts for*** more deaths than all other drugs, car accidents, suicides, homicides, and fires combined. ***Further***, nonsmokers who inhale smoke from other people's cigarettes face an elevated risk for lung cancer and other illnesses related to the lungs, a fact that has ***given rise to*** a nonsmokers' rights movement in the United States.

4. 解决问题型

段落开头提出一个问题，然后提出解决问题的方案或假设。

提出问题的**标志词**：problem, need, difficulty, dilemma, enigma, challenge, issue。

解决问题的**标志词**：answer, propose, suggest, indicate, solve, resolve, improve, plan, respond to。

例：The growth of urban areas exacerbated many ***problems***, including the absence of clean drinking water, the lack of cheap public transportation, and most importantly, poor sanitation. Sanitation problems led to heavy urban mortality rates and frequent epidemics of typhoid, dysentery, typhus, cholera, and yellow fever. Government officials, recognizing the ***need*** for improvement, initiated the return to suburban and rural areas. The ***proposal*** involved several cost effective *solutions*. Local village water delivery systems were improved, and as villages were substantially smaller, almost everything was in walking distance, thereby eliminating the need for public transportation.

5. 比较与对比型

对提出的两种事物之间的相同点和不同点进行比较和对比。比较侧重两者的相同点，被比较的双方地位相同，而对比重在强调两者的不同之处，其中一方往往是作者强调的重点。

标志词：however, nevertheless, on the other hand, but, similarly, although, also, in contrast, different, alike, same as, either/or , in the same way, just like, just as, likewise, in comparison, whereas 等。

例：In temperament Lewis and Clark were opposites. Lewis was introverted, melancholic, and moody; Clark, extroverted, even-tempered and gregarious. The better educated and more refined Lewis, who possessed a philosophical, romantic and speculative mind, was at home with abstract ideas; Clark, of a pragmatic mold, was more of a practical man of action. Each supplied vital qualities which balanced their partnership.

6. 分类型

按照一定的标准，对提到的事物进行分类介绍。常见**标志词**有：categories, classifications, groups, classes, ways, elements, features, kinds, types, varieties, methods 等。

例：Body fat can be divided into two basic categories, essential fat and storage fat. Essential fat is the fat that is necessary for the body to function normally. It is stored in the tissues and major organs. Typically, essential fat makes up about 3 percent of body weight for men and between 10 and 12 percent for women. (Women need more essential fat in order to maintain hormonal and reproductive functions.) The second kind of fat is called storage fat. Storage fat protects the internal organs and helps keep the body warm during periods of extreme cold. It accumulates around the stomach, buttocks, hips, thighs, and upper arms. Although the body needs some storage fat for protection, most people carry around a good deal more storage fat than they need.

7. 列举型

对并列的几个事物进行列举，常见的**标志词**有：first，second, next 等。

例：According to Maslow's theory of needs, human beings have five different kinds of needs that can be ranked in order of importance. First, humans have psychological needs such as the needs for food, air, and water. Next comes security needs, which reflect the desire for physical and emotional safety from harm. Third in rank are needs for belonging. These include the desire for love and affection. Next comes esteem needs, which include the need for recognition and respect. Finally, at the top of the list are self-actualization needs like the need to grow, develop, and expand one's abilities.

8. 空间顺序型

按照方位顺序来组织段落，这种结构在说明文中比较常见。

例：Where the mountains meet the sea is the official motto of Camden, Maine, a New England town known for its splendid harbor. No wonder, behind the harbor, not far from where the schooners are anchored, Ragged Mountain rises precipitously.

9. 转折型

段落开头先提出一种貌似合理的观点，接着作者笔锋一转，指出该观点的不正确之处或直接引出作者的观点。常见**标志词**有：however，but，on the other hand 等。

例：It was once assumed that improvements in telecommunications would lead to more dispersal in the population as people were no longer forced into cities. However, the ISTP team's research demonstrates that the population and job density of cities rose or remained constant in the 1980s after decades of decline. The explanation for this seems to be that it is valuable to place people working in related fields together. 'The new world will largely depend on human creativity, and creativity flourishes where people come together face-to-face.'

10. 混合型

很多情况下，文章中的段落会综合运用多种结构类型来组织句子，如下面的段落：

①Given the question of how to maneuver in the dark, what solutions might an engineer consider? ②The first one that might occur to him is to manufacture light, to use a lantern or a searchlight. ③Fireflies and some fish (usually with the help of bacteria) have the power to manufacture their light, but the process seems to consume a large amount of energy. ④Fireflies use their light for attracting mates. ⑤This doesn't require a prohibitive amount of energy. ⑥A male's tiny pinprick of light can be seen by a female from some distance on a dark night, since her eyes are exposed directly to the light source itself. ⑦However, using light to find one's own way around requires vastly more energy. ⑧Since the eyes have to detect the tiny fraction of the light that bounces off each part of the scene, the light source must therefore be immensely brighter if it is to be used a headlight to illuminate the path, than it is to be used as a signal to others. ⑨In any event, whether or not the reason is the energy expense, it seems to be the case that, with the possible exception of some weird deep-sea fish, no animal apart from man uses manufactured light to find its way about.

上面段落的句①提出问题，句②提出一个解决方案。句③通过举例指出此方案可能存在的问题。句④、⑤、⑥对所举出的例子进一步阐释和说明。句⑦和句⑧是因果关系，再次指出方案存在的问题。句⑨是对全段的总结，强调段首提出的方案是行不通的。

认识文章和段落的内部组织结构可以帮助我们很快找到重要的信息，记忆关键信息，理解作者的写作思路。

二 专题演练

练习 1：下列每题中给出了两个句子，请为这两个句子之间的关系选择合适的选项。

1. Up until the early 1970s, researchers thought that chimpanzees were gentle animals that occasionally defended their territories but otherwise lived in harmony with their neighbors.

Then, from 1974 to 1977, researchers Jane Goodall and Richard Wrangham observed how a large group of chimps repeatedly attacked a smaller neighboring group until every male in that smaller group was dead.

Sentence Relationship:

a. addition

b. spatial order

c. time order

d. statement/reversal

2. Noise is much more than just an annoyance.

In fact, noise can be a type of pollution that produces serious hearing impairments, prevents people from getting adequate rest, contributes to high blood pressure, interferes with productivity, and reduces the overall quality of life.

Sentence Relationship:

a. statement/clarification

b. comparing two topics

c. spatial order

d. time order

3. President Abraham Lincoln is widely considered to have been a good leader who utilized his resources wisely.

Lincoln's counterpart during the Civil War, Confederate president Jefferson Davis, is viewed as a less effective leader because he shielded incompetent people and refused to make use of talented individuals if he disliked them.

Sentence Relationship:

a. statement/clarification

b. statement/reversal

c. comparing two topics

d. contrasting two topics

4. For decades , environmental groups have been painting a grim picture of our planet's health.

In his book The Skeptical Environmentalist, however, Bjorn Lomborg argues that the Earth is actually getting healthier, with less pollution, more forests, and more food.

Sentence Relationship:

a. addition

b. spatial order

c. statement/reversal

d. contrasting two topics

5. Visitors enter the sunken plaza of Washington, D.C.'s World War II Memorial on ramps that pass by two giant arches representing the two fronts of the war, the Atlantic and the Pacific.

In the center of the plaza, fifty-six pillars symbolizing the unity of American states and territories during the war surround a reflecting pool with fountains and a Freedom Wall covered with 4,000 gold stars, where each star represents 100 Americans who gave their lives in the conflict.

Sentence Relationship:

a. addition

b. statement/clarification

c. spatial order

d. time order

6. Serving as a caregiver for an ailing loved one can be enormously rewarding because it provides a sense of fulfillment and may lead to deeper and more meaningful relationships.

But new research has revealed that caregivers tend to have weaker immune systems, suffer from depression more than non-caregivers, and are 63 percent more likely than non-caregivers to die prematurely.

Sentence Relationship:

a. addition

b. statement/reversal

c. contrasting two topics

d. statement/clarification

7. The planet Neptune has a rocky core surrounded by a mantle of water, methane, and ammonia ice, followed by an atmosphere composed mainly of hydrogen and helium, and—finally—eight satellites and five rings.

Its neighbor, the planet Uranus, is considered Neptune's twin because it has the same size, a similar internal structure and atmosphere, and similar rings and satellites.

Sentence Relationship:

a. spatial order

b. addition

c. comparing two topics

d. time order

8. Classicism, the predominant style of the 18th century, was not very interested in nature and celebrated reason, order, and restraint.

The 19th century romantics, in contrast, were enchanted by nature and believed the natural world to be a source of spiritual inspiration.

Sentence Relationship:

a. statement/clarification

b. contrasting two topics

c. statement/reversal

d. addition

9. In 1950, 7 percent of middle-class women were employed outside their homes and earned wages.

By 1960, 25 percent of middle-class women were part of America's workforce.

Sentence Relationship:

a. time order

b. spatial order

c. addition

d. statement/reversal

10. President Richard Nixon pursued his goal of world stability by visiting the leaders of China and the Soviet Union in order to reduce the tensions between the United States and those two countries.

He was also responsible for a peace settlement with North Vietnam that ended America's involvement in the Vietnam War.

Sentence Relationship:

a. comparing two topics

b. statement/clarification

c. addition

d. time order

练习 2：阅读下列段落，为段落选择合适的组织结构类型。

1. Relatively unknown to the general public, war correspondent Kate Webb (1943-2007) was a legend among her fellow war reporters, famous not just for her skills as a writer but also for her amazing courage in the face of danger. A New Zealander, Webb began her storied career in Indonesia in the 1960s during the bloody overthrow of President Sukarno. Webb legend truly began, however, during the war in Vietnam. Arriving in Vietnam in 1967, Webb felt mostly terror at the thought of covering a war, but she refused to let fear stop her from doing her job. And it didn't take long for her to become famous for her bravery and determination to tell readers what was happening in the war. In 1971, when she was just twenty-eight years old and the bureau chief in Phnom Penh, Cambodia, enemy forces captured Webb and marched her through the jungles bare foot until her feet were bloodied and blistered. Webb was held for so long that The New York Times published her obituary. Kate Webb, however, wasn't dead. Twenty-three days after being captured, one of the North Vietnamese soldiers holding her prisoner helped her escape, asking only that Webb "tell the truth about us." Emaciated, bloody, and sick with two different strains of malaria, Webb recuperated briefly and went right back to the war front. In the 1980s, while she was covering Kabul, Afghanistan after the Russians had abandoned their effort to control the country, an Afghan warlord assaulted Webb with the intent of raping her. He smashed her head into the floor of a hotel lobby and was dragging her by the hair across the floor when two other journalists rescued her. Afterwards Webb said only, "There is something very humiliating about having your head bashed. " Webb retired in 2001. She died in 2007 of cancer.

Organizational pattern or patterns:

a. definition

b. simple listing

c. comparison and contrast and definition

d. sequence of dates and events

2. "Flashbulb memories" is a term used to describe those memories of events so horrible or so tragic that we remember exactly where we were and what we were doing when the events occurred. Many people who came of age in the 1960s, for instance, know to this day where they were when they heard that President John F. Kennedy had been assassinated by Lee Harvey Oswald in 1963. Similarly, many people have flashbulb memories of what they were doing when Martin Luther King was killed by James Earl Ray in the same year. Flashbulb memories don't, however, occur only when famous or celebrated people die violently. We also have

flashbulb memories of where we were and what we were doing when a loved one died. And for everyone except those who were small children at the time, September 11, 2001 was an event that created millions of flashbulb memories all across the nation.

Organizational pattern or patterns:

a. definition

b. classification

c. comparison and contrast and process

d. sequence of dates and events and classification

3. Some medical myths just will not die no matter how often they are debunked. Take, for instance, the claim that hair and finger nails continue to grow after death. There is absolutely no truth to it, but the belief survives nonetheless. As the body shrivels after death, the hair and fingernails start to look longer by comparison, and that the reason why it has, for so long, been thought that hair and nails continue to grow. Another medical myth is that getting wet in cold weather causes colds. But weather doesn't cause colds. Viruses do. You can go out in the freezing cold with your hair soaking wet or get caught in an icy rain storm and still stay healthy as long as you don't make contact with a cold virus while out of doors. Yet another medical myth is that eating sweets causes diabetes. It doesn't, at least not directly. Eating sugar can and often does lead to weight gain, and it's being overweight that is a high risk factor for Diabetes 2 (adult onset in contrast to diabetes that occurs in childhood). It's also not true that eating chocolate causes acne. Most acne is hormone-related. What you eat doesn't affect the production of the hormones that produce acne. Yet another myth is that touching a frog will produce warts on your hand. Warts are caused by the papilloma virus. The virus is passed from person to person and enters the body through small cuts or cracks in the skin of the hand. Feel free to touch as many frogs as you want. No matter how many you touch, you still won't get any warts.

Organizational pattern or patterns:

a. definition

b. comparison and contrast

c. classification and process

d. simple listing

4. A study in Romania suggests that children who are abandoned at birth and placed in state-run institutions can eventually thrive if they leave the institution and are placed in foster care. In fact, children in the study who were placed in foster homes ended up on par emotionally, intellectually, and physically with children of the same age who had grown up with their biological families. In contrast, orphaned children who never left the state-run institutions showed steady declines in their emotional and mental health over the course of their stay. While the study supports the idea that foster care for abandoned children is better than institutional life, it's worth noting that Romanian institutions have a particularly horrific reputation for neglect. This may well account for the effects of long-term and unrelieved institutionalization upon

abandoned children.

Organizational pattern or patterns:

a. sequence of dates and events

b. classification

c. cause and effect and comparison and contrast

d. simple listing

5. Although the oft-repeated notion that people are right-brained or left-brained is close to complete nonsense, it is true that the two hemispheres, or halves, of the brain are dominant, or more proficient, in different areas. The left brain is more detail-oriented whereas the right-brain is better at seeing the global, or broader, more general, picture. When it comes to processing language, the left hemisphere is the one in charge, although it appears to be limited to processing literal meanings. Tell someone with damage to the right hemisphere to "Go jump in a lake." and they just might do it because the right side of the brain is better at coming up with figurative meanings. The left side processes the dictionary definitions and leaves the suggested meanings—in this case, "get out of my sight"—to the right side. Someone who has right hemisphere damage, then, is likely to take the command to jump in a lake at face value. Overall, the left side has better analytical abilities whereas the right side excels at recognizing spatial relationships and interpreting visual images. That being said, the two halves of the brain are connected by a fibrous bundle of nerves called the corpus callosum. Thanks to the corpus callosum, the two sides of the brain are able to communicate and work together in unison rather than opposition.

Organizational pattern or patterns:

a. classification

b. process

c. comparison and contrast and definition

d. definition

三 专题答案

练习 1：1. c　2. a　3. d　4. c　5. c　6. b　7. c　8. b　9. a　10. c

练习 2：1. d　2. a　3. d　4. c　5. c

星期六 学会略读和查读

雅思阅读考试归根结底是考察考生获取文本信息的能力，不管这种信息是大意还是细节。而且阅读部分的三篇文章的篇幅都较长，阅读量大，时间往往比较紧，这时候我们就不能像精读那样逐字逐句地阅读，而要根据文章的不同部分综合运用略读、查读和速读的策略。

一 策略点拨

1. 略读

当我们想获取文本的大意而不是细节信息时，我们会使用到略读（skimming）。在雅思阅读考试中，有的阅读题目要求你理解段落的大意，你就没有必要在一些与题目无关的细节上浪费时间；有的题目尽管是寻找细节的题目，但是你需要先找到可能包含该细节的相应段落，这些情况下你都要用到略读技巧。

当我们需要在有限的时间内完成大量的阅读材料，略读可以帮助我们在较短的时间内找到段落的大意，节省时间，提高阅读的效率。那么如何进行略读呢？下面给您几条建议：

1）阅读文章的标题和副标题

2）迅速阅读文章的首尾段落

3）阅读文中每个段落的首尾句

4）注意任何斜体的、大写的、黑体的单词或词组

5）扫描文章中的一些连接词，如 for example, however 等

阅读文章的标题和首尾段落能帮助我们迅速抓住文章的主要内容，因为很多文章会在开头和结尾处揭示文章的重点和中心内容。同样的道理，很多段落会在开头或结尾就点明段落的大意，阅读文中段落的首尾句能够帮助把握文章的脉络。文章中的一些连接词往往揭示了段落和句子之间的逻辑关系，它们可以帮助我们预测接下来的内容，让我们能够有选择地阅读文中重要的部分。

阅读文中段落的首尾句还可以帮助我们迅速定位答案在文中的相应位置。

练一练： 现在我们来看下面一篇短文。文后有这样一个简答题的题目：

How many way are there to pay the congestion charge?

请用略读法迅速找到答案可能在文中出现的段落。

London congestion charging

The charge was introduced on Monday 17 February 2003 to encourage people to leave their cars behind and use public transport when travelling in central London. It was introduced due to the high pollution levels and traffic congestion.

The Inner Ring Road forms the congestion zone boundary and includes roads such as Marylebone Road, Euston Road, Park Lane and Edgware Road. Drivers can travel along these roads without incurring the charge. Maps of this zone are published in the national press and are available from a range of outlets as well as online.

Commuters have to pay £5 for: each day they wish to travel through or within the charge zone between the hours of 7:00 a.m. and 6:30 p.m., Monday to Friday. Commuters have a choice about how they pay the £5. They can pay online, via the Internet, phoning, texting on their mobile phones and over the counter at petrol stations and convenience stores.

Commuters also have a choice about how often they pay. They can pay daily, weekly, monthly or annually.

Not everyone has to pay the £5. Those exempt include residents, emergency services, registered-disabled drivers, taxis and those using alternative energy vehicles. These people/organisations have to apply for exemption, which can be done online.

The London Congestion Charge works by using around 900 cameras at the boundary and within the zone. The cameras read the registration plates and send the information to a computer, which checks whether the owner has paid the charge and, if not, whether the owner has claimed exemption. If drivers have not paid the charge by 10 p.m. that day (and are not exempt) a penalty notice is sent to his/her home address. The longer that the penalty is not paid, the larger the fine. Persistent offenders have their vehicles clamped and removed.

答案在第三段，因为第三段出现了 Commuters have to pay £5…我们再仔细阅读本段，可以发现一共有 4 种，它们分别是 via the Internet, phoning, texting on their mobile phones and over the counter at petrol stations and convenience stores。

在雅思阅读中，我们经常要用到略读技巧。尤其对于考查段落大意的题目，我们只需要阅读包含重要信息的、概括性的句子，而对于无关的支撑性的细节则可以大胆地跳过。

练一练：我们再来看下面一段：

All these activities may have damaging environmental impacts. For example, land clearing for agriculture is the largest single cause of deforestation. Chemical fertilisers and pesticides may contaminate water supplies. more intensive farming and the abandonment of fallow periods tend to exacerbate soil erosion; and the spread of monoculture and use of high-yielding varieties of crops have been accompanied by the disappearance of old varieties of food plants which might have provided some insurance against pests or diseases in future. Soil erosion threatens the productivity of land in both rich and poor countries. The United States, where the most careful measurements have been done, discovered in 1982 that about one-fifth of its farmland was losing topsoil at a rate likely to diminish the soil's productivity. The country subsequently embarked upon a program to convert 11 percent of its cropped land to meadow or forest. Topsoil in India and China is vanishing much faster than in America.

如果后面的题目是找标题或者问这个段落的大意是什么，那么我们阅读时就应该把注意力放在概括性的句子上而忽略一些细枝末节。比如上面这一段，读过第一句后，我们发现 for example，说明第二句是对第一句提出的 idea 进行的举例。这些例子便是支撑本段第一句的细节，可以加快阅读速度，只读关键性的字眼，有时甚至可以跳过。读到本段的中间部分我们可以看到"Soil erosion threatens the productivity of land in both rich and poor countries."又是一句概括性的句子。紧接着下面开始再次提一些典型的国家进行举例，这时候只需要注意读到的国家的名字就行了。

2. 查读

查读（scanning）是当我们阅读时为了从材料中获取具体的信息而要用到的一种策略。比如平时查字典或者看列车时刻表时，我们会跳过不相关的内容，直到找到我们要查的那个词或者车次。在雅思阅读中，查读是要经常用到的另一种重要的阅读策略。

我们在做雅思的阅读题目时，由于我们大脑的瞬时记忆容量所限，很多情况下需要根据题目再回到原文中找可能包含题目答案的相关段落，经过精确定位后才有可能做出题目。为了提高做题效率，我们可以利用题目中已经给出的信息作为线索，然后回原文找答案。而题目中的人名、地名、年代日期、大写字母和斜体黑体的字句等往往是一些最为直接的、最容易定位的线索。

那么我们该如何进行查读呢？以下给您一些建议：

- 始终牢记你要寻找的关键信息。
- 先预测一下答案可能以什么样的形式出现（数字、人名、地名还是动词、形容词）以及你可能运用什么样的线索帮助你迅速找到答案。
- 运用标题或其他信息（比如每段的首尾句）来帮助你辨别文章的哪一部分可能包含要找的题目答案。
- 有选择性地阅读并且迅速跳过不相关的部分。
- 当你找到包含目的信息的句子时，仔细阅读整个句子甚至整个段落。

练一练：现在我们来看下面一篇文章以及文后的三个题目：

The Discovery of X-rays

Except for a brief description of the Compton effect, and a few other remarks, we have postponed the discussion of X-rays until the present chapter because it is particularly convenient to treat X-ray spectra after treating optical spectra. Although this ordering may have given the reader a distorted impression of the historical importance of X-rays, this impression will be corrected shortly as we describe the crucial role played by X-rays in the development of modern physics.

X-rays were discovered in 1895 by Roentgen while studying the phenomena of gaseous discharge. Using a cathode ray tube with a high voltage of several tens of kilovolts, he noticed that salts of barium would fluoresce when brought near the tube, although nothing visible was emitted by the tube. This effect persisted when the tube was wrapped with a layer of black cardboard. Roentgen soon established that the agency responsible for the fluorescence originated at the point at which the stream of energetic electrons struck the glass wall of the tube. Because of its unknown nature, he gave this agency the name X-rays. He found that X-rays could manifest themselves by darkening wrapped photographic plates, discharging charged electroscopes, as well as by causing fluorescence in a number of different substances. He also found that X-rays can penetrate considerable thicknesses of materials of low atomic number, whereas substances of high atomic number are relatively opaque. Roentgen took the first steps in identifying the nature of X-rays by using a system of slits to show that (1) they travel in straight lines, and that (2) they are uncharged, because they are not deflected by electric or magnetic fields.

The discovery of X-rays aroused the interest of all physicists, and many joined in the investigation of their properties. In 1899 Haga and Wind performed a single slit diffraction experiment with X-rays which showed that (3) X-rays are a wave motion phenomenon, and, from the size of the diffraction pattern, their wavelength could be estimated to be 10-8 cm. In 1906 Barkla proved that (4) the waves are transverse by showing that they can be polarized by scattering from many materials.

There is, of course, no longer anything unknown about the nature of X-rays. They are electromagnetic radiation of exactly the same nature as visible light, except that their wavelength is several orders of magnitude shorter. This conclusion follows from comparing properties (1) through (4) with the similar properties of visible light, but it was actually postulated by Thomson several years before all these properties were known. Thomson argued that X-rays are electromagnetic radiation because such radiation would be expected to be emitted from the point at which the electrons strike the wall of a cathode ray tube. At this point, the electrons suffer very violent accelerations in coming to a stop and, according to classical electromagnetic theory, all accelerated charged particles emit electromagnetic radiations. We shall see later that this explanation of the production of X-rays is at least partially correct.

In common with other electromagnetic radiations, X-rays exhibit particle-like aspects as well as wave-like aspects. The reader will recall that the Compton effect, which is one of the most convincing demonstrations of the existence of quanta, was originally observed with electromagnetic radiation in the X-ray region of wavelengths.

Answer the following questions:

1. When were X-rays discovered?
2. How many characteristics were X-rays found to have?
3. Who postulated the main properties of X-rays?

以上三个题目都是细节性题目，我们不必仔细阅读整篇就可以回答。首先，我们要确定需要去找的信息是什么类型。可以利用题目中关键性的动词、名词等来确定。比如，这里第一个问答题中的 when 揭示了答案应该是一个年代，那么我们去文中搜索答案的时候，就要注意所有表示年代的数字；题目后面的动词“discovered”是另外一个关键信息。这时回到文章中寻找的信息就已经非常的简单明了，我们只需要把 when 和 discover 牢记心中，再去文中搜索，阅读效率就会大大提高，做起题目自然也就会加快。同样，第二道题中的“how many”说明答案仍然是个数字，另外一个关键信息是 characteristics。现在请你用同样的方法来回答第三题。

二 专题演练

练习 1：阅读下文，运用略读和查读法完成文后的练习。

Pulp Friction

1. Every second, 1 hectare of the world's rainforest is destroyed. That's equivalent to two football fields. An area the size of New York City is lost every day. In a year, that adds up to 31 million hectares—more than the land area of Poland. This alarming rate of destruction has serious consequences for the environment; scientists estimate, for example, that 137 species of plant, insect or animal become extinct every day due to logging. In British Columbia, where, since 1990, thirteen rainforest valleys have been clear-cut, 142 species of salmon have already become extinct, and the habitats of grizzly bears, wolves and many other creatures are threatened. Logging, however, provides jobs, profits, taxes for the government and cheap products of all kinds for consumers, so the government is reluctant to restrict or control it.

2. Much of Canada's forestry production goes towards making pulp and paper. According to the Canadian Pulp and Paper Association, Canada supplies 34% of the world's wood pulp and 49% of its newsprint paper. If these paper products could be produced in some other way, Canadian forests could be preserved. Recently, a possible alternative way of producing paper has been suggested by agriculturalists and environmentalists: a plant called hemp.

3. Hemp has been cultivated by many cultures for thousands of years. It produces fibre which can be made into paper, fuel, oils, textiles, food, and rope. For centuries, it was essential to the economies of many countries because it was used to make the ropes and cables used on sailing ships; colonial expansion and the establishment of a world-wide trading network would not have been feasible without hemp. Nowadays, ships' cables are usually made from wire or synthetic fibres, but scientists are now suggesting that the cultivation of hemp should be revived for the production of paper and pulp. According to its proponents, four times as much paper can be produced from land using hemp rather than trees, and many environmentalists believe that the large-scale cultivation of hemp could reduce the pressure on Canada's forests.

4. However, there is a problem: hemp is illegal in many countries of the world. This plant, so useful for fibre, rope, oil, fuel and textiles, is a species of cannabis, related to the plant from which marijuana is produced. In the late 1930s, a movement to ban the drug marijuana began to gather force, resulting in the eventual banning of the cultivation not only of the plant used to produce the drug, but also of the commercial fibre-producing hemp plant. Although both George Washington and Thomas Jefferson grew hemp in large quantities on their own land, any American growing the plant today would soon find himself in prison—despite the fact that marijuana cannot be produced from the hemp plant, since it contains almost no THC (the active ingredient in the drug).

5. In recent years, two major movements for legalization have been gathering strength. One group of activists believes that ALL cannabis should be legal -- both the hemp plant and the marijuana plant -- and that the use of the drug marijuana should not be an offense. They argue that marijuana is not dangerous or addictive, and that it is used by large numbers of people who are not criminals but productive members of society. They also point out that marijuana is less toxic than alcohol or tobacco. The other legalization movement is concerned only with the hemp plant used to produce fibre; this group wants to make it legal to cultivate the plant and sell the fibre for paper and pulp production. This second group has had a major triumph recently: in 1997, Canada legalized the farming of hemp for fibre. For the first time since 1938, hundreds of farmers are planting this crop, and soon we can expect to see pulp and paper produced from this new source.

Questions:

Select the answer you think is correct.

Skimming

1. The main idea of paragraph one is ____.
   A. scientists are worried about New York City
   B. logging is destroying the rainforests
   C. governments make money from logging
   D. salmon are an endangered species

2. The main idea of paragraph two is ____.
   A. canadian forests are especially under threat
   B. hemp is a kind of plant
   C. canada is a major supplier of paper and pulp
   D. canada produces a lot of hemp

3. The main idea of paragraph three is ____.
   A. paper could be made from hemp instead of trees
   B. hemp is useful for fuel
   C. hemp has been cultivated throughout history
   D. hemp is essential for building large ships

4. The main idea of paragraph four is ____.
   A. hemp is used to produce drugs
   B. many famous people used to grow hemp
   C. it is illegal to grow hemp
   D. hemp is useful for producing many things

5. The main idea of paragraph five is ____.
   A. hemp should be illegal because it is dangerous

B. recently, many people have been working to legalize hemp
C. hemp was made illegal in 1938
D. marijuana is not a dangerous drug

Scanning

6. How many species of salmon have become extinct in BC?
A. 27.
B. 31.
C. 137.
D. 142.

7. How much of the world's newsprint paper is supplied by Canada?
A. 31%.
B. 49%.
C. 34%.
D. 19%.

8. What equipment on a ship was made from hemp?
A. Ropes.
B. Waterproof cloth.
C. Engine fuel.
D. Life rafts.

9. What drug can be obtained from a relative of hemp?
A. Cocaine
B. Heroin
C. Amphetamine
D. Marijuana

10. Where was hemp farming recently legalized?
A. USA.
B. Canada.
C. Singapore.
D. Netherlands.

练习 2：请运用查读策略完成下列问题。

Scanning for Detail: Bad Weather Driving

Choose the correct answer from the text. The answers may be in any order, and chosen more than once.

When should a driver... ?

01. drive in the middle of the road
02. open a window

03. ask his passenger to sit in the back of the car
04. be most careful steering
05. avoid worn tyres
06. not drive on if there is another vehicle in front of him
07. wait for a larger vehicle to overtake him
08. definitely keep his headlights on
09. go as fast as the conditions will allow him
10. grip the wheel quite firmly
11. use his engine to help him break
12. stop to clean the car

A. When the Road is Wet

On wet roads, drivers should double the recommended distance between their car and the one in front, allowing two car lengths for every 10 mph. They should reduce their speed and steer with a gentle touch. However, they should at the same time grip the wheel firmly enough to resist the steering deflection that may occur when the front wheels, travelling at speed, hit a pool of water. These pools are often not easy to detect when the road surface is shiny with rain.

Modern tyres are designed to keep their grip on the road surface by squeezing water on the road out of their path, but at high speeds there is not always time for the water to escape. A car travelling at 60 mph on a quarter of an inch of water may lose practically all adhesion as the tyre aquaplanes along the road on a cushion of water. Worn tyres lose their grip at lower speeds on a thinner water film.

B. When the Road is Flooded

Drivers should not attempt to drive through a flooded stretch of road if there is a danger that the engine, especially the ignition system, will be under water. Drivers should get out and check on foot, or wait until a bus or lorry goes through the water and indicates the depth. If a crossing seems possible, take the crown of the road, and enter the water carefully to avoid a splash. Maintain a steady speed, not so fast that the water surges through the radiator grill, but fast enough to create a slight bow wave which will reduce the depth of water in front of the engine and help to keep the fan clear. Keep the engine revving hard to prevent water entering the exhaust pipe.

C. When the Road is Icy

When ice makes road adhesion minimal, drivers should brake, steer, accelerate and change gear with an extremely delicate touch. Most skids start when wheels lock or spin, and so drivers need to be careful with acceleration as well as braking. Double or even treble the distance from the vehicle in front, and use high gear to lessen the chances of wheel spin and skids. As much weight as possible should be kept directly over the wheels, and any passengers should sit in the back. If driving alone, weights such as bags of sand should be put on the back floor of front-engined cars, and in the front luggage compartment of rear-engined cars.

D. When the Road is Snow-Covered

To climb a hill in deep snow, gain as much speed as possible before the slope and avoid over-revving during the ascent, even if it means letting the engine over-work. If a gear change-down becomes essential, make it quickly to keep up forward movement. When you go down a snow-covered hill, use a lower gear to make use of engine-braking rather than the wheel brakes, which may lock and slide. If a slide does occur, release the brakes at once, steer a straight course, and then apply gentle braking by dabbing at the pedal. Try to avoid climbing a snow-bound hill if there is already a vehicle on it, because of the danger of collision if the other driver loses control.

E. In Falling Snow

When there is thick falling snow, drivers should use headlights and anything else which will help them to see and be seen. Drivers should stop occasionally to clean away the build-up of snow at the limits of the windscreen wipers' travel, and clear the back windows, wing mirrors and lights at the same time. It is a good idea to carry a plastic or rubber-bladed scraper in the car of this purpose. Keep the de-froster working and, if necessary, open a window to cut down interior misting. The road surface quickly becomes slippery as snow falls, so the driver should accelerate, steer and brake gently and allow extra braking distance.

三 专题答案

练习1：1. B 2. C 3. A 4. C 5. B 6. D 7. B 8. A 9. D 10. B

练习2：1. B 2. E 3. C 4. C 5. A 6. D 7. B 8. E 9. D 10. A 11. D 12. E

星期日

识别转述

雅思阅读部分的文章长，且题型多样，题数较多，但大部分的题目考查的是细节题（为文章的段落选小标题的文章除外）。做这些细节题目的第一步是看到题目后能迅速找到与题目中的信息相照应的文章的位置，然后再进行细读、分析和判断。完成这个任务需要两个步骤：一是找到题目中的关键词；二是带着关键词回到文中运用查读法迅速辨认出与关键词照应的信息。第一步我们在第二周进行阅读题型专项训练的时候再讨论，今天我们主要来了解题目中的关键信息在文中是如何被转述或照应的，这有助于我们发现雅思阅读题目的规律。

一 知识点拨

雅思题目中的信息与文中的信息照应的方式通常有以下几种：

1. 重现

重现即文章中的某些词汇等在题目中以原貌重现，通常这些重复性词汇有专有名词、数词、黑体词和连体词和部分词汇等。有时，题目中的词会以原文中的同根词的形式出现，如communicate 和 communication。以它们为线索词可以帮助我们迅速找到文章相应的信息所在的位置。请看下面的例子：

例 1

题目：In **Melbourne**, people **prefer** to **live** in the outer **suburbs.** （判断 TRUE，FALSE or NOT GIVEN）

原文：The explosion in demand for accommodation in the inner **suburbs** of **Melbourne** suggests a recent change in many people's **prefer**ences as to where they **live**.

分析：从题目和原文的对比中我们可以看出，题目和原文中的句子共有四处完全一致的照应，Melbourne、live 和 suburbs，另外题目中的动词 prefer 在原文中以它的同根词 preference 的形式出现。像此处有这么多重现的词汇，我们就可以确定答案就在这句话中。

例 2

题目：The territory of **Nunavut** consists of little more than **ice, rock** and a few…（完成摘要题——片断）

原文：**Nunavut** is 1.9 million square kilometers of **rock and ice,** and a handful of islands around the North Pole.

分析：题目和原文完全照应的有 Nunavut，ice，rock，只不过原文中的 rock and ice 在题目中出现的顺序颠倒了一下。此题是句子填空，原文中的 a few 是 a handful of 的近义表达，答案就是原文中 a handful of 之后的 islands。

例 3

题目：**Cheap labour** guarantees effective **trade** conditions. （判断 TRUE，FALSE or NOT GIVEN）

原文：**Cheap labour** may make Chinese clothing competitive in America, but if delays in shipment tie up working capital and cause winter coats to arrive in spring, **trade** may lose its advantages.

分析：题目和原文中都有 cheap labour 和 trade，但题目中的 guarantees effective trade conditions（保证有利的贸易条件）和原文中的 trade may lose its advantages（贸易可能会失去其优势）。

例 4

题目：The history of Europe has been documented since **3,000 BC**.（判断 TRUE，FALSE or NOT GIVEN）

原文：Conventional historical sources begin only with the introduction of written records around **3,000 BC** in western Asia, and much later in most other parts of the world.

分析：题目中的 3,000 BC 是最明显的信号词，我们带着这个信号词去文中查读，可以很快定位到包含 3,000 BC 的文中的相应部分。虽然文中没有出现题目中的 Europe，但是文中的“much later in most other parts of the world”说明欧洲的历史被记录的年代更晚。

文中的原词在题中重现可以帮助我们很快定位，但在雅思题目中像这种完全照应的情况还是属于少数，为了增加阅读题目的难度，出题者往往会使用其他的词汇和表达方式来表达文中同样的信息。

2. 近义表达

雅思题目中比较常见的是关键词在文中以同义词或同根词、或用其他词来转述的方式。

例 1

题目：Radar is an **inaccurate** term when **referring to** bats **because** ...... are not used in their navigation system. （句子填空）

原文：It is technically **incorrect** to **talk about** bat “radar”, **since** they do not use radio waves.

分析：题目中的 inaccurate 和文中的 incorrect 是近义词，referring to 照应 talk about，because 照应 since，并且题目和原文都出现了 use，只不过原文中是用 use 的主动态，而题目是被动态，因而答案应该是原文中 use 的宾语。

例 2

题目：However, even **before this was understood**, the principle had been **applied** in the design of instruments which **calculated** the ...... of the **seabed**. （完成摘要题——片断）

原文：**Before this was discovered**, engineers had already built instruments to **exploit** the principle, for example, to **measure** the depth of **the sea under a ship**.

分析：题目中的 before this was understood 照应 before this was discovered，applied 照应文中

的 exploit，calculated 照应文中的 measure，答案即文中 measure 后面的名词 depth。

例 3

题目：It has been **suggested** that children **hold mistaken views** about the 'pure' **science that they study at school.** （判断 TRUE，FALSE or NOT GIVEN）

原文：Many studies have **shown** that children **harbour misconceptions** about 'pure', **curriculum science.**

分析：题目中的 suggest 与文中的 show 是近义词，hold mistaken views 和 harbour misconceptions 是近义短语，curriculum science 的意思即为 science that they study at school。

3. 运用上义词或下义词

如果某个词的词义包含另一个词的词义，如 furniture 包括 sofa，那么我们把前者称为上义词，后者称为下义词。一个上义词往往有多个下义词，如 color 的下义词有：white、black、red、green、yellow 等。在雅思阅读中，文中表达某些信息的词汇在题目中以其上义词的方式出现，也比较常见。我们来看以下的例子：

例 1

题目：In fact, the sensation is more **similar** to the way in which pain from a …… **arm or leg** might be felt.（完成摘要题——片断）

原文：the sensation may be referred to the front of the face, **like** the referred pain in a phantom **limb**

分析：原文和题目完全照应的词 the sensation，pain，近义表达有 similar 和 like，而原文中的 limb 是"四肢"的意思，它的下义词即为 arm、leg，因此答案是原文中 limb 前面的形容词 phantom。

例 2

题目：In seventh-century Europe, the ability to count to **a certain number** was necessary in order to fulfil **a civic role**. （匹配题，黑体部分是答案）

原文：The average person in the seventh century in Europe was not as familiar with numbers as we are today. In fact, to qualify as **a witness in a court of law** a man had to be able to count to **nine**!

分析：原文和题目完全照应的表达有 in seventh-century Europe 和 in the seventh century in Europe，the ability to count 和 be able to count，而 a certain number 与 nine 是上义词和下义词的关系，同理 a witness in a court of law（法庭上的证人）属于 a civic role（公民角色）。

例 3

题目：Examples of **wildlife** other than bats which do not rely on vision to navigate by（信息定位题）

原文：Obviously **the night-flying insects** that they prey on must find their way about somehow. **Deep-sea fish and whales** have little or no light by or by night.

分析：题目的 wildlife 包括 the night-flying insects 和 deep-sea fish and whales。

4. 其他转述方式

其他转述方式还有改变词序和改变语态，如主动语态变为被动语态等。

例 1

题目：One characteristic is present in all of these explanations. （判断 TROE，FALSE or NOT GIVEN）

原文：All of these explanations share one characteristic.

分析：虽然原文中的 explanations 和 characteristic 与在它们在题目中出现的顺序相反，两个句子的结构也不太一样，但它们表达的意思完全一样。

例 2

题目：They set witnesses who do not intervene apart from the rest of us.

原文：Witnesses who do not intervene are separated from the rest of us.

分析：题目只是把原文中的被动语态改为主动语态，意思保持一致。

从以上可以看出，只要我们能根据题目中的关键词识别出文中被转述的相应信息，我们就基本上找到了解题的钥匙。而识别转述的根本在于能够识别雅思阅读中常见的词汇的近义词、上义词、下义词等相关表达。下面就列出在雅思阅读中常见的一些词汇的近义词。

雅思阅读高频同义替换表达

表示根据，依照，按照	according to, in accord with , consistent with, as said, as indicated by
表示影响	affect, influence, have effect on, impact
表示要求	demand, require, ask for, order, need, claim
表示下降、变差	decline, decrease, drop, fall, recession, depression, reduction, slump, worsening
表示难题、困惑	troubled, confused, puzzled, perplexed, mystified, at a loss
表示阐释、解释、澄清	make …clear, account for, clarify, elucidate, explain, justify, explicate, expound, illustrate, interpret
表示传统的、一般的	conventional, traditional, historical, past, accepted, common, regular, routine, mainstream, ordinary
表示发展	develop, evolve, advance, grow, improve, progress, flourish
表示困境	difficulty, handicap, hardship, adversity, challenge, complication, dilemma, perplexity, plight, trouble
表示最初的、最早的	early, first, old, ancient, primitive, previous, former, remote
表示发现、注意到	find, discover, come across, encounter, hit on, expose, notice, note, observe, recognize, spot, uncover
表示将来的、未来的	in the future, what's next, prospect, approaching, expected, destined, forthcoming
表示阻碍、障碍	obstacle, bar, barricade, barrier, block, blockage, check, obstruction, problem, snag, hurdle
表示表明、显示、发现	suggest, show, indicate, discover, reveal
表示某人的主张、观点	hold, maintain, claim, assert, believe, propose, posit, put forward, state, argue, contend
表示某人提出反对意见	objection, challenge, defy, disapproval, opposition, protest, question
表示盛行的、普遍的	prevalent, common, usual, prevailing, widespread, general, popular
表示商业的	commercial, business, economic, financial, mercantile, profitable, pecuniary
表示减少	reduce，curtail, cut, decrease
表示角色、职能、任务类	role，function, job, position, duty, post, task, contribution

（续）

与最近的、当今的相关的	recent，modern, current, now, nowadays, today, contemporaneous, new, novel, present, up-to-date
表示模仿类的	act like, imitate, copy, echo, simulate, duplicate, reproduce, follow example, follow suit, mimic, mirror, mock, model
表示重要性的	significance, importance, milestone, impact, justification, gist, implication, point, purport, vital
表示范围广泛的	worldwide，international, cosmopolitan, global, universal, ubiquitous, widespread, around the world
表示解决	solve, resolve, deal with, cope with, handle, tackle
表示消除	get rid of, eradicate, eliminate
表示依赖	rely on, depend on, count on
表示十分	very much, immensely, hugely, largely, greatly, enormously, tremendously
表示损害	damage, hurt, injure, harm, impair
表示给予	give, offer, render, impart, provide
表示发展	develop, cultivate, foster
表示优势	advantage, merit, virtue, benefit, upside, strength
表示缺陷	disadvantage, detect, demerit, drawback, downside, weakness
表示进步、提高的动词	improve, ameliorate, better, develop, remedy, revise, enhance, enrich, upgrade, refine
表示重要、关键	important, significant, consequential, momentous, considerable, essential, valuable, distinctive, great, weighty, major, serious, grave, vital, capital, substantial, material, conspicuous, striking, prominent, eminent, noticeable
表示正确的、无误的	correct, rectify, accurate, precise, proper, undistorted, right, impeccable
表示建立	to build up; to establish; to set up; to found; to take root; to strike root
表示消除	to eliminate; to clear; to remove; to clear up; to take away; to smooth away
表示导致	to lead to; to bring about (or on); to result in; to cause; to spark off; to conduce to; to procure; to induce; to generate

4周攻克

雅思阅读周计划

第二周　雅思阅读题型专项训练（一）

星期一

找小标题（list of headings）

一 题型描述

list of headings 的题目通常出现在文章的前面，通常是一个方框里罗列出一系列的小标题，方框下面给出考生需要为其选择标题的段落号。方框中的标题数目往往要多于指定的段落数目，也就是说有的段落可能有好几个标题，但考生需要为每个指定段落选择最合适的标题。

二 题型透视

题目中所给的小标题实际上都是对段落大意中的总结和概括，通常的形式是以主题词为中心的名词短语，因而这类题目实际上是考查考生找段落大意的能力。我们在第一周已经讲过如何寻找主题、大意和细节的技巧，这类题目就需要充分运用这种技巧。

三 解题步骤

Step 1：划去已选标题，开始阅读文章中与题目相照应的第一个段落或部分，阅读时跳过已选题目的段落。

Step 2：找出第一个段落的主题句（比较概括性的句子），跳读文中的例子、数据等一些具体细节。注意转折词后的句子，注意阅读文章中的首、尾句。

Step 3：提炼主题句的主题词，并想一下主题词的其他同义表达，然后回到题目中寻找出现主题词或主题词的近义表达的标题。

Step 4：对于确定的段落标题，选定并在标题框将其划去，以便不断缩小题目选择范围；对于难以确定题目的段落，可以留到最后再做，注意排除题目中没有出现相关信息的标题和包含段落中细节内容的标题。

四 技巧点拨

1. 划去已选标题；
2. 直接看文章，寻找每个段落的主题句或主题词，并作下记号；
3. 对于十分确定的段落标题，划去以便缩小选择范围，降低难度；
4. 对于不太确定或比较相近的标题，先画虚线，留到最后再做。

五 例题精讲

例题

The following passage has six sections **A– F**.

*Choose the correct heading for sections **A–D** and **F** from the list of headings below.*

*Write the correct number **i–ix** in boxes 1–5 on your answer sheet.*

List of Headings

i	The probable effects of the new international trade agreement
ii	The environmental impact of modern farming
iii	Farming and soil erosion
iv	The effects of government policy in rich countries
v	Governments and management of the environment
vi	The effects of government policy in poor countries
vii	Farming and food output
viii	The effects of government policy on food output
ix	The new prospects for world trade

1. Section **A**
2. Section **B**
3. Section **C**
4. Section **D**

Example	*Answer*
Section **E**	**vi**

5. Section **F**

Section A

The role of governments in environmental management is difficult but inescapable. Sometimes, the state tries to manage the resources it owns, and does so badly. Often, however, governments act in an even more harmful way. They actually subsidise the exploitation and consumption of natural resources. A whole range of policies, from farm-price support to protection for coalmining, do environmental damage and (often) make no economic sense. Scrapping them offers a twofold bonus: a cleaner environment and a more efficient economy. Growth and environmentalism can actually go hand in hand, if politicians have the courage to confront the vested interest that subsidies create.

Section A 分析：主题句一般是包含概括性字眼的文字，而且往往是位于段首。细节一般是支撑主题句的例子、事实、数据等，也就是说明 who，where，when，how，why 的。读完第一句 The role of governments in environmental management is difficult but inescapable，我们可以提出这样几个问题：What is the role of governments? How do they manage environment? Why is their role difficult and inescapable? 这说明这句话比较概括，但是否就是本段的中心句呢？我们再接着往下看。后面四个句子中的 sometimes，often，actually 和 a range of policy 都是在说政府在 environmental management 方面实际上是如何做的，也就是对第一句中提到的 government 在 environmental management 方面的具体表现，因而是细节。本段的最后两句是作者为政府在提供环境管理方面的解决思路。看完整段，我们可以发现主题就是第一句，这句话的主语是 the role of governments in environmental management，而且反复出现的字眼是 government 和 environmental management，因此我们回到标题框中去找出现这两个主题词的标题。很快可以发现选项 v（Governments and management of the environment）正好包含了全部关键字眼，因此可以判断此项正是 section A 的标题。

Section B

No activity affects more of the earth's surface than farming. It shapes a third of the planet's land area, not counting Antarctica, and the proportion is rising. World food output per head has risen by 4 per cent between the 1970s and 1980s mainly as a result of increases in yields from land already in cultivation, but also because more land has been brought under the plough. Higher yields have been achieved by increased irrigation, better crop breeding, and a doubling in the use of pesticides and chemical fertilisers in the 1970s and 1980s.

Section B 分析：第一句可以概括为 the effect of farming on earth's surface，第二句是对第一句的举例说明。第三句说世界粮食产量（world food output）增长及其原因，第四句仍然是在说粮食增长的原因。因此这一段有两个大意，一个是农业对地球表面的影响，一个是粮食增长的原因。两者的主语分别是农业和粮食增长。带着这两个主题词再回到题目中，看一下是否有包含这两个词组或近义词组的标题。很快我们就可以发现标题 vii（Farming and food output）正好包含了本段的两个主题词，因此 section B 选 vii。

Section C

All these activities may have damaging environmental impacts. For example, land clearing for agriculture is the largest single cause of deforestation. Chemical fertilisers and pesticides may contaminate water supplies. more intensive farming and the abandonment of fallow periods tend to exacerbate soil erosion; and the spread of monoculture and use of high-yielding varieties of crops have been accompanied by the disappearance of old varieties of food plants which might have provided some insurance against pests or diseases in future. Soil erosion threatens the productivity of land in both rich and poor countries. The United States, where the most careful measurements have been done, discovered in 1982 that about one-fifth of its farmland was losing topsoil at a rate likely to diminish the soil's productivity. The country subsequently embarked upon a program to convert 11 percent of its cropped land to meadow or forest. Topsoil in India and China is vanishing much faster than in America.

Section C 分析：本段的首句是一个大意句（main idea），原因是 damaging environmental impacts 非常概括。For example 是支撑大意的细节，类型是举例，第三句、第四句全都是在举例说明什么样的 activities 导致了什么样的 environmental impacts。这些 activities 分别有 land clearing，chemical fertilisers and pesticides，more intensive farming and the abandonment of fallow periods，the spread of monoculture and use of high-yielding varieties of crops。damaging environmental impacts 分别有 deforestation，contaminate，soil erosion，disappearance of old varieties of food plants。接着第五句 Soil erosion threatens the productivity of land in both rich and poor countries. 又是一个比较概括的句子，后面的句子举例说明穷国和富国土壤流失的具体情况，因而是支撑第五句的细节。本段的大意句有两个：第一句和第五句，它们的主题分别是 damaging environmental impacts of these activities 和 soil erosion，其中 activities 指的是各种农业活动。回到标题列中，可以发现标题 ii（The environmental impact of modern farming）和标题 iii（Farming and soil erosion）似乎都可以，但仔细分析可以看出第三个标题没有把本段最重要的主题词 environmental impacts 包括进去，而 soil erosion 实际上属于 the environmental impact of modern farming 的一种，因此应该选择 ii。

Section D

Government policies have frequently compounded the environmental damage that farming can cause. In the rich countries, subsidies for growing crops and price supports for farm output drive up the price of land. The annual value of these subsidies is immense: about $250 billion, or more than all World Bank lending in the 1980s. To increase the output of crops per acre, a farmer's easiest option is to use more of the most readily available inputs: fertilisers and pesticides. Fertiliser use doubled in Denmark in the period 1960-1985 and increased in The Netherlands by 150 percent. The quantity of pesticides applied has risen too: by 69 percent in 1975-1984 in Denmark, for example, with a rise of 115 per cent in the frequency of application in the three years from 1981.

In the late 1980s and early 1990s some efforts were made to reduce farm subsidies. The most dramatic example was that of New Zealand, which scrapped most farm support in 1984. A study of the environmental effects, conducted in 1993, found that the end of fertiliser subsidies had been followed by a fall in fertiliser use (a fall compounded by the decline in world commodity prices, which cut farm incomes). The removal of subsidies also stopped land-clearing and overstocking, which in the past had been the principal causes of erosion.

Farms began to diversify. The one kind of subsidy whose removal appeared to have been bad for the environment was the subsidy to manage soil erosion. In less enlightened countries, and in the European Union, the trend has been to reduce rather than eliminate subsidies, and to introduce new payments to encourage farmers to treat their land in environmentally friendlier ways, or to leave it fallow. It may sound strange but such payments need to be higher than the existing incentives for farmers to grow food crops. Farmers, however, dislike being paid to do nothing. In several countries they have become interested in the possibility of using fuel produced from crop residues either as a replacement for petrol (as ethanol) or as fuel for power stations (as biomass). Such fuels produce far less carbon dioxide than coal or oil, and absorb carbon dioxide as they grow. They are therefore less likely to contribute to the greenhouse effect. But they are rarely competitive with fossil fuels unless subsidised and growing them does no less environmental harm than other crops.

Section D 分析：这部分比较长，包含 3 个自然段。在时间比较有限的情况下，我们可以灵活运用速读和跳读策略迅速定位主题句。第一个段落的第一句话的意思是：政府政策常常加剧了农业对环境造成的破坏，概括起来就是政府政策对环境的影响。第二句紧接着具体阐明富国采取的哪些政策对环境造成了哪些影响，接下来的一些数字和年代表明作者在提供一些事实和数据来举例说明。第二段举例说明上个世纪 80 年代到 90 年代政策上的一些变化，第三段重点说明这些政策对农民的农业活动带来的变化及对环境的间接影响。现在看来这三段都是围绕政府政策对环境的影响而展开的。标题列包含政府政策的小标题有 iv（The effects of government policy in rich countries），vi（The effects of government policy in poor countries）和 viii（The effects of government policy on food output）。但 vi 是 section E 的标题，同时 viii 的标题范围过窄，因而只有标题 vi 最符合，因为这部分举的例子全都是发达国家的政府政策对环境的影响。

Section E

In poor countries, governments aggravate other sorts of damage. Subsidies for pesticides and artificial fertilisers encourage farmers to use greater quantities than are needed to get the highest economic crop yield. A study by the International Rice Research Institute of pesticide use by farmers in South East Asia found that, with pest-resistant varieties of rice, even moderate applications of pesticide frequently cost farmers more than they saved. Such waste puts farmers on a chemical treadmill: bugs and weeds become resistant to poisons, so next year's poisons must be more lethal. One cost is to human health. Every year some 10,000 people die from pesticide poisoning, almost all of them in the developing countries, and another 400,000 become seriously ill. As for artificial fertilisers, their use worldwide increased by 40 percent per unit of farmed land between the mid 1970s and late 1980s, mostly in the developing countries. Overuse of fertilisers may cause farmers to stop rotating crops or leaving their land fallow. That, in turn, may make soil erosion worse.

Section F

A result of the Uruguay Round of world trade negotiations is likely to be a reduction of 36 percent in the average levels of farm subsidies paid by the rich countries in 1986-1990. Some of the world's food production will move from Western Europe to regions where subsidies are lower or nonexistent, such as the former communist countries and parts of the developing world. Some environmentalists worry about this outcome. It will undoubtedly mean more pressure to convert natural habitat into farmland. But it will also have many desirable environmental effects. The intensity of farming in the rich world should decline, and the use of chemical inputs will diminish. Crops are more likely to be grown in the environments to which they are naturally suited. And more farmers in poor countries will have the money and the incentive to manage their land in ways that are sustainable in the long run. That is important.

To feed an increasingly hungry world, farmers need every incentive to use their soil and water effectively and efficiently.

Section F 分析：本段的第一句说 the Uruguay Round of world trade negotiations 可能导致杀虫剂的使用水平下降，第二句又说对世界粮食生产的影响。后面的部分都是在讨论 the Uruguay Round 可能带来的 environmental effects，因此我们可以判断本段的大主题是 the possible effects of a result of the Uruguay Round of world trade negotiations。小标题中的 i（The probable effects of the new international trade agreement）正好吻合了本部分的主题，其中 the new international trade agreement 指的正是 the Uruguay Round of world trade negotiations。

六 专题演练

Exercise 1

The following reading passage has eight sections, **A–H**.

*Choose the correct headings for sections **B–H** from the list of headings below.*

NB There are more headings than paragraphs, so you will not use them all.

List of Headings

i	First successful example of using nonfossil sources
ii	A promising future
iii	Better solution for recycling bioplastics
iv	Problems with degradable additives
v	Quick development of technology in using new materials
vi	Estimates about the future development
vii	Other products made from the biodegradable material
viii	A return to bio-based sources
ix	Advantages of the new materials
x	Limitation of biosourced materials
xi	Possible problems with biobased plastics

Example	*Answer*
Section **A**	**viii**

1. Paragraph **B**
2. Paragraph **C**
3. Paragraph **D**
4. Paragraph **E**
5. Paragraph **F**
6. Paragraph **G**

Bioplastics Boom

A Although the plastics industry has depended predominantly on petrochemicals for feedstocks throughout most of its history, some early plastics were plant based. Parkesine, the first human-made polymer, was created by inventor Alexander Parkes in 1856 out of chloroform and castor oil. Henry Ford unveiled the now-legendary "soybean car", with soy-based plastic body panels, in 1941. Now, as the price of petroleum rises and concern mounts about the environmental effects of petrochemicals, the plastics industry is racing to create renewable polymers from bio-based sources.

B At the ninth annual Bioplastics Conference, sponsored by European Plastics News and held last December in Cologne, Germany, the Brazilian petrochemical company Braskem received the top honor in the second Bioplastics Awards. Braskem announced last summer that it has developed a "green polyethylene" sourced entirely from sugarcane—a natural choice given that Brazil is the world's largest producer of sugar. Despite the recent bioplastics boom, this is the first time a substance exactly equivalent to petrochemical polyethylene has been produced from nonfossil sources. "What's taken everybody by surprise," says John Williams, technology-transfer manager at the U.K.'s National Non-Food Crops Center, "is the speed of development" of this material. "If you look back a few years, estimates put the development of polyethylene from nonpetrochemical sources at 2020."

C "You can't argue with the fact that a bio-based plastic offers better possibilities for end-of-life treatment," says Williams. The carbon released from these plastics represents no net addition to the atmosphere, whereas the production and incineration of petrochemical plastics boosts CO_2 levels. Because Braskem's polyethylene is identical to fossil-based plastics, it can be recycled along with them, making it possible to integrate the new material into established recycling systems. This trait also makes it easier for producers to adopt the new polymer. According to Morschbacker, it can be processed using the same equipment and settings that companies use for petroleum-based polyethylene. The machinery will never know the difference. Incineration at high temperatures (900 degrees Celsius) also shows promise. And though the technology is still new and the number of plants small, some companies are also using catalysts or microwaves to convert the polymers into gasoline or diesel. This could be good news for the biofuels sector as well: Recycling bioplastics into fuel could allay concerns about the use of food crops in biofuels production.

D Still, compared with biodegradable and largely biosourced polymers such as Mater-Bi, produced by the Italian company Novamont, Braskem's green polyethylene has slightly fewer end-of-life options. And Braskem's baby comes with the same toxicity issues as petrochemical plastics. Francesco Degli Innocenti, Ecology of Products and Environmental Communication Manager at Novamont, takes an equitable view: "Generally speaking, nonbiodegradable polymers seem to be more suitable for durable products (as durability could be impaired by biodegradability). For disposable items, biodegradability and compostability can be an advantage."

E Novamont fared well at the Bioplastics Awards too. Several award-winning products, including sanitary pads and a printable plastic film for use in packaging, use Mater-Bi (the name stands for "Material Biodegradable") as a component. Plastic shopping bags—traditionally made with polyethylene—are another product being made with the material. This is great news for consumers who want to compost their food wastes—placing scraps in a biodegradable bag and chucking it in the compost pile eliminates the task of cleaning out the compost bucket.

F As with any rapidly developing technology, the potential for false starts is there. Billiard balls coated with the early plastic collodion exploded on contact with one another. A recent example whose potential concerns Williams is that of degradable additives. Added to fossil-based plastics, they are designed to cause the plastics to fragment more quickly and prepare them for biodegradation by soil microbes. But Williams is not convinced they're a good idea. "The last thing you want is for a petrochemical plastic to degrade into CO_2," he says. "Why would you want to do that? It's like taking oil out of the ground and burning it—except in between you get to use plastic." And he has another worry: "I haven't seen any unbiased work that guarantees 100 percent degradation," he says. Small plastic fragments are hydrophobic and attract other hydrophobic particles—including pesticides and heavy metals—which can lead to bioaccumulation of toxic substances. If degradable additives were proved to be completely effective, however, they could be useful in providing end-of-life solutions for biobased plastics.

G Williams is optimistic about future developments: "Let's face it—biobased plastics at the moment are in their infancy. As you scale up, efficiencies and energy balances become better." Morschbacker agrees. "We have a big road to build," he says. "We'll look to life-cycle analysis to find the best options." Braskem is already hard at work: It has been operating pilot plants, which produce samples of the polymer for companies to test, for two years; large-scale commercial production is scheduled to begin in 2009. If both industry and independent research groups continue to show interest in these technologies, the results could be very promising indeed.

Keys:

1. i   2. ix   3. x   4. vii   5. xi   6. ii

Exercise 2

The following reading passage has eight sections, **A－F**.

*Choose the correct headings for sections **A－F** from the list of headings below.*

NB There are more headings than paragraphs, so you will not use them all.

List of Headings

i	The importance of smell to mammals
ii	Dealing with olfactory information
iii	Why some smells can activate our past memories
iv	The function of odor sensors
v	Evolutional basis for retrieving memory instantly
vi	Questions about the association between smell and memory
vii	"Nurture" or "nature"
viii	The role of smell in recalling memory
ix	Failure to recognize the complexity of the olfactory system
x	Features and mechanism of the olfactory system
xi	Insufficient knowledge about smell and more to be discovered
xii	Why smell is more important than other senses

1. Section **A**
2. Section **B**
3. Section **C**
4. Section **D**
5. Section **E**
6. Section **F**

Smell and Memory

Section A

Of all the senses, smell could be said to be the sense that is best at bringing back memories. When you smell a certain scent it feels as though you slipped back in time and that you are actually at that scene again. If it was not for the other senses of your body, you might really feel as though you are back there again. But why is it that smell has this ability to instantaneously trigger memories of events, places or people that you usually would not "think" of?

Despite the tendency of humans to underestimate the role of smell in our every day lives, for most mammals, smell is the most important sense. Dogs are probably the most obvious example of this. It is through the use of the olfactory system that animals are able to find food, reproduce, and even communicate. While being one of the oldest and important parts of the brain, our failure to fully realize the importance of the olfactory system resulted in it being surrounded by numerous questions. How does it work? How do we identify smells? While these are only a few questions out of a whole list, research has progressed in recent years that we know much more about the olfactory system than before, but the fact remains that much remains to be found.

Section B

Through research conducted on mice, it is approximated that humans have 1000 different sensors in their nose. While this might seem like a large amount of sensors, it is not enough considering mice and humans can identify about 10,000 odors. The mystery surrounding this ratio can be explained through the unique features of the olfactory system. Odors are molecular so the method used is different from light or sound that comes in waves.

Inside your nose about the level of your eyes is a small patch of tissue containing millions of nerve cells. The odor receptors (sensors) lie on these nerve cells. Each of the receptors recognizes several odors, and likewise a single odor could be recognized by several receptors. Thus similar to codes, what happens is that different combinations of the 1,000 receptors result in our ability to identify 10,000 different odors. Linda Buck, an associate professor at Harvard, makes an analogy of this quite efficient system to letters being used in different combinations to make individual words. She goes on to say that this system "greatly reduces the number of sensors needed to code for the smells".

An important quality of the olfactory system is that information travels both to the limbic system and cortex. The limbic system is the primitive part of the brain that includes areas that control emotions, memory and behavior. In comparison the cortex is the outer part of the brain that has to do with conscious thought. In addition to these two areas, information also travels to the taste sensory cortex to create the sense of flavor. Because olfactory information goes to both the primitive and complex part of the brain it effects our actions in more ways than we think.

Section C

Many wonder how certain smells able to trigger memories of events taking place several years ago despite the fact that sensory neurons in the epithelium survive for about only 60 days. The answer is that the neurons in the epithelium actually have successors. As the olfactory neurons die, new olfactory neurons generated by the layer of stem cells beneath them, which eventually takes the role of the old neuron as it dies. Linda Buck points out that the key point to the answer is that "memories survive because the axons of neurons that express the same receptor always go to the same place". The memories are stored in the hippocampus, and through relational memory certain smells trigger memories.

Section D

Another popular question is the reason behind smell having such a strong role in instantaneously recalling memory. Despite our belief that sight and hearing are the two most important senses to our survival, from an evolutionary perspective smell is one of the most important senses. To recognize food or to detect poison, smell is the sense that almost all other mammals use. Because of this basic feature yet vital role, smell is one of the oldest parts of our brain. Trygg Engen, a psychology professor at Brown University notes that smells serve as "index keys" to quickly retrieve certain memories in our brain. This primitive yet essential role is probably why smells trigger memory more than does seeing or hearing.

Section E

Professor Engen goes on in attempting to further explain the relation of odor and memory. His controversial views basically state that the way we sense odors are all results of "nurture" and not "nature". He says that initially all smells are neutral, and that whether an odor is pleasant or unpleasant has to do with the initial condition in which the smell is perceived. It follows from this that when we smell odors, it triggers a certain memory that has to do with that particular odor and thus is decided whether it is pleasant or unpleasant. Engen's views are controversial because of the lack of convincing data to back his views up. Although certain points about Engen seem to make sense, such as how odor serve to trigger memories like index keys, his views about the "nurture" vs. "nature" are a little harder to understand. If odors are decided by "nurture", it leaves the question of how so many people have a similar view towards many odors. There is probably nobody who would say that the smell of rotten food is good. Yet Engen's views are definitely worth considering because for some odors like gasoline, some people say it is good while others detest it.

Section F

It is said that people can identify about 10,000 different smells, but have many smells can you name off the top of your head? In comparison, look at how many colors there are in a crayon box, or the many varieties of music existing. This lack of understanding and appreciation of odors is a result of our over reliance on our eyes and ears, even to the extent that we suppress our awareness of what our nose tells us. Our underestimation of the role of smell results in our lack of extensive knowledge concerning many aspects of the olfactory system. But as Proust stated, smell has such a strong power to vividly bring back memories, it is definitely more important than we realize. To a large extent smell is more personal than other senses so it brings back memories of people, not just places, or things.

Keys:

1. vi 2. x 3. iii 4. v 5. vii 6. xi

星期二

判断题（T/F/NG）

一 题型描述

通常出现在文后，共有 3～8 道题目不等，以陈述句的形式呈现。考生需要根据文章内容判断陈述句与文中所提供的信息或作者的主张一致、矛盾，还是文中没有提到相关信息或者无法判断作者的主张正确与否，并相应地选择 true /yes、false /no 或 not given。

二 题型透视

这种题型属于细节题，目的是考查考生依据文章中所给的信息进行归纳、推理和判断的能力。

三 解题步骤

Step 1：划出题目中的关键词，方便回到原文定位。如果题目中有数字、大写的词（表人名、地名、机构名等专有名词）、黑体词、斜体词、连体词、加引号的词等，我们应该把它们优先作为关键词，因为这些词在文中一般会以原貌出现且比较容易辨认。如果没有的话，那么我们要找出句子中重要的主题词，并想想这些主题词的同义表达，然后快速记忆。

Step 2：带着关键词及它们的同义表达回到原文中查找答案的大致位置，然后精读关键词所在的句子，有时为了找出答案，你往往需要精读不止一个句子，有时甚至是整个段落。

Step 3：仔细比较文中和题目中的信息，判断题目的信息与原文是一致，矛盾还是未提及。

四 技巧点拨

1．当无法判断某题目是 false/no，还是 not given 时，看一下题目与原文中的信息是否兼容，兼容则 not given，不兼容则 false/no。

2．题目出现的顺序与文中相应信息出现的顺序是一致的，因而某题目的答案一定是在下一道题目出现之前，记忆相邻的两道题目的关键词可以缩小寻找答案的范围和时间。

五 例题精讲

现在我们来对雅思阅读题目中的判断题出现的 true（yes）、false（no）和 not given 的几种情况进行一下总结，从而把握这类题目设计的规律。

True 或 Yes 的情况

1. 题目是原文信息的同义表达

题目运用同义词、改变语序等方式转述原文中的信息。例如，假设原文是 he has a pretty wife，而题目是 his wife is good-looking 就判断为正确，因为 pretty 和 good-looking 是近义词，两者的主语也都一样。现在我们以雅思真题为例，来看判断为 true 或 yes 的情况。

例 1

原文：But since 1980, the amount of water consumed per person has actually decreased, thanks to a range of new technologies that help to conserve water in homes and industry.

题目：Modern technologies have led to a reduction in domestic water consumption.

分析：原文中的 thanks to 意思是 because of，正好照应了题目中同样表示因果关系的 led to。题目中的 modern techonologies 照应原文中 new technologies。而 the amount of water consumed per person 即是指 domestic water consumption。因而题目是运用同义词和转换语序的方式传达了原文的信息。

例 2

原文：By the age of three, the children in the programme were significantly more advanced in language development than their peers, had made greater strides in problem solving and other intellectual skills, and were further along in social development.

题目：Most 'Missouri' programme three-year-olds scored highly in areas such as listening, speaking, reasoning and interacting with others.

分析：题目中的 most 'Missouri' programme three-year-olds 照应原文中的 by the age of three, the children in the programme，scored highly 照应原文中的 were significantly more advanced 和 had made greater strides，而题目中的 listening, speaking 照应原文中的 language development, reasoning 属于 problem-solving 的智力技巧，interacting with others 又属于 social development。题目是运用近义词和同义词手段来转述原文信息。

2. 题目是原文信息的推理（常见）

我们先来看一个简单的例子，假设原文是 some of my friends like music，那么题目 not all of my friends like music 就是对原文的自然推理，因为 some 就暗含了 not all。还有一种情况是 my friend likes music, art, sports, 那么 my friend likes music 就是正确的。

例 1

原文：He was also helped by six assistants, two of whom died whilst the Dictionary was still in preparation.

题目：Not all of the assistants survived to see the publication of the Dictionary.

分析：原文中说"有六个助手帮他的忙，但其中两个助手在字典还在筹备期间就去世了"。题目中说"并不是所有的助手都看到了字典的出版，"因而是基于原文的正确推理，选 TRUE。

例 2

原文：All S.K.I programs have charged interest on the loans, primarily to get the entrepreneurs used to the concept of paying interest on borrowed money. Generally the rates have been modest (lower than bank rates).

题目：The children have to pay back slightly more money than they borrowed.

分析：题目中的 the children 指的是原文中的 the entrepreneurs（年轻的创业者）。原文说“所有的 S.K.I 项目对所有的贷款都收取利息，主要是为了让这些创业者们适应偿还借款利息的概念。这些利息一般不高（比银行利息低）。”偿还利息加借款，也就是偿还比借款更多的钱，这是利息这个词的内在含义决定的。同时文中又强调利息并不高，因此题目中说“这些孩子必须偿还比借款更多的钱”是文中的正确推理。

例 3

原文：Archaeology is partly the discovery of the treasures of the past, partly the careful work of the scientific analyst, partly the exercise of the creative imagination.

题目：Archaeology involves creativity as well as careful investigative work.

分析：原文提到说考古学包括了三个方面的工作，而题目中提到了两个部分，但题目中的 creativity 照应了原文中的 the exercise of the creative imagination，careful investigative work 照应了原文中的 the discovery of the treasures of the past，它们表达的意思都是一样的，因而题目判断正确。

3．题目是原文信息的概括（常见）

题目中的一句话往往是原文中几句话的归纳和总结。比如假设原文中提到 he is not only an actor but also a singer, a pianist, and a director，那么我们由此可以总结出 he is a versatile man。

例 1

原文：Beyond the practical need to make order out of chaos, the rise of dictionaries is associated with the rise of the English middle class, who were anxious to define and circumscribe the various worlds to conquer-lexical as well as social and commercial.

题目：The growing importance of the middle classes led to an increased demand for dictionaries.

分析：题目中的the growing importance of the middle classes照应原文中的the rise of the English middle class。原文中说“字典的兴起是和英国的中产阶级的兴起联系在一起的”，接着用一个非限制性的定语从句接着补充说明他们当时的需求。因而我们可以得出是因为资产阶级的兴起导致了字典需求量的增长。

例 2

原文：Culture in this sense includes what the anthropologist, Edward Tylor, summarized in 1871 as “knowledge, belief, art, morals, custom and any other capabilities and habits acquired by man as a member of society”. Anthropologist also use the term “culture” in a more restricted sense when they refer to the ‘culture’ of a particular society, meaning the non-biological characteristics unique to that society, which distinguish it from other societies.

题目：Anthropologists define culture in more than one way.

分析：原文中提到人类学家给 culture 的意义有 knowledge, belief, art, morals, custom and any other capabilities and habits acquired by man as a member of society，另外一种是比较狭

义的概念（in a more restricted sense），因而题目说"人类学家给文化的定义不只一种"则是对原文的概括。

False 或 No 的情况

1．题目与原文某部分的意思相反或矛盾

题目借助反义词或其他手段提供的信息与原文所给的信息相反，举个简单的例子，如果原文说 he likes swimming，那么题目 he doesn't like any sports 则与原文是矛盾的，因为 swimming 属于 sports 的一种。

例 1

原文： Beforehand, the students have been carefully prepared for the language learning experience. Through meeting with the staff and satisfied students they develop the expectation that learning will be easy and pleasant and that they will successfully learn several hundred words of the foreign language during the class.

题目： Prior to the suggestopedia class, students are made aware that the language experience will be demanding.

分析： 题目中的 prior to the suggestopedia class 照应文中的 beforehand 和 prepared for the language learning experience。同时，原文中说"学生们通过和教学人员和满意的学生会面，产生学习非常容易和快乐的期待"。而题目中说"会让学生们意识到语言（学习）经历会很难"，很明显是与原文的相反表达。在这里，题目的 demanding 与原文中的 easy 是反义词，而且它们的主语在原文和题目中指的都是同一个事物，即课堂学习语言的经历。

例 2

原文： At the height of the Roman Empire, nine major systems, with an innovative layout of pipes and well-built sewers, supplied the occupants of Rome with as much water per person as is provided in many parts of the industrial world today.

题目： Water use per person is higher in the industrial world than it was in Ancient Rome.

分析： 原文中的 as much water per person as 说明古罗马居民的用水量和现代工业世界的很多地方的人们用水量是一样的。而题目中说"现代工业世界中的人均用水量要比古罗马的高"，与题目正好相反。

2．题目与原文在某事物的范围、数量和频率等方面不一致。

例 1

原文： A new study conducted for the World Bank by Murdoch University's Institute for Science and Technology Policy (ISTP) has demonstrated that public transport is more efficient than cars. The study compared the proportion of wealth poured into transport by thirty-seven cities around the world.

题目： The ISTP study examined public and private systems in every city of the world.

分析： 原文中说"这项研究比较了世界上 37 个城市把资金投入到交通上的比例"，而题目中说"该研究调查了世界的每座城市的公共和私有交通设施"，城市范围大于原文，因而是错误的。

例 2：

原文：The lack of ability of some cultures to deal with large numbers is not really surprising.

题目：All cultures have been able to express large numbers clearly.

分析：原文中说“一些文化缺乏处理较大数目的能力并不让人吃惊”，暗含的意思是有些文化不会处理较大数目，而题目中说“所有文化都能够清楚地表达较大数目”，数量不一致。

3．题目是原文某部分信息的错误推理或概括（常见）

例 1

原文：The rich mixture of danger and detective work has also made it the perfect vehicle for fiction writers and film-makers, from Agatha Christie with *Murder in Mesopotamia* to Stephen Spielberg with *Indiana Jones*.

题目：Movies give a realistic picture of the work of archaeologists.

分析：原文中说“危险和侦探性的工作也成为小说家和电影制作家的最好的素材”，暗含的意思是这类小说或电影以考古学家的工作为蓝本然后又加以改编和加工，因而已经不是对考古学家工作的真实反映，而题目中“电影真实地描绘了考古学家的工作”，是对原文的错误推理，因而是判断为 FALSE。

例 2

原文：Thus, in this explanation the subject merges his unique personality and personal and moral code with that of larger institutional structures, surrendering individual properties like loyalty, self-sacrifice and discipline to the service of malevolent systems of authority.

题目：In a sociological explanation, personal values are more powerful than authority.

分析：原文中说“在这样一个解释中，受试人把他的个性，个人和道德准则融入到更大的一个体制结构中，把个人的一些品质如忠诚、自我牺牲和自制等都投入服务权威的充满恶意的体制中”。言外之意是权威的力量完全压倒了个人的价值观和道德观，而题目说“个人的价值观比权威更有力量”，是与原文完全相反的推理。

Not Given 的情况

1．无中生有型

题目中主语或（和）宾语在文中出现，但题目所陈述的关于主语或（和）宾语的行为、事件或关系在文中却没有出现，属于典型的无中生有型

题目 1：Archaeology is a more demanding field of study than anthropology.

题目 2：Opponents of smoking financed the UCSF study.

分析：题目 1 中 archaeology 和 anthropology 在原文中均出现了，但文中根本没有对两者的难易度进行比较，无法判断 T 或 F，这时就只能选 NOT GIVEN。题目 2 中只有 the UCSF study 出现在了文中，但研究是否由吸烟的反对者们资助的，文中却没有提供相应的任何信息或线索。

2．偷梁换柱型

原文中提到了某两个事物之间存在的一些关系或联系或动作，但题目中呈现的是这两个

事物之间的另外一种关系，两种关系不呈相反关系，可以并存，但文中没有提供任何相关信息来判断它的对错，这种情况下我们也要选 NOT GIVEN。举一个简单的例子，假设原文中提到 Mary is more beautiful than Lucy，而题目中说 Mary is more outgoing than Lucy 则为 not given。

例 1

原文： Yet there is a dark side to this picture: despite our progress, half of the world's population still suffers with water services inferior to those available to the ancient Greeks and Romans.

题目： Modern water systems imitate those of the ancient Greeks and Romans.

分析： 题目中说“现代的水利系统是模仿（imitate）古希腊和古罗马那个时候的”，但原文只提到说“现代的水利服务设施还不如（inferior）古罗马和古希腊的”，因为原文没有比较孰优孰劣，因而我们判断为 NOT GIVEN。

例 2

原文： As an illustration of the health risks, in the case of a married couple where one partner is a smoker and one a nonsmoker, the latter is believed to have a 30 percent higher risk of death from heart disease because of passive smoking.

题目： If one partner in a marriage smokes, the other is likely to take up smoking.

分析： 原文中说“结婚的双方如果有一方吸烟，那么另一方由于被动吸烟会有高于对方 30% 的患上心脏病的风险”。而题目中说“结婚的双方如果一方吸烟，另一方也可能吸烟”，这种关系和文中提到的两者之间的关系不矛盾，但文中没有提到，因此我们选未提及。

3. 题目增添了原文中没有的细节

题目和原文中都提到的事物以及关于事物的行为、动作、关系，但题目中呈现的信息在某方面比原文更加具体或添加了原文中没有的细节。假设原文是 he bought a book yesterday，而题目若是 he bought a math book yesterday 则是未提及。另一个例子是 she is one of the tallest students in her class，那么 she is the tallest students in her class 则是未提及，因为 one of the tallest 只给出了一个范围，但并没有具体说明在最高的同学中她的身高排在第几位。

例 1

原文： But it is also the painstaking task of interpretation, so that we come to understand what these things mean for the human story.

题目： Archaeologists must be able to translate texts from ancient languages.

分析： 文中提到“这（指考古工作）也是一个辛苦的解读的过程”，而题目中说“考古学家必须能够翻译古代语言的文字”。本题解题的关键在于对 interpretation 的正确理解，需要翻译古代的文字是一种 interpretation，但 interpretation 并不一定就是 translate texts from ancient languages，因而判断 NOT GIVEN。

例 2

原文： A comedian will present a situation followed by an unexpected interpretation that is also apt.

题目： Most comedians use personal situations as a source of humour.

分析： 原文中说“一个喜剧演员会给出一个情景，接着会给出一个出乎意料却又恰当的诠释”。

题目说“大多数喜剧演员会把个人情景作为幽默的来源”，题目和原文中的主语和主语的行为都是一致的，但题目中的 personal situation 把原文中 a situation 具体化了，因而本题是 NOT GIVEN。

六 专题演练

Exercise 1

The Role of Biology in Environment

Biology is the study of life and comprises all levels from the molecular to the global. Biology is the study living organisms, their organization and their functions and biology is a large part of the way our environment evolved from simple organisms and is thus intimately part of our environment. Biology is a very broad field, covering the minute workings of chemical machines inside our cells, to broad scale concepts of ecosystems and global climate change. Biologists study subjects which range from intimate details of the human brain, the composition of our genes, and even the functioning of our reproductive system to the building blocks of the simplest organisms on earth which created our oxygen rich atmosphere capable of supporting higher life forms. Without biological processes you and I would not exist, nor the planet as we know it.

Biological systems in contrast to physical are vastly more complex, their function based on small numbers of units (atoms, molecules, cells) that are not at equilibrium. There are no biological laws of nature the way we find them in physics; the first and second law of thermodynamics, Heisenberg's uncertainty principle, Newton's law of gravity etc.

The supreme importance of the role of biology in environment can be seen if we consider biotechnology. Biotechnology, as Aldous Huxley foresaw in Brave New World, can usher in as profound a revolution as industrialization did in the early 19th century. It will parallel vast other themes like the expansion of artificial intelligence, the opening of the inner solar system to economic use, and much more.

Biologists tolerate a level of mystery in their work that would drive your average engineer or computer programmer crazy. Biologists can see that role of biology in environment has shaped our very nature and being. Just look at the human genome studies that have been done. The biologists have put together a complete rough draft of the human genome but they have little understanding of how those 40,000 or so genes work together and interact with our environment to make a human.

Biologists, geneticists, and doctors have had limited success in curing complex diseases such as cancer, HIV, and diabetes because traditional biology generally looks at only a few aspects of an organism at a time. Again, we would suggest that this is due to the role of biology in environment which is so complex that the unraveling of these interactions is only now beginning to be discovered.

Biological processes of course are consequences of physics and chemistry, which is why we require biology students to study the physical sciences. But organisms are also historical entities molded by their environment both physical and social, and that's where the complexities arise.

Synthetic Biologists build artificial biological systems in an analogous way, using individual components such as single genes and enzymes for which the reactivity and the products formed are accurately known. Synthetic biology will catch up even faster when it appreciates the role of biology in environment. Assembly of simple synthetic circuits using DNA fibers has been demonstrated.

Systems Biology is the application of mathematical/physical modeling to understand the functions of biological processes. It describes a multi-component approach, combining theoretical modeling with real data about the interaction between genes and their products within the environment. Arising from this is the need to interpret large datasets of complex biological information. It seeks to integrate the knowledge derived from the study of individual components of cells to their performance as integral elements of cells, tissues and populations.

So, in summary we are suggesting that the role of biology in environment cannot be ignored at any level, nor could the reverse be true. Throughout evolution environment has influenced the development of biological systems which in their turn have fed back into the environment and changed the environment to the one in which we live today. The role of biology in environment is simply to have made the environment in which we all live our lives.

Questions 1–10

Do the following statements agree with information given in Exercise 1?

In boxes 1–10 on your answer sheet, write

YES	*if the statement agrees with the writer*
NO	*if the statement contradicts the writer*
NOT GIVEN	*if there is no information about this in the passage.*

1. Biology study is one of the branches of study on the environment.
2. Biology is of great importance to we human beings.
3. Biology system is as complex as physical ones.
4. Laws found in physics could not apply to Biology.
5. It is impossible for biologist to work out the operating mechanism of our genes.
6. There some serious problems with the way biologists work on organisms.
7. Biology bears little relationship with physics and chemistry.
8. Synthetic Biologists have made a breakthrough in the study of DNA.
9. Systemic biology does not take the environment genes interact with each other into consideration.
10. Biology has helped to shape the environment we live today.

Keys:

1. NG　2. Y　3. N　4. Y　5. NG　6. NG　7. N　8. NG　9. N　10. Y

Exercise 2

Almost everyone with or without a computer is aware of the latest technological revolution destined to change forever the way in which humans communicate, namely, the Information Superhighway, best exemplified by the ubiquitous Internet. Already, millions of people around the world are linked by computer simply by having a modem and an address on the "Net", in much the same way that owning a telephone links us to almost anyone who pays a phone bill. In fact, since the computer connections are made via the phone line, the Internet can be envisaged as a network of visual telephone links. It remains to seen in which direction the Information Superhighway is headed, but many believe it is the educational hope of the future.

The World Wide Web, an enormous collection of Internet addresses or sites, all of which can be accessed for information, has been mainly responsible for the increase in interest in the Internet in the 1990s. Before the World Wide Web, the "Net" was comparable to an integrated collection of computerized typewriters, but the introduction of the "Web" in 1990 allowed not only text links to be made but also graphs, images and even video.

A Web site consists of a "home page", the first screen of a particular site on the computer to which you are connected, from where access can be had to other subject related "pages" (or screens) at the site and on thousands of other computers all over the world. This is achieved by a process called "hypertext". By clicking with a mouse device on various parts of the screen, a person connected to the "Net" can go traveling, or "surfing" through a part of the screen, a person connected to the "Net" can go traveling, or "surfing" through a web of pages to locate whatever information is required.

Anyone can set up a site; promoting your club, your institution, your company's products or simply yourself, is what the Web and the Internet is all about. And what is more, information on the Internet is not owned or controlled by any one organization. It is, perhaps, true to say that no one and therefore everyone owns the "Net". Because of the relative freedom of access to information, the Internet has often been criticised by the media as a potentially hazardous tool in the hands of young computer users. This perception has proved to be largely false however, and the vast majority of users both young and old get connected with the Internet for the dual purposes for which it was intended — discovery and delight.

Questions 1–10

Do the following statements agree with information given in Exercise 2?

In boxes1–10 on your answer sheet, write

TRUE	*if the statement agrees with the information*
FALSE	*if the statement contradicts the information*
NOT GIVEN	*if there is no information on this*

1. Everyone is aware of the Information Superhighway.
2. Using the Internet costs the owner of a telephone extra money.
3. Internet computer connections are made by using telephone lines.
4. The World Wide Web is a network of computerised typewriters.
5. According to the author, the Information Superhighway may be the future hope of education.
6. The process called 'hypertext' requires the use of a mouse device.
7. The Internet was created in the 1990s.
8. The 'home page' is the first screen of a 'Web'site on the 'Net'.
9. The media has often criticised the Internet because it is dangerous.
10. The latest technological revolution will change the way humans communicate.

Keys:

1. F 2. NG 3. T 4. F 5. T 6. T 7. F 8. T 9. F 10. T

Exercise 3

The Australian political scene is dominated by two major parties that have quite different political agendas. However, the policies of the Australian Labor Party and the Liberal Party have become much more difficult to tell apart in recent years. In fact, it would be true to say that both parties consist of conservative, moderate and radical elements, and therefore the general public is often perplexed about which party to vote for. Nonetheless, it is usual to find that an Australian will lean towards supporting one of these two parties and remain faithful to that party for life.

The Labor Party was formed early in the twentieth century to safeguard the interests of the common working man and to give the trade unions political representation in Parliament. The Party has always had strong connections with the unions, and supports the concept of a welfare society in which people who are less fortunate than others are financially, and otherwise, assisted in their quest for a more equitable slice of the economic pie. The problem is that such socialist political agendas are extremely expensive to implement and maintain, especially in a country that, although comparatively wealthy, is vast and with a small working and hence taxpaying population base. Welfare societies tend towards bankruptcy unless government spending is kept in check. The Liberal Party, on the other hand, argues that the best way to ensure a fair division of wealth in the country is to allow more freedom to create it.This, in turn, means more opportunities, jobs created etc., and therefore more wealth available to all. Just how the poor are to share in the distribution of this wealth (beyond being given, at least in theory, the opportunity to create it) is, however, less well understood. Practice, of course, may make nonsense of even the best theoretical intentions, and often the less politically powerful are badly catered for under governments implementing 'free-for-all' policies.

It is no wonder that given the two major choices offered them, Australian voters are increasingly turning their attention to the smaller political parties, which claim to offer a more balanced swag of policies, often based around one major current issue. Thus, for instance, at the last election there was the No Aircraft Noise Parry, popular in city areas, and the Green Party, which is almost solely concerned with environmental issues.

Questions 1–10

Do the following statements agree with information given in Exercise 3?
In boxes1-10 on your answer sheet, write

TRUE	*if the statement agrees with the information*
FALSE	*if the statement contradicts the information*
NOT GIVEN	*if there is no information on this*

1. Policies is support of the concept of a welfare society are costly.
2. Australians usually vote for the party they supported early in life.
3. The Labor Party was formed by the trade unions.
4. Radical groups are only found within the Labor Party.
5. The Liberal Party was formed after the Labor Party.
6. Welfare-based societies invariably become bankrupt.
7. According to the author, theories do not always work in practice.
8. Some Australian voters are confused about who to vote for.
9. The No-Aircraft-Noise Party is only popular in the city.
10. The smaller parties are only concerned about the environment.

Keys:

1. T　2. NG　3. NG　4. F　5. NG　6. F　7. T　8. T　9. NG　10. F

星期三

信息定位题（locating information）

一 题型描述

这种题型会给出一些包含文中部分信息的句子，考生需要从文章中辨别出那些段落包含题中所给的信息，并把代表段落的字母和相应的句子相匹配。有的段落可能包含题目中给出的止一种信息，有的段落可能没有包含题目中的任何信息，且题目中信息出现的顺序与文章段落先后的顺序毫不相关。

二 题型透视

题目所给的句子是对原文某些信息的转述或不同程度的概括，因此本题考查考生对原文细节部分的信息进行识别、提炼和概括的能力。但总体来看，本题型还是考查考生寻找细节的能力，不管是小的细节还是大的细节。

三 解题步骤

Step 1：迅速浏览题目，标出所有题目的关键词（若句子中有数字、大写的词、连体词、斜体词等较容易辨别的词我们把它们优先作为信号词），并联想与关键词所有相关的词，包括近义词、反义词、下义词和同根词等。

Step 2：带着信号词或关键词以及所能想到的关键词的相关词回到原文中顺序阅读，注意寻找信号词，关键词和关键词的同根词。

Step 3：当在原文中找到某个题目的信号词或关键词后仔细阅读该词所在的段落部分，确定该部分与题目中所给的信息相照应。

四 技巧点拨

1. 如果文章有标题和副标题的话，建议先浏览一下标题的内容，了解文章的主题。

2. 如果题目比较多，可以先阅读文章的首、尾段，然后再阅读题目，一般可以做出一两道题，由此减少记忆负担。

五 例题精讲

例 1

Questions 1-7

Reading Passage 1 has six paragraphs, A- F. Which paragraph contains the following information?

Write the correct letter ***A–F****, in boxes* ***1–7*** *on your answer sheet.*

NB *You may use any letter more than once.*

1. a reference to the exchange of expertise between different sports
2. an explanation of how visual imaging is employed in investigations
3. a reason for narrowing the scope of research activity
4. how some AIS ideas have been reproduced
5. how obstacles to optimum achievement can be investigated
6. an overview of the funded support of athletes
7. how performance requirements are calculated before an event

首先我们划出每道题目的关键词。找关键词时，跟所有细节题一样，如果有比较容易辨认的词，如数字、大写的词等时，我们要优先把它们作为关键词，如果没有的话，我们要找每个小题中的中心词和相对比较具体的词。

第 1 题中关键短语是 exchange of expertise，而 expertise 指“专门知识或技能”，它的近义词有 knowledge 和 skills，另外一个关键词是 different sports，这时我们就需要想想 sports 所有的下义词，当文中出现不同体育运动之间的技能转换的时候，我们就可以确定是该信息出现的位置。

第 2 题中 explanation 和 investigation 是比较概括的词，在文中可能不会直接出现，比较重要且相对具体的词有 visual imaging，还有动词 employ，文中可能会以 employ 的同义词出现，如 apply，use 等，因此我们在这里把 visual imaging 作为关键词，所有与这个词组相关的词我们都需要仔细阅读。

第 3 题的意思是“缩小研究活动范围的一个原因”，narrowing the scope 也就是 focus on one or two aims。

第 4 题中有一个很明显的大写的词 AIS，我们直接把它作为关键词，另外还有一个关键的动词 reproduce，它的近义词有 copy，duplicate, replicate 等。

第 5 题中关键词是 obstacles to optimum achievement，即“达到最佳表现的障碍”。

第 6 题中的关键词是 funded support, 我们要想想所有跟 fund 有关的词汇。

第 7 题中关键词组是 before an event, 即“在一场比赛开始之前”。现在开始阅读文章。由于题目中的信息在文中是乱序出现，我们就必须逐段阅读文章，同时注意题目涉及的具体信息。

READING PASSAGE 1

Australia's Sporting Success

A They play hard, they play often, and they play to win. Australian sports teams win more than their fair share of titles, demolishing rivals with seeming ease. How do they do it? A big part of the secret is an extensive and expensive network of sporting academies underpinned by science and medicine. At the Australian Institute of Sport (AIS), hundreds of youngsters and pros live and train under the eyes of coaches. Another body, the Australian Sports Commission (ASC), finances programmes of excellence in a total of 96 sports for thousands of sportsmen and women. Both provide intensive coaching, training facilities and nutritional advice.

分析：这一段我们注意到与 fund 相关的一个词 finances，sportsmen and women 的同义表达是 athletes，provide intensive coaching，training facilities and nutritional advice 表示 support，因此我们可以确定本段包含第 6 小题的信息。

B Inside the academies, science takes centre stage. The AIS employs more than 100 sports scientists and doctors, and collaborates with scores of others in universities and research centres. AIS scientists work across a number of sports, applying skills learned in one – such as building muscle strength in golfers – to others, such as swimming and squash. They are backed up by technicians who design instruments to collect data from athletes. They all focus on one aim: winning. "We can't waste our time looking at ethereal scientific questions that don't help the coach work with an athlete and improve performance," says Peter Fricker, chief of science at AIS.

分析：本段虽然多次出现 AIS，但是却没有出现与第 4 小题相关的内容。然而在本段的第 3 行我们可以发现 skills 和多项运动项目像 golfers, swimming, squash。同时包含这些词的句子说"把一种运动中学到的技巧应用到另一种"，因此本段包含第 1 小题中的信息。我们再继续往下看发现有一个 focus on one aim，即"只集中一个目标"，后面是 AIS 机构中的一个领导人给出的原因，因此本段还包含第 3 小题中的信息。

C A lot of their work comes down to measurement–everything from the exact angle of a swimmer's dive to the second-by-second power output of a cyclist. This data is used to wring improvements out of athletes. The focus is on individuals, tweaking performances to squeeze an extra hundredth of a second here, an extra millimetre there. No gain is too slight to bother with. It's the tiny, gradual improvements that add up to world-beating results. To demonstrate how the system works, Bruce Mason at AIS shows off the prototype of a 3D analysis tool for studying swimmers. A wire-frame model of a champion swimmer slices through the water, her arms moving in slow motion. Looking side-on, Mason measures the distance between strokes. From above, he analyses how her spine swivels. When fully developed, this system will enable him to build a biomechanical profile for coaches to use to help budding swimmers. Mason's contribution to sport also includes the development of the SWAN (SWimming ANalysis) system now used in Australian national competitions. It collects images from digital cameras running at 50 frames a second and breaks down each part of a swimmer's performance into factors that can be analysed individually – stroke length, stroke frequency, average duration of each stroke, velocity, start, lap and finish times, and so on. At the end of each race, SWAN spits out data on each swimmer.

分析：本段出现 3D，images 等与 visual imaging 相关的词汇，而且本段提到它们利用搜集到的图像来分析运动员的细微的运动表现，因此本段包含第 2 小题中的信息。

D "Take a look," says Mason, pulling out a sheet of data. He points out the data on the swimmers in second and third place, which shows that the one who finished third actually swam faster. So why did he finish 35 hundredths of a second down? "His turn times were 44 hundredths of a second behind the other guy," says Mason. "If he can improve on his turns, he can do much better." This is the kind of accuracy that AIS scientists' research is bringing to a range of sports. With the Cooperative Research Centre for Micro Technology in Melbourne, they are developing unobtrusive sensors that will be embedded in an athlete's clothes or running shoes to monitor heart rate, sweating, heat production or any other factor that might have an impact on an athlete's ability to run. There's more to it than simply measuring performance. Fricker gives the example of athletes who may be down with coughs and colds 11 or 12 times a year. After years of experimentation, AIS and the University of Newcastle in New South Wales developed a test that measures how much of the immune-system protein immunoglobulin A is present in athletes' saliva. If IgA levels suddenly fall below a certain level, training is eased or dropped altogether. Soon, IgA levels start rising again, and the danger passes. Since the tests were introduced, AIS athletes in all sports have been remarkably successful at staying healthy.

分析：本段的开头给出两位位于比赛第二名和第三名的运动员的表现数据，并指出实际上位于第三名的运动员游得更快，但为什么落后于第二名呢，是因为转身的速度慢了。接着说是如何利用一些特殊的技术手段来发现影响运动员发挥的因素的。在本段的后面又出现了 any other factor that might have an impact on an athlete's ability to run，因此我们可以确定本段包含第 5 小题中的信息。本题稍微有些难度，需要读懂文中的部分关键信息。

E Using data is a complex business. Well before a championship, sports scientists and coaches start to prepare the athlete by developing a "competition model", based on what they expect will be the winning times. "You design the model to make that time," says Mason. "A start of this much, each free-swimming period has to be this fast, with a certain stroke frequency and stroke length, with turns done in these times: All the training is then geared towards making the athlete hit those targets, both overall and for each segment of the race. Techniques like these have transformed Australia into arguably the world's most successful sporting nation.

分析：本段开头的第二句出现了一个短语 before a championship。championship 是"冠军赛"或"锦标赛"的意思，是 event 的近义词，而第 7 小题中正好包括 before an event。接着往下读可以发现，体育科学家们开发了一种 competition model 来计算获胜的时间。因此本段包含了第 7 小题中的信息。

F Of course, there's nothing to stop other countries copying – and many have tried. Some years ago, the AIS unveiled coolant-lined jackets for endurance athletes. At the Atlanta Olympic Games in 1996, these sliced as much as two per cent off cyclists "and rowers" times. Now everyone uses them. The same has happened to the "altitude tent", developed by AIS to replicate the effect of altitude training at sea level. But Australia's success story is about more than easily copied technological fixes, and up to now no nation has replicated its all-encompassing system.

分析：本段出现了 AIS，而且还出现 copying，replicate 等 reproduce 的近义词，因而本段包含第 4 小题中的信息。

六 专题演练

Exercise 1

A Magic Number?

An Australian team says it has figured out the minimum viable population for mammals, reptiles, birds, plants and the rest.

A Imagine how useful it would be if someone calculated the minimum population needed to preserve each threatened organism on Earth, especially in this age of accelerated extinctions. A group of Australian researchers say they have nailed the best figure achievable with the available data: 5,000 adults. That's right, that many, for mammals, amphibians, insects, plants and the rest. Their goal wasn't a target for temporary survival. Instead they set the bar much higher, aiming for a census that would allow a species to pursue a standard evolutionary lifespan, which can vary from one to 10 million years.

B That sort of longevity requires abundance sufficient for a species to thrive despite significant obstacles, including random variation in sex ratios or birth and death rates, natural catastrophes and habitat decline. It also requires enough genetic variation to allow adequate amounts of beneficial mutations to emerge and spread within a populace. "We have suggested that a major rethink is required on how we assign relative risk to a species," says conservation biologist Lochran Traill of the University of Adelaide, lead author of a *Biological Conservation* paper describing the projection.

C Conservation biologists already have plenty on their minds these days. Many have concluded that if current rates of species loss continue worldwide, Earth will face a mass extinction comparable to the five big extinction events documented in the past. This one would differ, however, because it would be driven by the destructive growth of one species: us. More than 17,000 of the 47,677 species assessed for vulnerability of extinction are threatened, according to the latest Red List of Threatened Species prepared by the International Union for Conservation of Nature. That includes 21 percent of known mammals, 30 percent of known amphibians, 12 percent of known birds and 70 percent of known plants. The populations of some critically endangered species number in the hundreds, not thousands.

D In an effort to help guide rescue efforts, Traill and colleagues, who include conservation biologists and a geneticist, have been exploring minimum viable population size over the past few years. Previously they completed a meta-analysis of hundreds of studies considering such estimates and concluded that a minimum head count of more than a few thousand individuals would be needed to achieve a viable population. "We don't have the time and resources to attend to finding thresholds for all threatened species, thus the need for a generalization that can be implemented across taxa to prevent extinction," Traill says.

E In their most recent research they used computer models to simulate what population numbers would be required to achieve long-term persistence for 1,198 different species. A minimum population of 500 could guard against inbreeding, they conclude. But for a shot at truly long-term, evolutionary success, 5,000 is the most parsimonious number, with some species likely to hit the sweet spot with slightly less or slightly more. "The practical implications are simply that we're not doing enough, and that many existing targets will not suffice," Traill says, noting that many conservation programs may inadvertently be managing protected populations for extinction by settling for lower population goals.

F The prospect that one number, give or take a few, would equal the minimum viable population across taxa doesn't seem likely to Steven Beissinger, a conservation biologist at the University of California at Berkeley. "I can't imagine 5,000 being a meaningful number for both Alabama beach mice and the California condors. They are such different organisms," Beissinger says. Many variables must be considered when assessing the population needs of a given threatened species, he says. "This issue really has to do with threats more than stochastic demography. Take the same rates of reproduction and survival and put them in a healthy environment and your minimum population would be different than in an environment of excess predation, loss of habitat or effects from invasive species."

G But, Beissinger says, Traill's group is correct for thinking that conservation biologists don't always have enough empirically based standards to guide conservation efforts or to obtain support for those efforts from policy makers. "One of the positive things here is that we do need some clear standards. It might not be establishing a required number of individuals. But it could be clearer policy guidelines for acceptable risks and for how many years into the future can we accept a level of risk," Beissinger says. "Policy people do want that kind of guidance."

H Traill sees policy implications in his group's conclusions. Having a numerical threshold could add more precision to specific conservation efforts, he says, including stabs at reversing the habitat decline or human harvesting that threaten a given species. "We need to restore once-abundant populations to the minimum threshold," Traill says. "In many cases it will make more economic and conservation sense to abandon hopeless-case species in favor of greater returns elsewhere.

Questions 1–7

The above reading passage has eight paragraphs, **A–H**.

Which paragraph contains the following information?

*Write the correct letter **A–H**, in boxes 1–7 on your answer sheet.*

***NB** You may use any letter more than once.*

1. initial research on calculating the number for a viable population
2. possible risks which might be encountered by a species
3. the potential impact of a threshold upon policy making
4. proportions of different kinds of endangered animals
5. concerns on smaller population sizes
6. the criteria for setting the minimum population size for the survival of a species
7. doubts cast on the viable population size

Keys:

1. D　2. B　3. H　4. C　5. E　6. A　7. F

Exercise 2

Amplifying with Acid

More carbon dioxide in the atmosphere means a noisier ocean

Carbon dioxide has gained notoriety as a "greenhouse gas"; it's one of the major waste products from human industrial activities that contribute to climate change. However, the gas that we release into the atmosphere is also absorbed into the oceans at a rate of about a million tons per hour. Seawater reacts with carbon dioxide to form carbonic acid, decreasing the pH of the oceans. This outcome has its own environmental impacts, such as damage to coral reefs and aquatic-animal respiration, but it also has a secondary consequence: It decreases the ocean's ability to absorb low-frequency sound.

Oceanographers Tatiana Ilyina and Richard Zeebe of the University of Hawaii, along with geochemist Peter Brewer of the Monterey Bay Aquarium Research Institute in California, report in the December 20 issue of Nature Geoscience that lowering the pH of the ocean by 0.6 units could decrease underwater low-frequency sound absorption by more than 60 percent. "Ocean acidification is not only affecting the chemistry of the ocean, but it also affects the basic physical properties," says Ilyina.

The ocean surface's average pH is currently estimated to be around 8.1, and to have dropped from about 8.2 since around 1800, before the industrial revolution took off, says Zeebe. A reduction of 0.1 units does not sound like much, but pH units are on a logarithmic scale, so a drop of one unit corresponds to a tenfold increase in acidity.

Using projections of fossil-fuel CO_2 emissions over the next century from the Intergovernmental Panel on Climate Change (IPCC), the researchers calculated changes for seawater pH at the surface and at a depth of 1 kilometer, along with the corresponding changes in sound absorption at several frequencies below 10 kilohertz. In the IPCC's "moderate" scenario, in which CO_2 emissions remain at a constant level, pH drops by about 0.6 units at the ocean's surface, and by about 0.2 to 0.4 units at depth.

The corresponding lowering of sound absorption depends on location and frequency. At a frequency of about 200 hertz, the drop ranges from about 10 to about 50 percent. Across all frequencies, the change is largest in the polar regions, because the colder water absorbs more CO_2 and thus has a greater pH change.

Changes in pH can impact the deep ocean because at about 1 kilometer down, the properties of temperature and pressure combine to produce a "channel" of water in which sound can propagate for many thousands of kilometers. Whales and other marine life make use of this channel for long-range communication. Most human-made ocean noise forms at the surface, but it can reflect and refract down into this channel as well.

Although the vast majority of sound loss in the ocean is due to distance, reflections and turbulence, the pH- dependent component of the ocean's sound absorbance comes from resonance reactions in natural salts, namely boric-acid compounds and magnesium sulfate. The reaction is similar for both, but it's more straightforward in magnesium sulfate, says Brewer: "The magnesium ion and the sulfate ion are attracted to each other—in human terms it's like they're dating—and in their normal state they exist with a single water molecule between them, like a courting couple would have a chaperone. When a sound wave comes through, it tends to squeeze that group together and the water molecule pops out, so our attracted couple just touches, ever so briefly. When the sound wave passes by, the water molecule jumps back in and separates the pair. And the work done to do that robs the sound wave of some energy." The problem is that as the ocean becomes more acidic, the ionized form of borate decreases, so there is less of the salt form to resonate and absorb sound.

Brewer emphasizes that this decreased-absorption effect is confined to a relatively small range of frequencies, between about 100 hertz and 10 kilohertz. He estimates that the effect will be most strongly felt around 200 to 600 hertz, over distances of roughly 100 miles. "We're talking 40 percent of a small effect, so it isn't a lot," he says. "On the other hand, 40 percent is a big number in itself; if any species is sensitive in that range, they would notice the change in that scale."

The affected range includes a large proportion of the frequencies used by marine organisms. Also, most human-generated ocean noise is in the range of 10 hertz to 1 kilohertz, and the volume is rising: The biggest component is shipping, and the number of ships worldwide has approximately doubled over the past 40 years. The researchers calculate that there could be "acoustic hotspots" that are most sensitive to changes in sound propagation, such as areas at the more extreme latitudes that also experience a lot of shipping.

"This effect has been off the radar screen, so to come along and say 'hey, what about this' is important," says Brewer. "It means there are new ways of looking at the Earth, it means we are nowhere near to running out of things that are going to change. We're fairly far down this greenhouse-gas road, and we're nowhere near to knowing what's going to happen to us. It's a strange new world we're getting into."

Questions 1–7

The above reading passage has six paragraphs, **A–F**.

Which paragraph contains the following information?

*Write the correct letter **A–F**, in boxes 1–7 on your answer sheet.*

***NB** You may use any letter more than once.*

1. initial research on calculating the number for a viable population
2. possible risks which might be encountered by a species
3. the potential impact of a threshold upon policy making
4. proportions of different kinds of endangered animals
5. concerns on smaller population sizes
6. the criteria for setting the minimum population size for the survival of a species
7. doubts cast on the viable population size

Keys:

1. D 2. B 3. H 4. C 5. E 6. A 7. F

Exercise 3

Extraordinary Perception

We think of people with autism as having a deficit in cognitive processing—but their distractibility could also result from having enhanced perceptual capabilities.

A When Pulitzer Prize–winning music critic Tim Page was in second grade, he and his classmates went on a field trip to Boston. He later wrote about the experience as a class assignment, and what follows is an excerpt: "Well, we went to Boston, Massachusetts, through the town of Warrenville, Connecticut, on Route 44A. It was very pretty, and there was a church that reminded me of pictures of Russia from our book that is published by Time-Life. We arrived in Boston at 9:17. At 11 we went on a big tour of Boston on Gray Line 43, made by the Superior Bus Company like School Bus Six, which goes down Hunting Lodge Road where Maria lives and then on to Separatist Road and then to South Eagleville before it comes to our school. We saw lots of good things like the Boston Massacre site. The tour ended at 1:05. Before I knew it we were going home. We went through Warrenville again, but it was too dark to see much. A few days later it was Easter. We got a cuckoo clock."

B Page received an unsatisfactory grade on his essay. What's more, his irate teacher scrawled in red across the top of the essay: "See me!" As he recalls in his new memoir Parallel Play, such incidents were not uncommon in his childhood, and he knew why he was being scolded: "I had noticed the wrong things."

C The subtitle of Page's memoir is Growing Up with Undiagnosed Asperger's, and indeed Page didn't learn until age 45 that he suffers from what is called autism spectrum disorder, or ASD. ASD is usually defined by impairments in social interaction and communication, but many people with autism and Asperger's syndrome (in which symptoms are milder) also tend to fixate on and remember seemingly irrelevant information in their world. Their attention seems to be awry, or to use Page's words, they notice the wrong things.

D But why? What's going on in the autistic mind that makes the details of bus routes infinitely fascinating? Why are people like Page so easily distracted from the main act? Psychologists at University College London think that it might be a mistake to consider such distractibility as simply a deficit. To the contrary, Anna Remington and John Swettenham and their colleagues speculate that people with ASD might have a greater than normal capacity for perception, so that what appears as irrelevant distraction is really a cognitive bonus. They decided to test the idea in the lab.

E Remington and Swettenham studied a group of people with autism spectrum disorder, most of whom had Asperger's, along with normal controls. They asked all the subjects to look at a computer screen, which displayed various combinations of letters and dots forming a ring. The subjects were instructed to very rapidly determine if the letters N or X were present in the ring and then hit the corresponding key on the keyboard. Some of the circles—those with more letters—were more difficult to process than others. There were also other letters floating outside the circle, but the subjects were specifically instructed to ignore those letters. Those floating letters were the laboratory equivalent of an irrelevant distraction in the real world.

F The psychologists were measuring perceptual capacity—that is why they varied the complexity of the task. As expected, everyone was slower at the task when the ring contained more letters. The researchers were also measuring distractibility. When a letter outside the ring was one of the target letters (N or X), the subjects often took a longer time finding the N or X in the ring—indicating they were distracted by the presence of a target letter in the location that they were supposed to ignore.

G The psychologists reasoned that as long as the subjects' total perceptual capacity was not exhausted, they would also process the irrelevant, distracting letters within their visual field. Once they had surpassed their perceptual capacity—once the ring of letters was sufficiently complex—irrelevant processing would stop. So if ASD subjects in fact have greater processing capacity, then they should process more distracting information even as the main task becomes increasingly complex.

H And that is exactly what they found. As the researchers reported online in the journal Psychological Science, although there was no difference among subjects in either reaction time or accuracy on the main task, those with ASD processed the irrelevant letters while solving much more complex problems. Their reaction times indicated that they were still noticing when the extra letter was an N or X, while also finding the target letter in the ring with the same speed and accuracy as the normal controls. Put another way, they weren't ignoring the main task, nor were they distracted away from it. Instead they were completing their work and moving on, using their untapped capacity.

I But here's the rub. Although this increased distractibility may be a talent rather than a deficit, as the psychologists point out, it nonetheless can have detrimental consequences in real-life situations. Just ask Tim Page about his uncanny facility for bus routes.

Questions 1–7

The above reading passage has nine paragraphs, **A–I**.

Which paragraph contains the following information?

Write the correct letter ***A–I****, in boxes 1-5 on your answer sheet.*

NB *You may use any letter more than once.*

1. speculation on greater perceptual ability of people with ASD
2. rationale behind the test
3. symptoms of peoples with ASD
4. page's impression of the field trip when he was still at school
5. laboratory environment for testing distraction

Keys:

1. D 2. G 3. C 4. A 5. E

星期四

完成摘要题（summary completion）

一 题型描述

在雅思阅读考试中，摘要题主要有两种命题形式。一种是填空式，这种形式是对文章中部分段落或全文给出若干个空格的一篇摘要，考生需要从文章中寻找对应的单词进行填空；另一种是选项式，即题目提供可选择的词库（其中包括若干选项），考生需要从词库中选择恰当的词汇填空。

二 题型透视

摘要题是对文章要点的总结和概括，但从本质上还是考查考生对文章主要细节的理解和归纳的能力，因而我们还是可以通过给出的摘要部分的线索迅速定位到文章的相关部分来找出答案。

三 解题步骤

Step 1：仔细阅读题目说明，确定是部分摘要还是全文摘要，是填空式摘要还是选择式摘要。如果是从原文中选词的填空式摘要，则看限定最多字数是多少（一般情况下是一个单词）；如果有被选项，则看是否可重复选择。

Step 2：略读 Summary，理解大意，根据空格前后的已有信息推测空格应填入的单词的词性和范围，并划出句子中的关键词和信号词。

Step 3：回到原文中寻找摘要中的关键词和信号词，确定答案所在的位置。

Step 4：精读定位后的答案所在语句，对照 Summary 中的对应信息，运用词汇及语法知识确定应填写的答案。

四 技巧点拨

1．很多摘要都带有自己的小标题，我们可以利用它的标题迅速定位摘要所对应的文章中的相应位置。

2．注意空格前后的词汇，看是否有一些比较容易查找的数字、单词，有的话，我们可以它们作为信号词，确定答案在文中出现的大致位置。

3．当找到关键词出现的位置后，仔细阅读包含关键词的句子以及之前和之后的句子，看是否与摘要部分照应。

五 例题精讲

首先，我们以剑 7 Test2 中的一篇文章后面的一道摘要题为例。

例 1

Questions 22-26

Complete the summary below.

*Choose **NO MORE THAN THREE WORDS** from the passage for each answer.*

Write your answers in boxes 22-26 on your answer sheet.

Professor Pretty concludes that our __22__ are higher than most people realize, because we make three different types of payment. He feels it is realistic to suggest that Britain should reduce its reliance on __23__. Although most farmers would be unable to adapt to __24__, Professor Pretty wants the government to initiate change by establishing what he refers to as a __25__. He feels this would help to change the attitudes of both __26__ and …

解析：本段摘要的第一句出现了一个人名 Professor Pretty，因此我们可以首先把它作为线索词去文章中定位，同时我们要划出空格前后的关键词，如 conclude，higher，payment，并同时思考一下它们的近义词、同根词等相关词汇。我们带着 Professor Pretty 回到原文中查读，可以迅速发现 D 段落首次出现这个人名，迅速略读包含该人名的句子以及之前和之后的句子之后，我们却找不到题目中空格前后的关键词，因此需要继续往下查读。接着，我们在 E 段中可以发现 Professor Pretty 再次出现，包含这个人名的句子是 “Professor Pretty draws a simple but memorable conclusion from all this: our food bills are actually threefold”。我们可以发现这句话中还包含关键词的同根词 conclusion，同时后面的 actually threefold 正好照应文章中的 higher than most people realise，因此可以确定答案就是位于 our 和 are 中间的那个词组：food bills。如果我们感觉还是不确定的话，可以接着再看下一句：we are paying for our supposedly cheaper food in three separate ways，此句正好与题目中的 because we make three different types of payment 相照应。第 23 空格所在的句子仍然有一个大写的词 Britain，空格前的关键词是 reduce 和 reliance。仍然是带着线索词和关键词去文章中查读，F 段中出现 Britain，仔细阅读带该词的句子：Breaking away from industrial agriculture as the solution to hunger may be very hard for some countries, but in Britain, where the immediate need to supply food is less urgent, and the costs and the damage of intensive farming have been clearly seen, it may be more feasible. breaking away from 就相当于 not rely on, 而 feasible 也正好照应了文中 realistic，因此答案是 industrial agriculture。第 24 个空所在句子的主语是 farmers，空格前的关键词是 adapt to，我们带着 farmers 去文中查找，很快发现 G 段的第二句的最后一个短词是 farmers，细读该句子：Professor Pretty feels that organic farming would be too big a jump in thinking and in practices for many farmers, 换句话说也就是 many farmers 难以适应 organic farming，因此答案即为 organic farming。第 25 个空格前的 a

决定了该答案是一个名词或名词词组，且这个事物是由 Professor Pretty 提出并希望政府使用的。继续往下读我们可以看到这一句“he is recommending the immediate introduction of a “Greener Food Standard”, which would ...”，recommend 是“提议、推荐”的意思，因此答案是 a 后面的“Greener Food Standard”。最后一个小题是两个名词或名词词组，而且因为前面有 change the attitudes，因此可以确定是表示某一类人的名词。继续查读文章，我们可以发现在文章的最后有这样一句话：it could go a long way, he says, to shifting consumers as well as farmers towards a more sustainable system of agriculture，其中 consumers 和 farmers 同时出现，而且它们都是表示一类人的名词，因此我们可以肯定答案就是这两个词。

我们现在再来看另一种完成摘要题，选择式摘要。与填空式摘要不同的是它不需要从原文中选词，而是给出一个词库。词库中的词要多于可选的词，因而考生需要从词库中选择最合适的词来完成摘要。做这种摘要题的步骤与填空式摘要基本相同，但由于考生还需要选词，因此要多出一个步骤，即选择文中原词的近义词，同时我们还可以根据运用排除法来缩小选择的范围。

接下来，我们以剑 5 Test1 中的一篇文章后的摘要题为例，详细讲讲解题步骤。

例 2

Questions 38–40

*Complete the summary with the list of words **A–I** below.*
*Write the correct letter **A–I** in boxes 38–40 on your answer sheet.*

GLOBAL WARMING

The writer admits that global warming is a __38__ challenge, but says that it will not have a catastrophic impact on our future, if we deal with it in the __39__ way. If we try to reduce the levels of greenhouse gases, he believes that it would only have a minimal impact on rising temperatures. He feels it would better to spend money on the more __40__ health problem of providing the world's population with clean drinking water.

A. unrealistic　　B. agreed　　C. expensive　　D. right
E. long-term　　F. usual　　G. surprising　　H. personal
I. urgent

解析：首先这个摘要有小标题，我们根据给出的小标题 global warming 去定位摘要的起始位置。通过查读，可以很快发现在文章的第二段出现了 global warming。研读该句子：one form of pollution — the release of greenhouse gases that causes global warming – does appear to be a phenomenon that is going to extend well into our future, but its total impact is unlikely to pose a devastating problem。其中 that is going to extend well into our future 的意思是“要延续到我们的未来”的意思，也就是相当长的一段时间内存在，它是 phenomenon 的同位语从句，而 phenomenon 指的正是 global warming，因此第 38 题应该是表示长期的意思，我们应选择 E. long-term。38 题和 39 题都在一个句子里，因此它的答案应该离第一个答案出现的位置不远，我们接着读出现 global warming 的句子

后面的一句：a bigger problem may well turn out to be an inappropriate response to it。这句话的意思是“如果我们对此反应不当，那么就可能产生更大的问题”。反过来说也就是如果能做出正确的反应、决策，那么就不会产生严重的后果，因此 39 题应该是 inappropriate 的反义词，也就是 D. right。40 题后面的词是 health problem，可以以它为关键词，继续查读。在文章中间我们可以发现一个 most pressing health problem，整句话是 yet the cost of reducing carbon dioxide emissions, for the United States alone, will be higher than the cost of solving the world's single, most pressing health problem: providing universal access to clean drinking water and sanitation。这句话中 provide，clean drinking water 相继出现，与摘要中最后一句话中出现的词一致，因此我们可以确定答案应该是 pressing 的近义词。词库中只有 urgent 是表示“紧急的，急迫的”意思，因此我们选 I。

六 专题演练

Exercise 1

Transforming wastewater from a major health and environmental hazard into a clean, safe and economically-attractive resource is emerging as a key challenge in the 21st century. It is a challenge that will continue to intensify as the world undergoes rapid urbanization, industrialization and increasing demand for meat and other foods unless decisive action is taken, says a new United Nations report released March 22.

Urban populations are projected to nearly double in 40 years, from current 3.4 billion to over six billion people–but already most cities lack adequate wastewater management due to aging, absent or inadequate sewage infrastructure.

The new report, called Sick Water, says some two million tons of waste, estimated to equal two or more billion tons of wastewater is being discharged daily into rivers and seas spreading disease to humans and damaging key ecosystems such as coral reefs and fisheries. Wastewater is a cocktail of fertilizer run-off and sewage disposal alongside animal, industrial, agricultural and other wastes.

The report says that the sheer scale of dirty water means more people now die from contaminated and polluted water than from all forms of violence including wars. Dirty water is also a key factor in the rise of de-oxygenated dead zones that have been emerging in seas and oceans across the globe.

Yet many of the substances that make wastewater a pollutant—for example nitrogen and phosphorus- can also be useful as fertilizers for agriculture. Wastewater can also generate gases to fuel small power stations or be used for cooking. The report notes that already some 10 per cent of the world's population is being supplied with food grown using wastewater for irrigation and fertilizer and with better management and training of farmers this could be increased substantially.

The report, launched to coincide with World Water Day, goes so far as to say that the concentration of nutrients in wastewater "could supply much of the nitrogen and much of the phosphorous and potassium normally required for crop production. Other valuable micro-nutrients and organic matter contained in the effluent would also provide benefits".

Complete the summary below.

Choose ***NO MORE THAN THREE WORDS*** *from the passage for each answer.*

A report says it is necessary and possible to __1__ wastewater into a clean and safe energy in order to meet the increasing demands of the modern industrialized world. With the rapid growth of urban population and the lack of __2__ , wastewater is threatening human health as well as __3__ However, the substances in the wastewater can be useful as __4__, and wastewater can also produce gases for domestic use. The report even claimed that the wastewater can provide as much of the __5__ as needed for crop production.

Keys:

1. transform　　2. adequate sewage infrastructure　　3. key ecosystems
4. fertilizer　　5. nutrients

Exercise 2

Environmentally Friendly Homes

If the 3 little pigs where building houses today, what would they choose to build with?

What is an environmentally friendly home that will stand the test of time? Some would say it is a home that was designed to use natural systems such as sun in the winter and shade in the summer or perhaps even geothermal energy to limit reliance on electricity and fossil fuels for home comfort. Indeed these, and other factors such as energy efficient appliances, are; in fact, part of a design that limits a home's impact on the environment. But builders of truly environmentally friendly homes need also consider what the home is actually made of. What's holding it together?

Home building material options come roughly in three categories. Wood, concrete or steel are the main building blocks of houses today. As building materials, each of these has certain benefits and drawbacks. Each also has environmental costs. Consideration must be given to what it takes to get a load of 2x4's, concrete or steel framing to build a wall. From where do these raw materials come? How available are they? What does it take to extract and process these materials to provide us with useable building material?

Wood, concrete and steel are end products, processed from various natural resources. Wood, of course, comes from trees. Concrete is a mixture of sand, gravel and cement, which is made of burned lime and clay. Like concrete, steel also comes primarily from below the earth with the mining of iron-ore, which is then alloyed together with other materials to get certain properties. While each of these materials are extracted and processed differently, the environmental friendliness of each can be measured by keeping track of the total energy inputs for the product, from cradle to grave. The amount of energy required is a quantifiable tool to measure environmental impact.

Common sense suggests that if non-wood materials are used in place of wood, fewer trees have to be cut down. While demand for wood products does affect timber harvesting, the results of using other products have greater environmental costs. Steel ranks as the greatest energy consumer, with concrete second and wood as the least energy-demanding product to procure and process. Numerous studies have quantified this.

In the part of the world where one study was conducted, a typical steel house has a steel frame and corrugated iron roof with a concrete floor, brick veneer wall cladding and aluminum window frames. In actuality, the fraction of this house in steel is only 6% by weight but consumes up to 31% of the total energy! A house such as this requires approximately 525 units of energy measured in billions of Joules (GJ).

A typical concrete house ranks second, totaling almost 400 GJ. The concrete in this house accounts for approximately 26% of the total energy consumed.

A typical wood house (defined as a house where wood requires the largest percentage of energy of the 3 materials used) ranks number 1 in the amount of energy required to produce the building materials. The energy used to produce the wood used in a typical wood house totals less than 20% of the total energy required for the materials in that house. Overall, a wood house requires just over 300GJ to produce. This is greater than 10% savings in total energy in production when compared to a concrete house and savings of almost 40% when compared to a steel house! This means that wood is the most environmentally friendly building material if consideration is given to how much energy it takes to get and process various materials.

Not only is wood easier to produce in terms of total energy to process, but it also comes from a natural resource which is renewable! As was mentioned earlier, all three products originate from natural resources. Natural resources fall into one of two broad categories, renewable and non-renewable. Renewable resources, as the name suggests, are renewable. That is, within a reasonable time frame (a generation or two), the resources we harvest can be replenished. The best and most pure example of renewable natural resources is forests.

Non-renewable natural resources, on the other hand, cannot be replenished within a reasonable time frame. Materials such as iron and concrete are examples of products that come from primarily non-renewable resources. When sand and gravel are mined from an area, it will not be replenished by natural systems except in geologic time (thousands and millions of years). The same is true for iron-ore, the primary ingredient in steel, we can not to back to an area and get more in a few years unless there was more there to begin with.

Trees, as natural resources, grow very fast. Trees can be harvested for use in our homes and offices and more trees will grow. With a little bit of management, we can even encourage faster and better growth! Depending on the type of trees, a new stand ready for harvest can grow from the ground up in as little as 15 years to as great as 100 years. Even at this upper end, wood is a very renewable resource!

Wood, concrete and steel are all acceptable building materials in terms of strength and durability. But they are not created equal in terms of the impact to the environment. If the 3 little pigs where building houses today, what do you think they "WOOD" choose?

Questions 1–5

Complete the summary below.

Choose ***NO MORE THAN THREE WORDS*** *from the passage for each answer.*

Environmentally friendly homes are those which are designed to reduce its __1__ on the environment, and they are made of three major building materials: wood, concrete and steel. Each of the materials has different environmental impact, which can be measured by calculating the amount of __2__ for the product. Contrary to our common sense, many studies have shown that steel has actually the greatest __3__, with concrete second and wood the least. Wood is the most environmental friendly building material not only because it needs less energy to process, but also because it comes from a __4__. Iron and concrete are non-renewable in that they can not be replenished by __5__ with a reasonable period of time. With good management, trees can be encouraged to grow faster and better.

Keys:

1. impact　2. energy　3. environmental cost　4. renewable resource
5. natural systems

Exercise 3

Languages are wonderfully idiosyncratic. English puts its subject before its verb. Finnish has lots of cases. Mandarin is highly tonal. Yet despite these differences, one of the most influential ideas in the study of language is that of universal grammar. Put forward by Noam Chomsky in the 1960s, it is widely interpreted as meaning that all languages are basically the same and that the human brain is born language-ready, with an in-built program that is able to decipher the common rules underpinning any mother tongue. For five decades this idea has dominated work in linguistics, psychology and cognitive science. To understand language, it implied, you must sweep aside the dazzling diversity of languages and find the common human core.

But what if the very diversity of languages is the key to understanding human communication? This is the idea being put forward by linguists Nicholas Evans of the Australian National University in Canberra and Stephen Levinson of the Max Planck Institute for Psycholinguistics in Nijmegen, the Netherlands.

They believe that languages do not share a common set of rules. Instead, they say, their sheer variety is a defining feature of human communication - something not seen in other animals. And that's not all. Language diversity is the "crucial fact for understanding the place of language in human cognition", Levinson and Evans argue.

In recent years, much has been made of the idea that humans possess a "language instinct": infants easily learn to speak because all languages follow a set of rules built into their brains. While there is no doubt that human thinking influences the form that language takes, if Evans and Levinson are correct, language in turn shapes our brains. This suggests that humans are more diverse than we thought, with our brains having differences depending on the language environment in which we grew up. And that leads to a disturbing conclusion: every time a language becomes extinct, humanity loses an important piece of diversity.

Since the theory of universal grammar was proposed, linguists have identified many language rules. Although these are supposed to be universal, there are almost always exceptions. It was once believed, for example, that no language would have a syllable that begins with a vowel and ends with a consonant (VC), if it didn't also have syllables that begin with a consonant and end with a vowel (CV). This universal lasted until 1999, when linguists showed that Arrernte, spoken by Indigenous Australians from the area around Alice Springs in the Northern Territory, has VC syllables but no CV syllables.

Other non-universal "universals" describe the basic rules of putting words together. Take the rule that every language contains four basic word classes: nouns, verbs, adjectives and adverbs. Work in the past two decades has shown that several languages lack an open adverb class, which means the number of adverbs available is limited, unlike in English where you can turn any word into an adverb, for example soft into softly. Others, such as Lao, spoken in Laos, have no adjectives at all. More controversially, some linguists argue that a few languages, such as Straits Salish, spoken by indigenous people from north-western regions of North America, do not even have distinct nouns or verbs. Instead they have a single class of words to encompass events, entities and qualities.

Even apparently unassailable universals have been found wanting. This includes recursion, the ability to infinitely embed one item in a similar item, such as "Jack thinks that Mary thinks that... the bus will be on time". It is widely considered to be a characteristic that sets human language apart from the communications of other animals. Yet Dan Everett at Illinois State University recently published controversial work showing that Amazonian Pirahã does not have this recursive quality.

The more we learn about languages, the more apparent the differences become (see "Tower of Babel"). While most linguists have somehow lived with these anomalies, Evans and Levinson believe they cannot be ignored. "The haul of clear and empirically impeccable universals, after decades of searching, is pitiful," Evans notes. He and Levinson argue that the idea of universal grammar has sent researchers down a blind alley. We should embrace linguistic diversity, they say, and try to explain the forms that languages actually take. To that end, they published a paper outlining their theory in Behavioral and Brain Sciences last year (vol 32, p 429). Everett has described it as "a watershed in the history of linguistic theory".

If languages do not obey a single set of shared rules, then how are they created? "Instead of universals, you get standard engineering solutions that languages adopt again and again, and then you get outliers," says Evans. He and Levinson argue that this is because any given language is a complex system shaped by many factors, including culture, genetics and history. There are no absolutely universal traits of language, they say, only tendencies. And it is a mix of strong and weak tendencies that characterises the "bio-cultural" hybrid we call language.

Questions 1–6

*Complete the summary with the list of words **A–R** below.*

Universal grammar, __1__ by Noam Chomsky, holds that all human languages share some common rules and this idea has generated far-reaching __2__ in different fields. However, recently some linguists began to __3__ this belief by claiming that language __4__ is a feature that distinguishes human language from those of animals and it is also __5__ for understanding the role of language in human cognition. According to them, language can shape our brains. The also found some __6__ that shows the exceptions to the universal rules claimed to underlie all human languages. They even published a paper putting forward their theories by arguing that influenced by various factors languages are more different than alike.

A. differences B. challenge C. domination D. share
E. necessary F. questioned G. proposed H. words
I. similarity J. diversity K. helpful L. critical
M. traces N. influence, O. express P. characteristic
Q. evidence R. asked

Keys:

1. G 2. N 3. B 4. J 5. L 6. Q

星期五

选择题（multiple choice）

一 题型描述

选择题是最为常见的一种出题形式，也为广大中国考生所熟悉。在雅思A类阅读考试中选择题主要有单选和多选两种形式，因此考生一定要看清题目说明。如果是单选题，一般是给出四个选项，考生需要选择一个最佳选项。如果是多选题，题目会提供四个以上的选项并告诉考生需要选取几个正确选项。

二 题型透视

多数情况下，选择题考查的是考生对文章细节信息的理解能力，因此考生可以根据提干中的关键字眼，通过查读来定位答案在文中的相应位置，然后再研读目标句，选择时注意要善于排除明显错误或文中未提及的干扰项。

三 解题步骤

Step 1：仔细阅读题目说明，确定是单选题还是多选题。如果是单选题，迅速浏览题干，划出关键字和信号词（容易辨认的特殊字体），并思考关键词的相关词。

Step 2：带着关键词和信号词回到文章中迅速查读，直到找到关键词和信号词在文中的相应位置。

Step 3：仔细研读目标句和目标段落（必要时）。

Step 4：仔细阅读题目，选择答案。

四 技巧点拨

1. 首先阅读题目，分析是细节题还是大意题，然后再读文章。
2. 当不好作出选择时，运用排出法，去除干扰项。

五 例题精讲

我们以剑5 Test3中的一篇文章后面的题目为例。

Questions 38-40

Choose the correct letter ***A***, ***B***, ***C*** *or* ***D***.

Write your answers in boxes 38–40 on your answer sheet.

38. According to researchers, in the late 1980s there was a feeling that______.
   A. a general theory of AI would never be developed
   B. original expectations of AI may not have been justified
   C. a wide range of applications was close to fruition
   D. more powerful computers were the key to further progress
39. In Dr Leake's opinion, the reputation of AI suffered as a result of______.
   A. changing perceptions
   B. premature implementation
   C. poorly planned projects
   D. commercial pressures
40. The prospects for AI may benefit from______.
   A. existing AI applications
   B. new business models
   C. orders from internet-only companies
   D. new investment priorities

分析：

38 题：本题的题干中有一个非常明显的信号词 late 1980s，我们回到文章中查读，定位该信号词在文中出现的段落，以下是该段：

Most researchers agree that AI peaked around 1985. A public reared on science-fiction movies and excited by the growing power of computers had high expectations. For years, AI researchers had implied that a breakthrough was just around the corner. Marvin Minsky said in 1967 that within a generation the problem of creating "artificial intelligence" would be substantially solved. Prototypes of medical-diagnosis programs and speech recognition software appeared to be making progress. It proved to be a false dawn. Thinking computers and household robots failed to materialize, and a backlash ensued. "There was undue optimism in the early 1980s," says David Leake, a researcher at Inidana University. "Then when people realized these were hard problems, there was retrenchment. By the late 1980s, the term AI was being avoided by many researchers, who opted instead to align themselves with specific sub-disciplines such as neural networks, agent technology, case-based reasoning, and so on."

首先我们找出含有 1980s 的句子。在本段的后半部分分别出现 early 1980s 和 late 1980s。文中说，"在上个世纪 80 年代早期弥漫着一种过度的乐观主义，但是当人们意识到存在着一些难题后，就开始尽量避免使用 AI。到了 80 年代后期，许多研究者都避免使用名词 AI"。在段落的开头也提到公众有着很高的期待，接着开始举例说明这些期待都是什么，但在段落中间笔锋一转，提到 it proved to be a false dawn，因为很多原来的猜想都没有实现。现在我们再来看题目和选项。题目中说，根据研究者们所说，20 世纪 80 年代后期有一种感觉是：A 人工智能的一般性理论永远不会有所发展；B 对人工智能最初的期望可能不是那么理由充分；C 广泛的应用很快就要取得成果；D 更加强大的计算机是进一步发展的关键。根据我们上面对段落的分析，很明显答案是 B。

39 题：题干中仍然有一个大写的人名：Dr Leake。我们以它为线索词继续查读文章。紧接着下一段就出现了题目的人名。

Ironically, in some ways AI was a victim of its won success. Whenever an apparently mundane problem was solved, such as building a system that could land an aircraft unattended, the problem was deemed not to have been AI in the first place. "If it works, it can't be AI," as Dr Leake characterizes it. The effect of repeatedly moving the goal-posts in this way was that AI came to refer to "blue-sky" research that was still years away from commercialization. Researchers joked that AI stood for "almost implemented". Meanwhile, the technologies that made it onto the market, such as speech recognition, language translation and decision-support software, were no longer regarded as AI. Yet all three once fell well within the umbrella of AI research.

段落开头提到"人工智能在某种程度上是它自己胜利的牺牲品。当一个看似非常平常的问题解决后，人们也绝不会认为它属于人工智能问题"。接着 Dr Leake 总结道："如果问题解决，也绝不可能是人工智能"。接着提到"这样做的后果是人工智能被认为是无价值的研究，距离商业化还有很多年。同时一些使它走入市场的技术也不再认为是人工智能，而这些技术曾经都属于人工智能方面的研究。"

题目中问道人工智能的名誉受损是由于：A：变化的看法；B 过早的实施；C 计划不周的项目；D 商业压力。答案应该是 A，因为段落的首尾部分都提到人们对人工智能的态度的转变，中间是这种转变给人工智能带来的影响，而 B 文中并没有提到或暗示过早的实施，C 在文中也没有提到，商业压力也没有提到。

40 题：人工智能的前景可能从什么中获益：A 现有的人工智能的应用；B 新的商业模式；C 来自网络公司的订单；D 新的投资重点。我们以 the prospects for AI 为线索词，接着查读，很快在接下来的段落可以发现这样一句话：another factor that may boost the prospects for AI in the near future is that investors are now looking for firms using clever technology, rather than just a clever business model, to differentiate themselves。因此我们应该选 D。

六 专题演练

Exercise 1

The Language Playing Field

To improve your communication abilities, try taking up hockey

When a hockey player hits the ice, practicing his skills until they are second nature, he's probably not aware that he's also improving his language cognition aptitude. Experience doing an activity, such as playing hockey, may allow the brain to recruit areas that are usually devoted to skilled action to the task of comprehending speech, particularly when the words relate to the activity in question. And the phenomenon holds not only for players, but also for fans who have experience watching the sport but none playing it.

Sian Beilock, a psychologist at the University of Chicago, and her colleagues gathered a group of hockey players from college and minor-league teams, as well as avid fans and "novices" with no hockey experience whatsoever. The participants underwent a magnetic resonance imaging (MRI) scan while they passively listened to a set of sentences that related either to everyday activities ("The individual pushed the cart") or hockey actions ("The hockey player saved the shot"). The researchers recorded which areas of the brain the sentences activated in the three groups of participants.

After the scan, the participants heard the same sentences again, but this time they were asked to perform a matching task: After each sentence, they were shown a picture and selected, as quickly as possible, whether or not the illustration showed the action being described in the sentence.

Previous research has established that responses should be faster when the picture matches the sentence. "The idea is that if you understand the sentence better, then you should be better at discriminating between people performing actions that match versus people performing actions that don't," Beilock explains. This result was true of all the participants for the everyday actions. But for the hockey-related sentences, only players and fans showed the effect.

Looking at the MRI scans, Beilock and her colleagues were able to account for the increased comprehension of hockey-related sentences in players and fans. Those two groups showed activation in the part of the brain called the left dorsal premotor cortex, an area that lights up as a person plans to perform a well-learned action—and not usually a brain region implicated in language comprehension.

"Everyone really can understand the sentences at some level, but what we're showing is that a deeper understanding seems to arise from experiencing and doing the action described in the sentence," Beilock says. "We think that a better comprehension arises because those people with those experiences are essentially relying on areas of the brain involved in 'doing' when they're just listening to the language."

Fans look a lot like experts in terms of how they activate these brain regions. "So just having some seeing experience seems to sort of rev up the 'doing' system," Beilock says. "We think that active mental picture involves some motor plan to act, which is really neat considering that they've never acted in that way."

In contrast, novices' brains instead showed activation in an area used for more general-purpose movement. "Novices don't have plans in their motor skill repertoire to act on the actions they've heard, either through seeing or doing," says Beilock. "But they may still be trying to understand the sentences in a sense through embodying the action, so they seem to call upon sensory-motor areas involved in simpler actions."

Fans 'brains also showed activity in this second region, but players' brains did not. "It's almost as if our fans are activating extra stuff they don't need and are doing more work," Beilock says. "Even though they look like the experts in terms of their patterns of performance, the fans are slower at doing the comprehension task in general, not only than the experts but slower than the novices. And it's not just that our fans are drinking beer all the time because they don't look slow when responding to non-hockey sentences."

The results cannot be explained simply as fans having, say, a greater hockey vocabulary than novices, Beilock says: "By looking in the brain we can say it's not just merely abstract conceptual understanding, it has something to do with how those areas of the brain involved in selecting actions are more highly activated for these fans than for novices."

Beilock thinks this phenomenon is not specific to hockey or even to sports, but may be found across a wide range of experiences, such as playing or appreciating music. The results could also help explain why sometimes people remember things better when they act them out. "It may be that's because this acting out allows these people to call on these motor systems when they then have to remember," Beilock says.

Another implication is that adult language-processing mechanisms might not be so impervious to change as previously thought. It might be possible to alter these systems with activities completely unrelated to language.

Beilock also suggests that students could benefit from a more active experience in learning subjects with action components, such as physics or math. "Rather than having kids at a desk," she says, "getting them about and moving and experiencing some of the concepts they're going to learn about, such as momentum, may actually help jump-start their comprehension when it comes time to read about it in the textbook."

Choose the correct letter A, B, C or D for the following questions.

1. According to the passage, playing hockey can______.
   A. perfect the hockey playing skill
   B. improve one's language aptitude
   C. activate certain areas of the brain
   D. deepen the understanding of sports
2. The results of MRI scan experiment showed that______.
   A. hockey players and fans had better language comprehension
   B. the same brain region is responsible for a well-learned action and language comprehension
   C. hockey players and fans understood hockey-related language better
   D. novice hockey players showed difficulty in understanding hockey-related language
3. Which of the following can best explain the different performance between hockey fans and novices in the experiment?
   A. Hockey fans are quicker to make response than novices.
   B. Different areas of the brain are activated for fans and novices.
   C. Hockey fans have larger hockey vocabulary than novices.
   D. The brain areas of fans are more activated than novices.

4. Which of following implication is not mentioned in the passage?
   A. Doing things leads to better memory.
   B. Adult language-processing mechanisms can be altered.
   C. Students may have better learning results in active learning experience.
   D. It can help change traditional subject teaching method.

Keys:

1. B　　2. C　　3. D　　4. D

Exercise 2

Last fall, Professor Adam Anderson began arriving at his office much earlier than usual, at an hour when the psychology department on the St. George campus was deserted. He didn't turn on his computer or even flick on the lights. Each morning, he just shut the door, sat down and closed his eyes. He could have used the time to get a head start on the work piled on his desk, but instead he took half an hour to concentrate on nothing at all.

Anderson, an expert on how the brain produces positive and negative emotions, began his daily ritual because he was studying the mental health benefits of meditation and wanted to test them firsthand. He is one of a growing number of researchers at U of T who are investigating the biological, psychological and circumstantial causes of happiness.

Anderson's early-morning meditation sessions didn't induce Zen-like bliss: a construction project was going full tilt outside his office window. "It wasn't like an idyllic setting with a babbling brook," he says with a laugh. "I heard jackhammers and saws. So I just said, 'I'm going to find peacefulness in the din.'"

While practising mindfulness, people learn how to find calm in a difficult world. Being mindful means paying attention to moment-by-moment experiences. It means observing physical sensations and the mind's thoughts and feelings, both positive and negative, without suppressing them or letting oneself be engulfed by them. A mindfulness response to anger would be "This is anger, and it will pass" rather than "I am really angry".

Students of mindfulness begin by focusing on their breathing. Inevitably, the mind wanders. The challenge, says Anderson, is to keep bringing your attention back to your breath as a means of anchoring yourself in the present moment. Mindfulness instructors suggest meditating for 20 to 45 minutes every day. These sessions are the foundation of the whole practice, but the objective is to be mindful throughout all of life.

"Rather than labelling your daily experiences as good or bad," says Anderson, "you just experience them for what they are." When you wake up in the morning feeling down, for example, you monitor the dark thoughts and any related bodily symptoms such as heaviness or tension while getting on with your day. You simply note the sadness. You don't ruminate on how you could possibly feel like this when the sun is out, who is to blame, whether it's ruining your life and so on. "Mindfulness is a childlike sensibility. It's more sensory," he says. It's what Buddhists call the "beginner's mind".

People who master this skill are less prone to get upset when unpleasant feelings arise. Everyday mindfulness has helped Anderson, a Canada Research Chair in Cognitive Neuroscience who came to U of T from Stanford University in 2003, handle the pressures of being a new professor. "When I'm working on something, I feel guilty because I know it's taking me away from working on something else. But I'm able to have those thoughts now without the anxious feelings that would normally accompany them," he says. "I feel more composed." Meditation, he adds, is like fitness for the brain. "It's like training any other muscle in your body. You're developing your brain to cope better with the world."

New research has found that mindfulness can help people who suffer from depression. Professor Zindel Segal, the Morgan Firestone Chair in Psychotherapy at U of T and Mount Sinai Hospital, combines the principles of mindfulness with cognitive behavioural therapy, a form of psychotherapy that helps people see the connection between their thoughts and feelings. In people who have been depressed before, even mild sadness can trigger an excessive amount of negative thinking, which can, in turn, cause a recurrence of full-blown depression.

Professor Segal has discovered that mindfulness can keep people out of that harmful loop by teaching them to be aware of temporary unhappiness without being swallowed up by it. They learn that sad feelings are a part of life and usually transient, provided they don't dwell on them. In a study published in 2000 involving individuals who had recovered from several bouts of depression, Segal found that those who completed mindfulness-based cognitive therapy relapsed in the following year only half as often as those who did not receive the therapy. A subsequent study in the U.K. replicated these findings, and researchers concluded that mindfulness therapy is most effective in preventing the recurrence of depression in patients who have had three or more previous episodes.

Why does mindfulness meditation work? Neuroscientists from several North American universities have been studying Buddhist monks – the acknowledged world champions of meditation – to see how their brains differ from the average person's. Segal and other researchers at U of T, meanwhile, are using advanced medical imaging to examine how mindfulness and psychotherapy affect the brains of ordinary people struggling with depression.

Along with Dr. Helen Mayberg, who is now at Emory University in Atlanta, but is still an adjunct professor of psychiatry at U of T, Segal led a groundbreaking study in 2002 that compared the brains of people who had recovered from depression using cognitive behavioural therapy with those who had used a popular antidepressant. The patients who got well with the drug showed changes in the lower, more primal, part of the brain known as the limbic system, while those who received therapy demonstrated changes in the upper areas of the brain connected with higher thought. Both areas are implicated in depression. The hopeful message from this research, says Segal, is that there are different routes to mental health. Drugs are not the only solution; we can also feel better by altering how we think.

Evidence of the healing power of mental training is exciting for everyone interested in happiness, says Anderson, and not just for those who want to prevent depression. "This empowers us as individuals to understand and regulate our own emotions," says Anderson. "That's part of what's exciting about it—we're looking at untapped human potential."

1. Why does Professor Anderson practice meditation every day?
   A. He wants have a rest.
   B. He wants to study the effects of meditation.
   C. He wants to start working earlier.
   D. He wants to find out the causes of happiness.
2. Mindfulness means______.
   A. thinking something else
   B. talking to oneself secretly
   C. focusing on one's breathing
   D. experience what is on
3. Which of the following is not the benefit of mindfulness?
   A. It can help people handle pressure.
   B. It can help people fight depression.
   C. It can help you become more concentrated.
   D. It can improve people's mental health.
4. What did the author say about using drugs and therapy in healing depression?
   A. Drugs are more effective than therapy.
   B. Therapy is more effective than drugs.
   C. Drugs are as effective as therapy.
   D. Drugs and therapy work in different parts of the brain.

Keys:

1. B   2. D   3. C   4. D

Exercise 3

Tornadoes

Tornadoes are one of the most severe types of weather phenomena. While many people fear tornadoes and their destructive power, few people understand their real causes and effects, nor are they aware of how to protect themselves from their devastating force.

Tornadoes, violently rotating columns of air, occur when a change in wind direction, coupled with an increase in wind speed, results in a spinning effect in the lower atmosphere. These whirling movements, which may not be visible to the naked eye, are exacerbated when the rotating air column shifts from a horizontal to a vertical position. As the revolving cloud draws in the warm air that surrounds it at ground level, its spinning motion begins to accelerate, thereby creating a funnel that extends from the cloud above it to the ground below. In this way, tornadoes become pendent from low pressure storm clouds.

When a tornado comes into contact with the ground, it produces a strong upward draft known as a vortex, a spiraling column of wind that can reach speeds in excess of 200 miles per hour. Traveling across the landscape, the tornado wreaks a path of concentrated destruction. It is not uncommon for these twisters to lift heavy objects, like cars or large animals, and throw them several miles. Houses that succumb to the force of the tornado seem to explode as the low air pressure inside the vortex collides with the normal air pressure inside the buildings.

Tornadoes can occur at any time of the year, but are typically most frequent during the summer months. Equally, tornadoes can happen at any time during the day, but usually occur between 3:00 in the afternoon and 9:00 in the evening. While these fierce funnels occur in many parts of the world, they are most common in the United States. On average, there are 1,200 tornadoes per year in this vast nation, causing 70 fatalities and 1,500 injuries.

Although taking myriad shapes and sizes, tornadoes are generally categorized as weak, strong, or violent. The majority of all tornadoes are classified as weak, meaning that their duration is less than 10 minutes and they have a speed under 110 miles per hour. Comprising approximately 10 percent of all twisters, strong tornadoes may last for more than 20 minutes and reach speeds up to 205 miles per hour. Violent tornadoes are the rarest, occurring less than one percent of the time. While uncommon, tornadoes in this classification are the most devastating, lasting more than one hour and resulting in the greatest loss of life. Even though only violent tornadoes can completely destroy a well-built, solidly-constructed home, weaker ones can also cause great damage.

Owing to the powerful and destructive nature of these winds, there are, perhaps not surprisingly, a number of myths and misconceptions surrounding them. For instance, many people mistakenly believe that tornadoes never occur over rivers, lakes, and oceans; yet, waterspouts, tornadoes that form over bodies of water, often move onshore and cause extensive damage to coastal areas. In addition, tornadoes can accompany hurricanes and tropical storms as they move to land. Another common myth about tornadoes is that damage to built structures, like houses and office buildings, can be avoided if windows are opened prior to the impact of the storm. Based on the misunderstanding that open windows might equalize the pressure inside the structure and minimize the damage to it, this action can instead result in fatal injury.

Because of the profound effects that tornadoes have on communities and their inhabitants, safety measures are of paramount importance during adverse weather conditions. Drivers often attempt to outrun tornadoes in their cars, but it is extremely unsafe to do so. Automobiles offer very little protection when twisters strike, so drivers should abandon their vehicles and seek safe shelter. Mobile homes afford little shelter, so residents of these homes should go to an underground floor of the sturdiest nearby building. In the case of a building having no underground area, a person should go to the lowest floor of the building and place him or herself under a piece of heavy furniture. If no building is available, a person caught in a tornado should lie prostate in a nearby ditch or other depressed area of land and cover his or her head.

1. All of the following key facts about tornadoes are mentioned in the passage EXCEPT______.
   A. the number of deaths from tornadoes
   B. the time of day when tornadoes usually take place
   C. the time of year when tornadoes are most common
   D. the average wind speed of most tornadoes
2. Which of the following best explains the term waterspouts?
   A. Tornadoes that move away from coastal areas.
   B. Tornadoes that occur over oceans, rivers, and lakes.
   C. Tornadoes that occur onshore.
   D. Tornadoes that accompany tropical storms and hurricanes.
3. What is the safest place to be when a tornado strikes?
   A. An abandoned vehicle.
   B. Mobile homes.
   C. The basement of a building.
   D. Under a piece of sturdy furniture.

Keys:

1. D　　2. B　　3. C

星期六

综合训练（一）

READING PASSAGE 1

*You should spend about 20 minutes on **Questions 1–13**, which are based on Reading Passage 1 below.*

Secondhand smoke linked to mental distress

A Where there's secondhand cigarette smoke, there's emotional fire. As exposure to cigarette fumes increases among nonsmokers, so does their risk of developing serious psychological distress and of being hospitalized for mental ailments, a new study finds.

B Cigarette smokers have been shown to have more psychological problems than nonsmokers do, and new evidence suggests that nonsmokers who inhale high levels of secondhand smoke may experience nearly as much psychological distress as smokers, say epidemiologist Mark Hamer of University College London and his colleagues. Overall, these findings support the view, largely based on animal studies, that nicotine administered in large enough doses can induce sadness and other negative moods, the researchers propose in the August Archives of General Psychiatry.

C "Our data are preliminary, but there is a strong possibility that the observed association reflects a causal link," Hamer says. Previous research suggests that nicotine alters mood by disrupting immune responses, stress-hormone regulation and the transmission of dopamine, a chemical messenger in the brain. But little is known about nicotine's possible relationship to specific psychiatric disorders. The link between nicotine exposure and mood held up after statistically accounting for participants' social status, alcohol use, physical activity level, body mass index, chronic physical illness, level of psychological distress upon entering the study and previous hospitalizations for mental illness.

D A related study, published in the January Psychosomatic Medicine, found an increased risk for depression symptoms among nonsmokers exposed to modest or greater levels of secondhand smoke. A team led by epidemiologist David J. Lee of the University of Miami Miller School of Medicine examined data from a 2005–2006 survey of nearly 3,000 U.S. adults. Given widespread exposure to secondhand cigarette smoke, further research on its relation to mental health is warranted, Hamer asserts. A 2006 federal report estimated that 60 percent of nonsmokers in the United States display biological signs of having ingested at least low levels of nicotine via cigarette smoke.

E Despite Hamer's new evidence, scientists cannot rule out that people who experience especially stressful home and work lives are also most likely to encounter secondhand smoke and to develop serious psychological problems, Lee remarks. One promising research direction would be to examine whether policies that ban smoking in public or on the job lead to reductions in depression, anxiety and psychiatric hospitalizations, he says.

F Hamer's team studied 5,560 nonsmokers and 2,595 smokers, with average ages in the mid- to late 40s. Participants came from a nationally representative sample in Scotland that was surveyed in 1998 and 2003 about a variety of health issues. Volunteers completed a 12-item questionnaire that measured psychological distress by inquiring about sleep problems, general levels of happiness and symptoms of depression and anxiety in the previous month. Saliva levels of cotinine, a breakdown product of nicotine, allowed the researchers to identify nonsmokers who had experienced low, moderate or high exposure to secondhand smoke. Cotinine levels also served to confirm self-reported cigarette use.

G In 1998, psychological distress affected 9 percent of nonsmokers with low secondhand smoke exposure, 11 percent of nonsmokers with moderate secondhand smoke intake and 14 percent of those who frequently breathed secondhand smoke. Psychological distress occurred in 20 percent of smokers. Over an average follow-up period of nearly six years, 41 study participants were admitted to psychiatric hospitals, mostly for depression and substance abuse. Psychiatric cases clustered among current smokers and participants with high secondhand smoke exposure.

H Prior research has found that psychotic disorders occur at elevated rates among marijuana users. It's not clear whether marijuana smoking contributed to elevated cotinine levels and at least some mental ailments that were seen among cigarette abstainers in the new study, Hamer notes. Self-reports of marijuana use were not collected in the Scottish investigation.

Questions 1–7

Reading Passage 1 has eight paragraphs, ***A–H****. Which paragraph contains the following information?*

Write the correct letter ***A–F****, in boxes 1-6 on your answer sheet.*

NB *You may use any letter more than once.*

1. A useful tool for identifying the amount of second-hand smoke exposure.
2. Direction for future research.
3. The necessity to conduct further research.
4. The relationship between psychological problems and marijuana use.
5. How Nicotine can affect one's mood.
6. The relationship between nicotine and negative mood.

Questions 7–11

Complete the summary below.

Choose ***ONE WORD ONLY*** *from the passage for each answer.*

Write your answers in boxes 7–11 on your answer sheet.

A recent research found that there might be an __7__ between the amount of exposure of second-hand smoke and the risk of developing __8__ disorders. One of the possible explanations is that large doses of nicotine can cause negative mood on people, though the link between nicotine and the __9__ mental ailment has not been identified. Another study found that people who have higher level of second-hand exposure are prone to __10__ However, since people who live under tense __11__ are also likely to get depressed, further research is needed to clarify the relationship between various factors.

Questions 12 and 13

Answer the questions below.

Choose ***NO MORE THAN THREE WORDS AND/OR A NUMBER*** *from the passage for each answer.*

Write your answers in boxes 12 and 13 on your answer sheet.

12．In which country were the participants from in Hamer's study?

13．How many items did the questionnaire have in hamer's study?

READING PASSAGE 2

You should spend about 20 minutes on ***Questions 14–26****, which are based on Reading Passage 2 below.*

Questions 14–19

Reading Passage 2 has six marked sections, ***A–F****. Choose the correct heading for each section from the list of headings below. Write the correct number,* ***i-x****, in boxes 14–19 on your answer sheet.*

List of Headings

i	A public display
ii	The origin of calligraphy
iii	The necessity of learning to read and write
iv	Privilege enjoyed by a few
v	The power of writing
vi	Application in politics
vii	Private communications
viii	The art of reading and writing
ix	Literacy level of ancient Egyptians
x	Learning how to read and write

14 Section **A**
15 Section **B**
16 Section **C**
17 Section **D**
18 Section **E**
19 Section **F**

Literacy

A Until the advent of mass education in the Western world in the nineteenth century, most people could not read or write. Writing in most ancient civilisations was restricted to a fairly small and powerful elite. It was a useful tool in the creation of empires and kingdoms through administration and record-keeping.

B This great skill was used to record payments of taxes and tributes to kings and rulers, and to keep track of the numbers of tax-payers in censuses. It was used to record commercial contracts and transactions between individuals, of goods and services bought and sold, and of the cost involved. Some of the earliest written texts from Mesopotamia and Egypt are of this kind. Cuneiform tablets from ancient southern Iraq, for example, record the allocation of rations to workers. Therefore, writing has been a means of organisation and keeping wealth and power.

In ancient Egypt levels of literacy were very low, less than one per cent. However, in some places we have evidence that a lot of people in that particular place able to read and write. Deir el-Medina, a walled village was home to the high middle-class officials working on building and decorating the New Kingdom tombs in the Valley of the Kings.

A stone ostrakon found there records work attendance in 280 days of Year 40 of the reign of Ramesses II (about 1279-1213 BC), only about 70 seem to have been full working days.

The list of forty names is accompanied by the reasons for their absence, such as illness, the death of relatives and purifications - perhaps relating to childbirth. Occasionally a man is away “building his house”, or at “his festival” or even “drinking”.

C In order to make sure records were kept and understood, reading and writing have always been studied. In ancient Mesopotamia, schooling began at an early age.

Boys (and very rarely girls) learned how to make a tablet and handle the stylus used to make impressions in the clay. After learning the basic cuneiform signs students went on to learn the thousands of different Sumerian words. The teacher would write lines on one side of a tablet and students would turn it over and try to reproduce them. After training, students could call themselves dubsar or scribe and they became a member of a privileged class.

D Even though literacy has traditionally been only for the wealthy, writing has been consistently used throughout history as a means of recording ideas and information in public proclamations. Kings and emperors set up inscriptions proclaiming their titles and chronicling their victories over their enemies. The Greek city of Athens in the fifth century BC recorded the decisions of its democratic constitution in public inscriptions. This made the political process open and accountable.

E People have also used writing to record and communicate their thoughts and wishes in private or to friends and colleagues, even during periods of very limited literacy. Letters inscribed on clay and sealed in clay envelopes are preserved from ancient Mesopotamia and in the Egyptian, Greek and Roman worlds, ink and papyrus were widely used for private correspondence.

One of the oldest surviving handwritten documents in Britain is an invitation to a birthday party. It is one of the so-called Vindolanda tablets, a collection of letters and other pieces of writing on strips of tree bark from one of the main military outposts on the northern frontier of Roman Britain.

The invitation from Claudia Severa, wife of Aelius Brocchus, is for Sulpicia Lepidina, wife of Flavius Cerealis. It was mostly written by a scribe, but Severa's writing can also be seen. The tablet is one of the earliest known examples of writing in Latin by a woman.

F In many societies, a special room would be set aside within a wealthy household for private writing and study. In east Asian and Islamic cultures, the furniture of writing, pens and boxes, became extremely ornate, and the art of penmanship, or calligraphy, highly prized as a sign of learning or social prestige.

Until the end of the Edo period (AD 1868), every literate Japanese person had a personal writing-box containing brushes, ink-stone, ink-stick and water-dropper. The quality of the craftsmanship reflected the status of the owner.

Right up to modern times, literacy has been a highly prized skill. In China a simplified script was created to help improve literacy during the 1940s and 50s. But, while in developed countries most people learn to read and write at school, there are still people with very limited levels of literacy, if any at all, all over the world.

Questions 20–26

Do the following statements agree with information given in Reading Passage 2?

In boxes 20–26 on your answer sheet, write

TRUE	*if the statement agrees with the information*
FALSE	*if the statement contradicts the information*
NOT GIVEN	*if there is no information on this*

20. Mass education began in the nineteenth century in the Western world.
21. Ancient Egyptians had higher literacy level than people in other parts of the world.
22. In ancient Mesopotamia, learning to write and read was difficult for students.
23. Kings and emperors liked to have a detailed record of their accomplishment.
24. Britain has the oldest surviving handwritten document in the world.
25. The furniture of writing is a necessary part in people's life in east Asian and Islamic cultures.
26. Calligraphy became the symbol of a person's social status in Japan.

READING PASSAGE 3

*You should spend about 20 minutes on **Questions 27–40**, which are based on Reading Passage 3 on the following pages.*

Water Purification

Water purification, or drinking water treatment, is the process of removing contaminants from surface water or groundwater to make it safe and palatable for human consumption. A wide variety of technologies may be used, depending on the raw water source, contaminants present, standards to be met, and available finances.

Over time, ecosystems have developed sophisticated ways to process and store natural waste products such as sediments, nutrients, heavy metals, and bacteria. Water is the primary medium for transporting these materials through most ecosystems. The "water purification" process is accomplished to varying degrees in a variety of ecosystems including streams, wetlands, estuaries, and forests. Wetlands and streamside plant communities are particularly efficient at improving water quality. These communities act as buffers that filter and process sediment and debris from floods, waste products from aquatic and terrestrial plants and animals, and, minerals, metals, and microorganisms before they can reach faster moving water such as rivers.

The water emerging from some deep groundwaters may have fallen as rain many decades or even hundreds of years ago. Soil and rock layers will have naturally filtered the groundwater to a high degree of clarity even before it is pumped to the treatment plant. Such water may emerge as springs, artesian springs, or may be extracted from boreholes or wells. Deep groundwater is generally of very high bacteriological quality but may be rich in dissolved solids especially carbonates and sulphates of calcium and magnesium. Depending on the strata through which the water has flowed, other ions may also be present including chloride, and bi-carbonate and there may be a requirement to reduce the iron or manganese content of this water to make it pleasant for drinking, cooking, and laundry use. Disinfection is also required. Where groundwater recharge is practised, such groundwaters should be graded as being equivalent to lowland surface waters for treatment purposes. Shallow groundwaters — water emerging from shallow groundwaters are usually abstracted from wells or boreholes and the bacteriological quality can be variable depending on the nature of the catchment. A variety of soluble materials may be present including potentially toxic metals such as copper or zinc.

Upland lakes and reservoirs-typically located in the headwaters of rivers systems, upland reservoirs are usually sited above any human habitation and may be surrounded by some form of protection zone to restrict the opportunities for contamination. Bacterial and pathogens levels are usually low but some bacteria, protozoa and algae will be present. Where upland are forested or are peaty, humic acids can colour the water brown. Many upland sources have low pH which requires adjustment before the water is put into supply. Rivers, Canals and low-land reservoirs - lowland surface waters will have a significant bacterial load and may also contain algae, suspended solids and a variety of dissolved constituents. A municipal surface water treatment plant must first screen or sieve out large objects such as trash and leaves. Filtering is not sufficient to completely purify water, but it is often a necessary first step, since such particles can interfere with the more thorough purification methods. Water from rivers may also be stored in bankside reservoirs for periods between a few days and many months to allow natural biological purification to take place. This is especially important if treatment is to be by slow sand filters. The filtered water is then treated to remove any microscopic organisms including protozoa and bacteria. This is generally followed by a disinfection stage to eliminate any residual bacteria and viruses.

When a new slow sand filter bed is brought into use, raw water is carefully decanted onto the filter material until a water depth of 1 to 3m is achieved, dependant on the size of the filter bed. The water passing through the filter for the first few hours is recirculated through the filter and not put into supply. Within a few hours, a biological film comprised of bacteria, protozoa, fungi, and algae builds on the surface of the sand. This is the Schmutzedecke layer and it is this layer that removes all the impurities. An effective slow sand filter may remain in service for many weeks or even months if the pre-treatment is well designed and produces an excellent quality of water which physical methods of treatment rarely achieve. Disinfection - The finished water is then disinfected with chlorine gas, chloramine, sodium hypochlorite, chlorine dioxide, ozone, or ultraviolet light, before it is pumped into the distribution system of water mains and storage tanks on its way to consumers. Some plants also pre-chlorinate their raw water influent after the screening phase to reduce the incidence of biological films in the treatment cycle. Water utilities may choose to further boost chlorine levels (termed re-chlorinating) in the distribution system to counteract any pathogens that may occur. Bleach may be used for emergency disinfection at the rate of 2 drops of 5% bleach per liter or quart of clear water.

Many environmental and cost considerations affect the siting and design of water purification plants. Groundwater is cheaper to treat, but aquifers once depleted can take thousands of years to recharge. Surface water sources must be carefully monitored for the presence of unusual types or levels of contaminants. The treatment plant itself must be kept secure from vandalism or terrorism and the presence of large quantities of dangerous chemicals mandates special training for workers and emergency personnel. The facility must responsibly dispose of its settled and filtered solids and prevent them from contaminating the treatment components or the source waters. All facilities disinfect finished water, but the exact method of disinfection can be controversial, and the costs and benefits of different methods must be evaluated.

Questions 27–29

*Choose the correct letter, **A**, **B**, **C** or **D**.*
Write the correct letter in boxes 27–29 on your answer sheet.

27. Water purification______.
    A. is a complex process
    B. makes water drinkable to people
    C. involves the use of special technologies
    D. is the treatment of polluted water
28. Ecosystems______.
    A. can remove natural waste products from water
    B. can work as buffers,
    C. can finish water purification process independently
    D. are full of plants and animals
29. Sand filter bed______.
    A. is effective in purifying water
    B. can eliminate all bacteria and virus
    C. takes several months to form
    D. is slow than physical methods

Questions 30–36

Classify the following statements according to whether they belong to characteristics of the following:

A. Surface water
B. Ground water
C. Both

*Write the correct letter **A**, **B** or **C**, in boxes 30–36 on your answer sheet.*

30. Having a high degree of clarity
31. Bacterial level varied
32. Filtering is needed
33. Rich in ions
34. Requiring disinfection
35. Cheap to treat
36. Can be easily contaminated

Questions 37–40

Complete the table below using information from the reading passage. Write ***NO MORE THAN THREE WORDS*** *for each answer. Write your answers in boxes 37–40 on your answer sheet.*

Water Purification Process

phase	name	process
1	screening	screen or sieve out large objects; __37__ can also be used
2	purification	remove __38__
3	__39__	to get rid of any bacteria and viruses
4	Putting into use	pumped into the __40__ of water mains and storage tanks

Keys:

1. F
2. E
3. D
4. H
5. C
6. B
7. association
8. psychological
9. specific
10. depression
11. stress
12. Scotland
13. 12
14. iv
15. v
16. x
17. i
18. vii
19. viii
20. T
21. F
22. NG
23. T
24. NG
25. F
26. T
27. C
28. B
29. A
30. B
31. C
32. A
33. B
34. C
35. B
36. A
37. natural biological purification
38. microscopic organisms
39. disinfection
40. distribution system

星期日 综合训练（二）

READING PASSAGE 1

*You should spend about 20 minutes on **Questions 1–13**, which are based on Reading Passage 1 below.*

What's All the Flap About?

Butterflies need their hind wings not to stay aloft but to evade predators

It's not just poetic alliteration that makes the pat phrase "a butterfly fluttered by" so appropriate. The insects, although not always that speedy, often take a flight path that involves so many erratic dips and turns that they almost look out of control. But it's not because they can't do any better: such unpredictable flight is how butterflies evade birds and other predators. However, most butterflies are brightly colored, which would seem to counter their evasiveness by making them easier to spot and track. "The question always bothered me," says Thomas Eisner, a biologist at Cornell University. "Why are butterflies flaunting their visibility?" As Eisner and Benjamin Jantzen, a doctoral candidate now at Carnegie Mellon University, report in the October 28 issue of the Proceedings of the National Academy of Sciences, a butterfly's ability to evade and its blatant pigmentation may go hand in hand.

The first step was to find out what physical feature of butterflies allows them to move so erratically. It's been known for about a century that the front wings in butterflies are the ones driven by the insect's muscles; the hind wings are passively coupled to the front ones. Eisner decided to investigate just what the back wings were doing by trimming them away bit by bit. To his surprise, he found that if he removed the entire hind wing, the insects had no problem flying. Indeed, when Eisner went on to test an extensive list of butterfly and moth species, he found that without exception they were all capable of sustained flight with only their front wings. "It is pretty startling that they're that overendowed with lifting surface," says Jantzen.

Eisner was careful not to use any rare species in the study. For each species, he used only one or two individuals. "I have one of the monarch butterflies in my home who has lived four months with me," Eisner says. In the wild the insects often run into obstacles and cause their own wing rips and tears. "Wing breakage is very common in natural circumstances," Eisner says. "I've found butterflies that have literally one wing completely gone, and they can fly."

To determine just what the hind wings contribute to the flight, Jantzen and Eisner set up an enclosure with two video recorders. They used two pest species, the white cabbage butterfly and the gypsy moth. Jantzen wrote software that translated the video imagery into a three-dimensional trajectory of each insect's flight, first intact and then without the hind wings. With half their wing area, the insects flew more slowly and could not turn as quickly, but they could still follow similar flight paths. In other words, they could zigzag as usual, but had to do it at a slower pace.

So although butterflies and moths don't need their hind wings to stay aloft, the structures appear to be essential for evading predators. "Many other insects can go significantly faster than butterflies," says Jantzen. "But by having these massive wings, they can manage these pretty enormous turning accelerations. Whether or not something is faster than you in a straight line, if you can take the corner more sharply, you don't get eaten." The hind wings therefore function somewhat like the paddle of a canoe: A larger paddle has more surface to push against the water, which makes for sharper turns.

And this result gets back to Eisner and Jantzen's theory about why butterflies have such bright coloring. Nocturnal moths likely evolved evasiveness first to avoid predators such as bats. Butterflies evolved from moths into diurnal species. Moths have no reason to evolve colors for night life, but daytime butterflies are large and visible to birds. Since they are going to be spotted in any case, being showy about it isn't a drawback, but is potentially a defensive maneuver—to advertise that they are difficult to catch.

"If a young, inexperienced bird sees a butterfly at a distance farther than any other insect is visible, it says wow, look at that big thing there. The bird goes after it and finds that it's very difficult to catch. If the bird does catch it, it's slippery, because the butterfly wing is covered in scales. And then the bird realizes that it's all wrapper and no candy. If the bird tries again, with a different butterfly of a different color, but it's the same experience, then a bird learns that it's not worth chasing these colored things that are so easy to spot."

Butterflies, in a way, are therefore getting double duty out of their investment in large hind wings. "Those giant wings are just so brightly colored," says Jantzen, "and those are exactly what make it hard to get hold of them."

Questions 1–7

Do the following statements agree with information given in Reading Passage 1?
In boxes 1–7 on your answer sheet, write

TRUE	*if the statement agrees with the information*
FALSE	*if the statement contradicts the information*
NOT GIVEN	*if there is no information on this*

1. A butterfly's special way of flight protects itself from predators.
2. The hind wings of butterflies are separated from their front wings.
3. Rare Species of butterflies are forbidden from being experimented.
4. The hind wings of butterflies have little effects on their flight paths.
5. Moths have less risk of eaten by predators than butterflies.
6. Butterflies' brightly colored wings made them exposed to more dangers.
7. Experience birds are less likely to chase a butterfly.

Questions 8–13

Complete the summary below.

*Choose **ONE WORD ONLY** from the passage for each answer. Write your answers in boxes 8–13 on your answer sheet.*

Butterflies' colorful wings and their ability to __8__ themselves seem to be a contradiction to people. However, researcher found that the two are actually __9__ each other closely. Eisner, a biologist at Cornell University, examined the __10__ of the hind wings of butterflies and he found that all the butterflies could still stay in __11__ flight. With a more carefully designed experiment, Jantzen and Eisner found that the hind wings contribute to the speed of flight and quicker __12__ of butterflies, which can help them __13__ from predators.

A. disappear	B. related to	C. lofty	D. speedy
E. helping	F. defense	G. escape	H. avoid
I. attractive to	J. color	K. protect	L. corners
M. function	N. evasiveness	O. confuse	P. continuous
Q. cover	R. turns		

READING PASSAGE 2

*You should spend about 20 minutes on **Questions 14–26**, which are based on Reading Passage 2 below.*

Questions 14–19

*Reading Passage 2 has seven marked paragraphs, **A–G**. Choose the correct heading **B**, **C**, **D**, **E**, **F**, and **G** from the list of headings below. Write the correct number, **i–x**, in boxes 14-19 on your answer sheet.*

List of Headings

i	Following strict rules
ii	Limitations in clay construction
iii	Facial features
iv	Building muscles

v	Reconstruction in clay
vi	Acquiring the skeletal structure
vii	Beginning the reconstruction
viii	Making more life-like
ix	Measuring facial depth
x	Computer facial reconstruction
xi	The advantages of using 3D

Example	*Answer*
Paragraph **A**	v

14. Paragraph **B**
15. Paragraph **C**
16. Paragraph **D**
17. Paragraph **E**
18. Paragraph **F**
19. Paragraph **G**

Facial Reconstruction

A Once the skin and flesh has rotted away from the skull of a corpse, their character and physical appearance disappear along with it. It then becomes the job of forensic anthropologists, sculptors and creative artists, to reconstruct a life-like form of what the person looked like from the skeleton and sometimes, remaining parts of a skeleton. Clay is a common form of reconstruction.

B In order to reconstruct a life-like face, sculptors need to know the depth of skin that overlays the skull. Sculptors usually begin sculpting with 20 to 35 tissue layers, scattered all over the face. The main heavily concentrated depths are situated around the mouth and in between the eyes. Facial depth measurements are available for male and female, certain ages, racial groups, thin people and obese people. Small pegs are used as facial depth indicators and are fixed into the skull or otherwise into a cast of the skull. Strips of clay that have been made to match the height of the pegs are then placed between them and once the strips are in place, clay is used to fill the gaps between each peg.

C The sculptor is then able to start work on the eyes, mouth, ears, nose, chin, jaw and cheeks, as these are the aspects of the face that give the most character, but are also the parts that perish most quickly as the body decays. Sculptors rely on certain rules during the reconstruction of a face, for example, the width of the nose is the same as the distance between the inner corner of the eyes and the corners of a person's mouth lie below the inner boarders of the iris. Ears are seen as being roughly the same length as the nose, though elderly people usually have longer ears. Once the facial features are complete, the sculptor makes a mould from the clay head using a plaster of Paris silicone rubber.

D Now, the reconstruction of the face involves the task of building the muscles around it. Sculptors must approximate the muscle structures by noting the shape and size of certain facial bones, as these will directly affect the shape of the muscles previously attached to them. Using their experience, the sculptors are able to build the face by shaping each of the muscles and then fixing each one in its place on the skull. The final step is to cover the clay muscles with a layer of clay skin, which is smoothed over so that it resembles real skin.

E However experienced the sculptor is, there are certain accuracy limits that occur during the reconstruction of a face. Sculptors can only guess hairstyles and cannot create the expressions on a persons, face that make the sculpture completely life like. However, a sculpture is successful if it aids in jogging someone's memory or can narrow down a search by excluding anyone whose face does not resemble the reconstructed face.

F Computer facial reconstruction has developed far enough to allow a virtual form of reconstructing the face from a skull, making it easy and efficient to travel from computer to computer. Such software allows for a 3D image/structure of the finished face to be rotated and moved around on a monitor.

G Using computer facial reconstruction does not require artistic skill, but it does require skills of a different sort. There is no standard method of computer facial reconstruction but the initial data and facial shape comes from a 3D scan of the skull. This process is non-destructive to the skull and involves the skull rotating on a turning table whilst a laser scanner lights up a thin perpendicular strip. Mirrors located on either side of the turning table reflect the images from the lit up area to sensors. The data that the scan produces allows a controlling program to determine the distances of each point located on the skull. This then creates a digitalised model of the skull that is easily and freely rotated on the computer screen.

Applying muscle and skin to the bone requires computer *tomography* (CT) scans of actual living people, which acquire images showing where bones cast shadows onto the skull and record hard/soft tissue (bones and flesh) in a 3 dimensional view. Using CT scans, data files record the shape of the skull as well as the tissue depth. Forensic anthropologist's knowledge is also utilized in choosing an appropriate form of CT scan. Any clothing found with the bones can provide a clothing size, which is useful, as it allows scientists to adjust any tissue depth measurements to account for obesity or thinness. Merging the two scans, the CT scan is applied to the digital scan of the skull, becoming two skulls on top of each other. At this stage of the process, the two skulls are different shapes. The computer program distorts the skulls' marks on both so they match each other and at the same time, distorting the facial tissue properties, creating a facial shape that resembles the victim.

CT scans cannot record vital surface detail such as hair, skin and eye colour, so these aspects of persons face must be added. This involves borrowing the physical features of a living person in order to paint these features onto the 3D model. A person who has similar age, racial qualities, and build as the modeled skull is used in a 3D rendering process called 'colour mapping'. This process involves photographing the face of the person with similar qualities and using software to merge the three views into one strip that is put onto the computer to complete the reconstruction. The final result can be viewed and turned on the screen. Like clay facial reconstruction, the method does have its accuracy limitation. Nose, mouth and ear shape are largely down to guessing, however, lighting conditions and the ability to view the face from any angle makes computer facial reconstruction very lifelike and helpful during investigations.

Questions 20–26

Do the following statements agree with information given in Reading Passage 2?
In boxes 20-26 on your answer sheet, write

TRUE	*if the statement agrees with the information*
FALSE	*if the statement contradicts the information*
NOT GIVEN	*if there is no information on this*

20. Sculptors use small pegs for measuring facial depth.
21. The facial features are the most demanding part to reconstruct for a sculptor.
22. Experienced sculptors can reconstruct a face accurately in each aspect.
23. Computer facial reconstruction has replaced traditional clay facial reconstruction.
24. Computer facial reconstruction is based on information provided by 3D scan of the skull.
25. No specialized knowledge is needed in choosing the right form CT scan.
26. Computer facial reconstruction has to use real living person as a model.

READING PASSAGE 3

You should spend about 20 minutes on ***Questions 27–40****, which are based on Reading Passage 3 on the following pages.*

Human History Written in Stone and Blood

Two bursts of human innovation in southern Africa during the Middle Stone Age may be linked to population growth and early migration off the continent.

A Even by archaeological standards, Blombos Cave is a modestly sized shelter. Yet artifacts recovered from just 13 cubic meters of deposit inside transformed our understanding of when our species developed behavioral attributes we associate with "modern" humans. From this cramped hole in a sandstone cliff on the Southern Cape coast of South Africa, Christopher Henshilwood and his colleagues unearthed evidence of symbolic expression, in the form of abstract designs (carved ochre bars) and personal ornaments (shell beads) at least 70,000 years old. That is more than 35,000 years before anything comparable emerged in Europe.

B When these discoveries were first announced earlier this decade, they stood out as extraordinary and provocative—at odds with the prevailing wisdom about the time and place of emergence of symbolic behavior, a trait unique to Homo sapiens. Our modern anatomical features can be traced back almost 200,000 years, based on fossilized remains found in Ethiopia, but the making of the modern mind apparently lagged behind by more than 100,000 years. The remarkable finds at Blombos raised several intriguing questions. What triggered this watershed event in human prehistory? How geographically widespread was it? Did it occur simultaneously elsewhere in sub-Saharan Africa? And what role, if any, did such innovations play in the first steps of the worldwide dispersal of our species?

C Important clues come from the stone toolkit that accompanied the crosshatched ochres and deliberately perforated shells at Blombos. Stone tools commonly are the most ubiquitous items at archaeological sites because they survive longer than animal or plant remains. Archaeologists pay close attention to their method of manufacture and how they might have been used. Although much less heralded than engraved ochre and shell beads, the Middle Stone Age deposits at Blombos contained an important assemblage of stone tools known as Still Bay points. These finely shaped lanceolate, or narrow, points are flaked on both sides and probably formed spearhead parts. Discovered in 1866 by Sir Langham Dale near Cape Town, they were among the first type of stone tool described in South Africa. A. J. H. Goodwin, the father of South African archaeology, was the first to appreciate the technological sophistication of this stone-tool industry.

D The Still Bay cultural industry is now widely viewed as a phase of precocious and innovative technology within the Middle Stone Age of Africa, preceded by 200,000 years of much less sophisticated stone toolkits. It was followed by another episode of technological innovation—the Howieson's Poort industry—that includes bladelike tools made blunt on one side and attached to a wooden handle to produce a composite weapon. Like the Still Bay, Howieson's Poort vanished too. Technology of similar sophistication does not appear again in the archaeological record until the Later Stone Age in Africa and the Upper Paleolithic in Europe, many tens of millennia later.

E The importance of the Still Bay and Howieson's Poort lies not only in their enhanced technological sophistication with what looks like hunting tools, but also with the range of associated innovative behavioral artifacts. These include the Blombos finds in the south, engraved ochre at Klein Kliphuis and decorated ostrich eggshells at Diepkloof in the west, and bone points and shell beads at Sibudu to the east. These relics of human cognitive advancement imply that an increasingly complex technological and social organization coincided with what some archaeologists now consider a period of expanded human population size and settlement density in Africa. Comparably sophisticated stone-tool technologies also existed in North Africa (most notably the bifacially flaked and stemmed Aterian projectile points found throughout the Maghreb) and, possibly, in East Africa, the suspected launching ground for early human forays off their native continent. Personal ornaments occasionally have been found at those sites as well, including perforated ostrich eggshell beads and pierced shells of marine gastropods.

F Efforts to compare the timing of these technological and behavioral innovations to those in southern Africa have long been frustrated by uncertainties in the dating of evidence from each region. As a result, identifying the time and place of the emergence of modern human behavior has eluded us. So have the reasons for, and the immediate consequences of, our ancestors becoming "human". Solving these puzzles will require more finely resolved dating and chronologies for key archaeological sites across the continent. We started this quest with a systematic dating study of several sites in southern Africa. Our results hint at the possible role of population expansions in Africa as a trigger for these Stone Age innovations—and, maybe, for early migrations out of Africa about 60,000 years ago.

Questions 27–33

Do the following statements agree with information given in Reading Passage 3?
In boxes 27–33 on your answer sheet, write

TRUE	*if the statement agrees with the information*
FALSE	*if the statement contradicts the information*
NOT GIVEN	*if there is no information on this*

27. Expressing something abstractly is considered as one of attributes of modern humans.
28. Some fossilized remains of early humans were also found at Blombos.
29. Symbolic behavior emerged in Africa as early as in other parts of the world.
30. The stone tools found at Blombos are quite sophisticated.
31. Still Bay industry and Howieson's Poort industry did not last long in history.
32. The stone tools and personal ornaments help to determine the when and where modern human behavior first emerged.
33. Early migrations from Africa took place about 60,000 years ago.

Questions 34–36

Complete the following sentences by choosing ***ONLY ONE WORD*** *from the passage.*

34. Goodwin was the first to __34__ the sophisticated technology of the stone-tool industry.
35. Our modern anatomical features started from about __35__ years ago.
36. The still Bay, Howieson's Poort, Blombos, Klein Kliphuis are all important __35__ sites in Africa.

Questions 37–40

Complete each sentence with the correct ending, ***A–H****, below.*

*Write the correct letter, **A–H**, in boxes 37–40 on your answer sheet.*

37. The unearthed artifacts at Blombos
38. Still Bay points
39. The Still Bay cultural industry
40. The coexistence of the stone tools and the ornaments

A. were first discovered by Sir Langham Dale near Cape Town.
B. give archaeologist important clues on the emergence of modern human behavior.
C. changed our view of the emergence of symbolic behavior.
D. imply that human population expanded with the increasingly complex technological and social organization.
E. provided evidence for our modern anatomical features.
F. represents a phase of a more sophisticated technology.
G. are more sophisticated than the tools found at Blombos.
H. preceded by the episode of the Howieson's Poort industry.

Keys:

1. T	2. F	3. NG
4. T	5. NG	6. F
7. T	8. K	9. B
10. M	11. P	12. R
13. G	14. vii	15. iii
16. viii	17. ii	18. x
19. vi	20. F	21. NG
22. F	23. NG	24. T
25. F	26. T	27. T
28. NG	29. F	30. T
31. T	32. F	33. NG
34. appreciate	35. 200,000	36. archaeological
37. C	38. A	39. F
40. D		

4周攻克

雅思阅读周计划

第三周　雅思阅读题型专项训练（二）

星期一

匹配题（matching）

一 题型描述

在雅思阅读中，搭配题通常有三部分组成：题目说明、选项的集合、题目的集合。题目说明会要求你根据某种关系将每个题目与各自的选项相匹配。匹配题主要包含下列几种形式：文章中的重要概念和对这些概念的阐释配对；学者及其主要观点相配；错误观点（misconception）和反驳错误观点的论据（counterargument）相配；事件和事件的发展过程相配；原因和结果相配；某种标志性事物和其所在的时代相配；新产品和发明家、发明时间相配等。

二 题型透视

这种题型考查考生的查读和快速阅读能力，即迅速从文章中找到相关细节信息的能力。由于多数情况下是人名和地名与相应信息的匹配，我们以这些大写的单词为线索词汇会较快地找到相应信息的位置。但搭配题通常不具有顺序性，也就是说，题目的顺序和原文的顺序是不一致的，从而从另一方面增加了题目的难度。因而关键还是能精准地把握关键词。

三 技巧点拨

1．仔细阅读题目说明，因为有的题目和选项是一对一的关系，而有的是一对多的关系。

2．仔细阅读选项和题目，决定以哪个作为定位词，原则是容易辨认的简短的词优先。

3．一般情况下，选项和题目中提到的事物总有一组是顺序在文中是顺序出现的，考生需要仔细分析题目，然后确定哪些可能在文中顺序出现，再进行查读。

四 解题步骤

Step 1：仔细阅读题目说明和例题，看清题目要求，确定答题方式。

Step 2：划出题目中的中心词并回到原文寻找信息点，注意以大写、斜体、括号和引号方式出现的概念。

Step 3：对于有关人名与理论、新产品和发明家、时间的配对题，首先要快速找出人名、公司名和时间，然后在附近的上下文中找答案。

五 例题精讲

例 1

我们以剑 3 Test1 中的一篇阅读文章后面的 matching 题为例。下面是文章的相关部分和题目。

Questions 1–4

Look at the following items (Questions 1–4) and the list of groups below.
Match each item with the group which first invented or used them.
*Write the correct letter **A–E** in boxes 1–4 on your answer sheet.*
***NB** You may use any letter more than once.*

1. black powder
2. rocket-propelled arrows for fighting
3. rockets as war weapons
4. the rocket launcher

First invented or used by

A	the Chinese
B	the Indians
C	the British
D	the Arabs
E	the Americans

分析： 首先阅读题目说明。这道题要求把题目 1～4 列出的那些事物与首次发明或使用的人群相匹配。这些来自不同国家的人群在方框中一一列出。题目另外特别提醒方框中的某个选项可能要用上不止一次，也就是说某些国家的人民可能首次发明或使用了不止一种题目中提到的事物，这也说明有的选项有可能根本用不上。

策略： 题目一共有 4 道，而选项一共有 5 个，且有的选项可能要重复使用，虽然表示某个国家的人群的大写名词比较好定位，但由于有些选项可能用不上，因而我们需要从题目找关键词作为定位词。由于每道题目提到的事物名称都不算长，我们可以把它们全部记住，带着这些事物的名称回到原文当中快速查读。

解析：

题　目	原　文	解　析	答　案
1. black powder	The invention of rockets is linked inextricably with the invention of **"black powder"**. Most historians of technology **credit the Chinese with its discovery**. They base their belief on studies of ______.	文章一开始就提到了 black powder，然后很多技术方面的历史学家都相信中国人发明了它。接下来一句提供他们持有这种看法的依据，我们不用再继续往下看，就可以确定答案了。	A

（续）

题　目	原　文	解　析	答　案
2．rocket-propelled arrows for fighting	① By the thirteenth century, powder-propelled fire arrows had become rather common. The Chinese relied on this type of technological development to produce _______ to repel their enemies. ② Another weapon was the 'arrow as a flying sabre', which could be fired from crossbows. The rocket, placed in a similar position to other rocket-propelled arrows.	我们在文章接下来的部分中可以迅速发现 powder-propelled fire arrows，但这个与题目中的 rocket-propelled arrows for fighting 还不完全一致。接下来的一句说“中国人通过使用这种技术（由火药推动火箭的技术）发明了一系列的武器来击退敌人”。然后文章列举并详细介绍了两种使用这种技术的武器。在说明第二种武器时，出现了 rocket-propelled arrows，原文中这种武器的火箭与其他由火箭推动的箭一样，被置放在一个相似的位置。因此第二种武器就是题目中的 rocket-propelled arrows for fighting，这个事物同样是中国人发明的。	A
3．rockets as war weapons	It was not until the eighteenth century that Europe became seriously interested in the possibilities of using the rocket itself as a weapon of war and not just to propel other weapons. Prior to this, rockets were used only in pyrotechnic displays. The incentive for the more aggressive use of rockets came not from within the European continent but from far-away India, ______.	文章第二段的开始提到“直到 13 世纪，欧洲人才对把火箭用作战争武器而不是用来推动其他武器感兴趣”。这句非常具有迷惑性，性急的考生可能马上认为答案就是 European，但这句没有说他们是否首次发明和使用了它，且答案中也没有 European 的选项，我们继续向下，看到另外一句说“把火箭投入更具侵略性的用途的动机不是来自欧洲大陆，而是来自遥远的印度”。接下来又具体举例说明印度人如何用火箭作为武器来对付英国人的。因而是印度人首次使用火箭作为武器的。	B
4．the rocket launcher	The Americans developed a rocket, complete with its own launcher, to use against the Mexicans in the mid-nineteenth century.	这句话中有一个 launcher，整句话的意思是“美国人开发了一种带有自己发射器的火箭，用来对付 19 世纪中期的墨西哥人”，因而火箭发射器是美国人发明的。	E

例 2

Questions 11–13

Look at the following cities (Questions 11–13) and the list of descriptions below. Match each city with the correct description, ***A–F****.*

Write the correct letter, ***A–F****, in boxes 11–13 on your answer sheet.*

11．Perth

12．Auckland

13．Portland

List of Descriptions

A	successfully uses a light rail transport system in hilly environment
B	successful public transport system despite cold winters
C	profitably moved from road to light rail transport system
D	hilly and inappropriate for rail transport system
E	heavily dependent on cars despite widespread poverty
F	inefficient due to a limited public transport system

分析：题目中给出了三个城市的名字，选项中是关于这些城市的描述。题目要求把城市名和选项 A 到 F 中关于这些城市的正确描述相匹配，且每个城市只有一个正确选项。由于给出的选项数目大于正确选项数目，因此考生在选择时需要仔细分辨它们之间的差异，以便做出正确选择。

策略：由于题目中给出的城市名称简短且容易辨认，而给出的选项中的句子都较长，且数目比较多，有些描述可能在文章中找不到判断的依据，因此我们直接以题目中的城市名作为定位词，回到原文中迅速查读，找到文章中出现这些城市名的地方，然后再仔细阅读。

解析：

题　目	原　文	分　析	答　案
11. Perth	①A new study ________ has demonstrated that public transport is more than cars. …The study found that the Western Australian city of **Perth** is a good example of a city with minimal public transport. ②Newman notes that Portland has about the same population as **Perth** and had a similar population density at the time.	文中有两处出现了 Perth。第一处说“一项新研究发现公共交通工具比小汽车的效率更高，且发现澳大利亚西部城市 Perth 就是一个有着很少公共交通工具的城市的例子”。我们由此可以推理出 Perth 这个城市由于引入不发达的公共交通系统而效率不高。第二处说“Portland 和 Perth 的人口数量和密度在那个时期都差不多”。因而从文章我们可以得到关于 Perth 的两个信息：一个是它的交通工具，一个是人口。	F：由于有限的交通工具，效率低下。 易错选项 E：尽管普遍贫穷，但还是严重依赖小汽车。Perth 有可能过度依赖小汽车，但由于文中并没有关于 Perth 贫穷的信息，因而弃选该项。
12. Auckland	For example, Newman accepts it would be hard for a city as hilly as **Auckland** to develop a really good rail network.	文中出现 Auckland 的句子说，“Nerman 认为让一个多山的城市比如 Auckland 来发展一个优良的轻轨系统可能比较困难”。因此我们得到的信息是 Auckland 是一个多山的城市，因而不适合建轻轨。	D：多山，且不适宜建轻轨。 易错选项 A：提到了多山的环境，然而它还提到成功地运用了轻轨交通系统，这与原文提供的信息相反，因而排除该项。

（续）

题　目	原　文	解　析	答　案
13. Portland	In fact, Newman believes the main reason for adopting one sort of transport over another is politics: "The more democratic the process, the more public transport is favored." He considers **Portland**, Oregon, a perfect example of this. _______ whether to spend the money on **light rail** instead. The **rail proposal won** and the railway worked spectacularly well.	文章第一处出现 Portland 的地方说"实际上，Nerman 认为采取一种而不是另一种交通系统的主要原因是政治：'过程越民主，公共交通系统就会得到更多的支持。'他认为俄勒冈州的 Portland 就是一个最好的例子"。接下来具体介绍了轻轨系统是如何最终在这个城市建立的，且运行得非常好。	C：有利地从公路转向轻轨系统。 易错选项 A：虽然提到成功地使用了轻轨系统是正确的，但文中并没有说 Portland 也是一个多山的城市，因而排除该项。

六 专题演练

Exercise 1

Shedding Light on Dolphins

During the early 1970s, a Russian biologist named Y. G. Aleyev set out to explain a longstanding puzzle. Four decades before, James Gray, an English zoologist, had estimated the power that dolphins need to swim (according to some simple principles of fluid mechanics) and compared that figure with what their muscles can generate (according to some simple principles of physiology). Not only did the two numbers not match, but the power requirement was a full seven times the amount theoretically available.

Aleyev hypothesized that fatty skin folds, which form when a dolphin swims rapidly, have special hydrodynamic properties that substantially reduce drag. To test his idea, he assembled a team of professional women swimmers, dragging these volunteers through the water at high speeds either clad in tight-fitting body suits or au naturel. Because these swimmers had about the same thickness of subcutaneous fat as dolphins do, zooming around underwater while in the buff raised similar folds on their bodies. Yet Aleyev's measurements showed that these pleats created more drag, not less, leaving the mystery of dolphin energetics completely unresolved.

The persistence of Gray's paradox has more recently prompted Jim Rohr, a civilian physicist working for the U.S. Navy, and Michael Latz, a marine biologist at the Scripps Institution of Oceanography, to once again probe the hydrodynamics of dolphins in a novel way, which they reported last year in the Journal of Experimental Biology. Rather than enlisting the aid of immodest professional swimmers, they received help from some modest single-celled organisms that periodically bloom in the waters around San Diego, primarily dinoflagellates of the species Lingulodinium polyedrum.

It is well known that these marine plankton respond to mechanical stimulation by emitting light. Most reports in the scientific literature had indicated that turbulence is needed to set off the fireworks. But after studying these organisms in the lab, Latz and Rohr discovered that laminar flow too can trigger the bioluminescence, as long as the shear stress (for example, in the boundary layer that forms around a moving object) exceeds a critical threshold.

Armed with this understanding and a low-light video camera, Rohr and Latz boarded a friend's boat one moonless night and set sail into San Diego Bay to see whether they could learn something about the hydrodynamics of dolphins. Although they observed dolphins "lit up" by bioluminescent phytoplankton during their very first outing, the conditions proved difficult to reproduce. Not only must the bioluminescent organisms be adequately abundant and the dolphins sufficiently friendly, but the experiment also requires the darkness of a new moon. And even if nature cooperates fully, "the lights of the city can kill you," notes Rohr.

So Latz and Rohr engineered somewhat more controlled conditions by erecting a large tent over one of the floating pens used for the Navy's marine mammals program in San Diego Bay. With the help of the animals' military handlers, they directed trained dolphins to swim into the darkened pen, where they had positioned their low-light camera.

By recording the ghostly, blue-green bioluminescent halo around the moving dolphins, Latz and Rohr were able to examine the flow of water over the creatures as they coasted beneath the camera. The study revealed that the hydrodynamic boundary layer is typically quite thin up front and that, contrary to expectations based on simple fluid mechanics, the flow does not separate from the body of the animal along its flank.

The surprising lack of flow separation (and the concomitant drag that separation would cause) may help to explain why Gray's calculation was in error. But the full solution may in fact be more prosaic. "The simple answer is that they're not moving as fast as everyone said," says Frank Fish, a zoologist at West Chester University in Pennsylvania.

Gray had supposed that dolphins could swim at 20 knots, whereas modern estimates indicate that dolphins cannot sustain much more than 15 knots. Because the energy expended underwater scales with the cube of the speed, this difference alone more than halves the theoretical energy requirement. Other simple differences, for example, between the muscles of dolphins and the muscles of the human athletes on which Gray based his calculations, can also help reconcile the discrepancy. But a major question still remains: Why does water flow smoothly over the body of a dolphin without separating in the way that simple hydrodynamic theory predicts? Fish is eager to join with Rohr in solving that riddle using natural bioluminescence, but he is guarded about their prospects, given the many experimental difficulties involved: "If we have some money," says Fish, "and the planets are aligned correctly, maybe we can pull it off."

Questions 1–7

Look at the following statement (Questions 1 – 7) and the list of researchers below.
Match each statement with the correct researcher(s), A–E.
Write the correct letter, A–E, in boxes 1–7 on your answer sheet.
***NB** You may use any letter more than once.*

1. Bioluminescence can also take place while there is a laminar flow.
2. Skin folds actually generated more resistance in swimming.
3. Dolphins do not swim that fast as people have believed.
4. The muscles of dolphins are different from those of the human athletes.
5. Fatty skin folds can help lessen resistance generated by rapid swimming of dolphins.
6. Water flow and body of the dolphin along its flank do not keep apart.
7. The amount of power required by dolphins is far more than those their body could generate.

List of Researchers

A	Aleyev
B	Gray
C	Rohr and Latz
D	Fish
E	None of the above

Keys:

1. C　2. A　3. D　4. E　5. A　6. C　7. B

Exercise 2

Plasticity in the Adult Brain

The dogma of neurophysiology up until the 1970s was that generation of new neurons was limited to the period of embryogenesis for most of the brain, with a few exceptions, including the granule cells of the olfactory bulb and hippocampus. After birth, regeneration of neurons was believed to be limited to the peripheral nerves. As it became clear that all cortical areas of the brain exhibit plasticity (changes over time), modulations in function and activity were ascribed to synaptic changes. However, recent studies have suggested that neurogenesis may also be in play. Following are nine reports that describe simple enlargement of the brain or an increase in the volume of specific cortical areas after various stimuli. In the first four reports neurogenesis was not considered by the researchers; in the latter five reports, it plainly occurred.

In the early 1980s, William Greenough and colleagues trained adult rats on multiple maze patterns and found that afterward: "visual cortex pyramidal neuron dendritic fields were larger" than in controls. Rats trained on complex motor tasks also showed greater "cerebellar cortex thickness" than control rats given "far more physical activity" using devices such as treadmills. According to the authors, the results "strongly implicate changes in the number of synapses in the memory process". They did not pursue a conclusive histological investigation.

In the 1990s, Gregg Recanzone and coworkers trained monkeys "to discriminate between two vibrating stimuli applied to one finger" and after several thousand trials found that "the cortical representation of the trained finger became more than twice as large as the corresponding areas for other fingers".

In 1995, Thomas Elbert used neuroimaging to study right-handed string musicians and found that "the cortical representation of the fingers of the left hand … was larger than that in controls".

In 2004, Bogdon Draganski and colleagues employed fMRI scans of young volunteers who had mastered over a three-month period "a classic three-ball cascade juggling routine" and found expansion in gray matter in the mid temporal area and left posterior intraparietal sulcus. Notably, the expansion decreased three months later.

In the following five reports, postnatal neurogenesis was explicitly addressed.

Studies by Fernando Nottebohn in birds may have relevance to neurogenesis in the human brain. In the early 1980s, Nottebohn's lab reported in several papers that in the female canary forebrain (hyperstriatum), the volume of two vocal control nuclei (functional collections of neurons and associated cells) increased markedly during the peak of the singing season, then declined, then increased again during the successive singing season. The song repertoire of the canaries changes each year. The birds were injected with 3H-thymidine, which becomes incorporated in the DNA of replicating cells. In birds that received the label, it was shown that the volume increase in one particular area was accompanied by labeled glial, endothelial and migrating neuronal precursor cells — all of which were interpreted as signs of neurogenesis.

The earliest neurological studies using radioactive labeling were done in 1962 by Joseph Altman, who injected 3H-thymidine into lesions created in the lateral geniculate body of adult rats. He found labeled glial cells, neuroblasts, and a few neurons in or near the lesion area. The presence of labeled neuroblasts was judged to support "a process of neurogenesis" in the area of repair.

In 1999, Elizabeth Gould and coworkers injected bromodeoxyuridine (BrdU, a synthetic nucleotide analog that, like 3H-thymidine, gets incorporated into DNA in replicating cells) into adult macaques and after one week found labeled mature neurons in the prefrontal, inferior temporal and parietal cortices, indicating that neurons "are added to primate neocortex in adulthood". The authors did not regard the prior studies by Altman and Nottebohn as definitive or as establishing neurogenesis.

Peter Ericksson and colleagues reported in 1998 on the injection of five terminally ill patients with BrdU. They found that after their deaths (from several weeks to two years later), cells in the hippocampal dentate gyrus were labeled with both BrdU and a neuron-specific marker. They interpreted their findings to indicate the "genesis" of new neurons from "dividing progenitor cells" in the gyrus.

Finally, work by Marian Diamond and colleagues indicated that the continued growth of human brain after birth is influenced by nutritional factors and environmental influences. They found that rats given playthings and treadmills ("an enriched environment") develop more glial cells per neuron in the occipital cortex. Other changes noted were "neuronal stroma size, neuronal density, length of dendritic branches, dendritic spine density, length of synapses and glial cell counts".

Questions 1–6

Look at the following statements (Questions 1–6) and the list of researchers below.

Match each statement about their findings with the correct researcher.

*Write the correct letter **A–H** in boxes 1–6 on your answer sheet.*

***NB** You may use any letter more than once.*

1. Signs of neurogenesis were found in the study.
2. Postnatal brain growth was affected by nutrition and environment.
3. Radioactive labeling were first used in the study.
4. The effect of training on the change of brain volume did not last long.
5. Cortex pyramidal neuron dendritic fields could become larger by doing complex motor tasks.
6. The cortical area of the trained finger were larger than those of other fingers.

List of Researchers

A	William Greenough
B	Gregg Recanzone
C	Thomas Elbert
D	Bogdon Draganski
E	Fernando Nottebohn
F	Joseph Altman
G	Elizabeth Gould
H	Marian Diamond

Keys:

1. E　2. H　3. F　4. D　5. A　6. B

Exercise 3

Though humankind has lived on this planet for several million years, it's only in the last 10,000 that people began to live together communally, and to raise animals and crops. Approximately 6000 years ago, as societies became more intricate and complex, they began to develop a system of written language to be able to record and pass down knowledge to the next generation. As the body of knowledge increased, people began to recognize the need for a more formal system of education and formed schools as a result.

Long before the Greeks and the Romans developed their schools, Eastern civilizations had highly developed and complex societies requiring formalized education. While the exact date when schools actually began will probably never be determined. Evidence exists that the ancient Sumerians of Mesopotamia, the fertile crescent between the Tigris and Euphrates Rivers in what is modern-Iraq, had cuneiform (a form of writing) texts for mathematics that have been dated to 2000 BC.

Schools probably existed in China almost 4,000 years ago. As a highly developed society, the Chinese designed their schools around the perpetuation of tradition, compliance and conventionality, to allow their youth to function in an increasingly formal and complex society. The individual was not deemed particularly important, rather it was the individual's acceptance of the cultural traditions and practices and his place in society that characterized educational practice. Females for the most part were not deemed worthy of a formal education.

As with many other cultures, the Japanese system of education evolved after they developed a written language. Adapting the Chinese form of writing, the Japanese aristocracy was the first to learn to read and write. Originally the Japanese borrowed heavily from the Chinese culture in providing a curriculum of study. However, eventually the needs of Japanese society became paramount and the educational system began to reflect a Japanese culture and belief system. Education was also used to provide for the societal needs such as the specific schools that were set up to train young men for civil service.

The Hebrews valued education and centered their instruction around the teachings of their bible. Harsh discipline also characterized educational practice along with a strict emphasis on following the laws of the Old Testament. Females were not formally educated, but instead were required to learn the skills associated with homemaking. Teachers were treated with great respect, indicative of the value that Hebrew society placed on education.

Ancient Hindu societies were based on a strict adherence to a proscribed system of familial status known as the caste system, whereby an individual's status is determined by his family's place in the society. Formal education helped perpetuate this system by only allowing access to boys from the highest or Brahmin caste. Priests were used as teachers resulting in a heavy emphasis on moral development, learning to write, and harsh discipline.

The Egyptians developed a very early, highly civilized society. They had a form of writing known as hieroglyphics, and were divided into castes. The priests were the most highly educated segment of society and provided the instruction for the privileged males deemed worthy of learning.

Each of these societies in their own way contributed to the development of schools and education. Many of the practices spread to other parts of the world through travel and conquest. Several important Greek philosophers, such as Plato, Pythagoras, Lycurgus, and Solon studied in Egypt.

The societies described above were quite similar in the design of their formal education systems in that all excluded females and were limited to mainly the upper classes. These practices helped perpetuate and sustain the existing class and power structure within each society by denying the disenfranchised the opportunity to access the information they needed to become members of the elite group. These customs were also part of European and American formal education up until the beginning of the 20th century.

Questions 1–5

Look at the following statements (Questions 1–5) and the list of groups below.
Match each statement about education with the correct group(s).
*Write the correct letter **A–F** in boxes 1–5 on your answer sheet.*
***NB** You may use any letter more than once.*

1. Instruction was around the bible.
2. Priest acted as teachers and gave instructions.
3. Harsh discipline was enforced.
4. Schools put an emphasis on tradition, compliance and conventionality.
5. Schools were originally developed by imitating a neighboring country.

List of Groups

A	The Sumerians
B	The Chinese
C	The Japanese
D	The Hindus
E	The Egyptians
F	The Hebrews

Keys:

1. F 2. D, E 3. D, F 4. B 5. C

星期二

分类题（classification）

一 题型描述

题目一般是一些事物或事物特征的集合，然后要求分别对这些事物或特征按照给定的标准进行分类。类别一般是二到四个，通常是三个类别，比如让你决定列出的特征中哪些是属于 A 事物的，哪些是属于 B 事物的，哪些是 A 和 B 两者共有的，哪些是 A 和 B 都没有的。事物特征的数目一般要大于事物类别的数目，因而每个字母都要用上。

二 题型透视

这种题型仍然属于细节题，考查考生迅速查找相关信息并进行仔细比较和分析的能力。由于给出的类别往往比较简短且通常是名词，因而考生可以以类别词为关键词回到原文查读，提高阅读的效率。

三 解题步骤

Step 1：首先明确分类的标准是什么，是不是有一些大写的词在里面，如果有的话，以它们为关键词，回到原文中查读。

Step 2：如果分类的标准不是专有名词，那么我们需要看题目中是否有容易辨认的单词，并把它们一一划下作为关键词，然后回到原文中查读。

Step 3：找到相关信息在文中的具体位置后仔细阅读，并与题目相比对，最后作出选择。

四 技巧点拨

1．仔细阅读题目要求进行分类的标准，注意这些标准之间的异同，找出关键词。

2．如果要求对其分类的事物比较长，划出中心词，并注意其他可能的转述形式。

五 例题精讲

例 1

我们首先来看剑 5 Test2 中的一篇阅读文章后的分类题：

Questions 8-11

Classify the following techniques according to whether the writer states they

A. are currently exclusively used by Australians.

B. will be used in the future by Australians.

C. are currently used by both Australians and their rivals.

Write the correct letter A, B or C, in boxes 8-11 on your answer sheet.

8. cameras

9. sensors

10. protein tests

11. altitude tents

分析：题目列出了4种技巧，然后根据它们是目前只被澳大利亚人使用，将来会被澳大利亚人使用，还是目前正在被澳大利亚人和他们的竞争对手使用进行分类。这四种事物分别是照相机、传感器、蛋白质测试和高地帐篷。

策略：首先我们需要注意三种类别之间的差异，其次我们发现题目中列出的4种事物都是简短的名词或名词短语，可以尽可能把它们迅速记在脑中然后在原文中查找它们的相应位置，再决定答案。

解析：

题　目	原　文	分　析	答　案
8. cameras	It collects images from digital **cameras** running at 50 frames a second and breaks down.	文中出现cameras的段落介绍了澳大利亚人如何使用这个技术研究运动员的运动的，而且这项技术已经被澳大利亚的研究人员在使用，同时文章没有提到这项技术在别的国家使用。	A
9. sensors	They are developing unobtrusive **sensors** that will be embedded in an athlete's clothes or running shoes to monitor heart rate, ______.	我们可以看到包含sensors的句子使用的是进行时态，且后面的是一个将来时态，说明传感器将来会被澳大利亚人使用在体育研究上。	B
10. protein tests	______ AIS and the University of Newcastle in New South Wales developed **a test** that measures how much of the immune-system **protein** immunoglobulin A is present in athletes' saliva… Since **the tests were introduced,** AIS athletes in all sports have been remarkably successful at staying healthy.	在文中，test和后面的protein是分开的，文中说“澳大利亚的研究机构开发了一种测量运动员的唾液含有多少免疫球蛋白A的测试”，接着又提到“自从这种测试被引进后，所有运动项目的AIS的运动员们都成功地保持了健康”。现在完成时态表明这种技术现在还在被澳大利亚人所使用，而且文中其他地方也没有提到这种技术目前在被别的国家使用着。	A

（续）

题　目	原　文	解　析	答　案
11. altitude tents	Of course, there's nothing to stop other countries copying – and many have tried. Some years ago, the AIS unveiled coolant-lined jackets for endurance athletes ________. Now everyone uses them. The same has happened to the **'altitude tent',**	首先我们可以注意到包含 altitude tent 的句子只提到："同样的事情也发生在高地帐篷上"，但 the same thing 指什么呢？我们需要继续往前面找答案。文中提到："当然这无法阻止其他国家模仿它们"。然后给出了一个例子：coolant-lined jackets，说现在大家都在使用这项技术，接着说同样的事情也发生在 altitude tent 上，说明这项技术目前既被澳大利亚也被其他国家使用着。	C

例 2

接下来我们看一下剑 7 Test 2 中的分类题。

Questions 5–10

Classify the following as typical of

A．both Chinese and Japanese pagodas

B．only Chinese pagodas

C．only Japanese pagodas

Write the correct letter, A, B or C, in boxes 5–10 on your answer sheet.

5．easy interior access to top

6．tiles on eaves

7．use as observation post

8．size of eaves up to half the width of the building

9．original religious purpose

10．floors fitting loosely over each other

分析：题目给出了 6 种塔的特征，然后要求考生根据这些特征是日本塔独有的，中国塔独有的，还是两者共有的，进行分类。

策略：分类比较好记忆，我们现在需要看这些特征的表述。值得注意的是，6 种特征的字面表述可能是原文相关信息的转述或概括，因此需要划出每个题目中的关键词，并思考一下这些关键词的相关词汇。5. 很容易到达塔顶的内部通道，关键词 interior access；6. 屋檐上有瓦，关键词 tiles；7. 作为瞭望台使用，关键词 observation post；8. 屋檐到达建筑物宽度的一半，关键词 half the width；9. 最初是为了宗教上的原因使用的，关键词 religious；10. 每一层都松散地架置在另一层的上面，关键词 loosely。

解析：

题　　目	原　　文	分　　析	答　案
5. easy interior access to top	The Chinese built their pagodas in brick or stone, with **inner staircases,** and used them in later centuries main as watchtowers.	题目中的 interior access 和文中的 inner staircases 相照应，因为 interior 和 inner 都是近义词，而 staircase 是用来帮助达到塔顶的，且文中告诉我们内部有楼梯是中国塔的构造特征。	B
6. tiles on eaves	For the same reason, the builders of Japanese pagodas seem to have further increased their weight by choosing to cover these extended eaves not with the **porcelain tiles** of many Chinese pagoda but with much heavier **earthenware tiles.**	文中 porcelain tiles 和 earthenware tiles 和题目中的 tiles 相照应。文中这句话的意思是："由于同样的原因，日本塔的建造者似乎又由于选择重得多的陶瓦而不是中国塔的瓷瓦来增加屋顶的重量"。这句话说明不管是中国塔的瓷瓦还是日本塔的陶瓦，它们的屋檐上都使用了瓦，因此这个特征应该是两者共有的。	A
7. use as observation post	The Chinese built their pagodas in brick or stone, with inner staircases, and used them in later centuries main as **watchtowers.**	文中的 watchtower 和题目中 observation post 相照应，都是"瞭望台"的意思，而这是中国塔的特征。	B
8. size of eaves up to half the width of the building	The **roof** a Japanese temple building can be made to overhang the sides of the structure by **fifty per cent** or more of the building's overall **width.**	文中的 roof 和题目中的 eaves 相照应，fifty per cent 和 half 相照应，the building's overall width 和 the width of the building 相照应，文中这句话的意思是"日本寺庙的屋顶可以延伸出塔的周边，长度达到整个建筑物的一半宽度甚至更多"。	C
9. original religious purpose	The multi-storey pagoda came to Japan from China in the sixth century. As in China, they were **first introduced with Buddhism** and were ______.	文中的 first 题目中的 original 相照应，Buddhism 又跟 religious purpose 相照应。文中这句话的意思是"多楼层的塔在 6 世纪从中国传到日本。跟在中国一样，它们最初被引进的时候是跟佛教联系在一起的"，因此这个特征是中国塔和日本塔所共有的。	A
10. floors fitting loosely over each other	What those early craftsmen had found by trial and error was that under pressure a pagoda's **loose stack of floors** could be made to slither to and fro independent of one another.	文中的 loose stack of floors 意思是"松散地叠放在一起的楼层"，这正好与题目中的 floors fitting loosely over each other 相照应，而这个是日本塔独有的建筑特征。	C

六 专题演练

Exercise 1

The Tickling Trigger

Tickling is a fascinating instance of the connection between playfulness and social bonding. It begins in early infancy, when parents tickle their babies to evoke laughter and pleasurable sensations in them. Although there are a few "unticklish" children and adults, tickling almost always produces laughter. Probably tickling and laughter evolved in part to help us relate to others.

One remarkable feature of tickling is that we do not laugh when we tickle ourselves, only when other people tickle us. This implies that the brain may have a different mechanism for responding to the two types of tickling. Charles Darwin first explored the link between tickling and social relations, arguing that tickling provokes laughter through the anticipation of pleasure. If a stranger tickles a child without any preliminaries, catching the child by surprise, the likely result will be not laughter but withdrawal and displeasure. Darwin also noticed that for tickling to be effective, you must not know the precise point of stimulation in advance. He reasoned that this is why you cannot effectively tickle yourself.

Researcher Sarah-Jayne Blakemore confirmed Darwin's propositions by investigating how the brain distinguishes between sensations we create for ourselves and sensations others create for us. She used robotic arms to tickle people and found them to be as effective as real people in provoking laughter. When her subjects used a joystick to control the tickling robot, however, they couldn't make themselves laugh. Her studies suggest that when you try to tickle yourself, your cerebellum sends to your somatosensory cortex precise information on the position of the tickling target and therefore what sensation to expect. Apparently some cortical mechanism then decreases or inhibits the tickling sensation.

Why is the brain built this way? "It may be that there is no point laughing to your own tickle because it is not biologically important," says Blakemore. But tickling by your playful companions is indeed socially important, as we have seen.

From these studies an apparent contradiction arises. If laughter can be triggered by stimulating highly developed cortical areas of the brain, how could laughter be, at the same time, a primitive feature of both human and nonhuman brains? The answer may lie in our prodigious human capacity for humor, which we do not seem to share with other animals.

The main argument here is that laughter induced by a joke or by watching something funny may be a highly evolved version of the laughter induced in our ancestors by play or tickling. Provine suggests that the human brain is able to enlarge the capabilities of one of its ancient, more primitive features by processing lower functions.

"When we hear laughter, we are hearing something that is very primitive. In the more modern version, laughter induced by jokes involves cognitive systems, something that evolved long after speech and language." Chimpanzees show laughterlike behavior in response to physical contact, such as wrestling, chasing, or tickling, but humans laugh more in response to conversational and visual stimuli.

Both Darwin and German evolutionist Ernst Haeckel theorized that jokes were essentially "psychological tickling." Haeckel believed that laughter was a kind of reflex, which relieved the irritation of vasomotor nerves brought on by physical or mental tickling. Ethnologist Glenn E. Weisfeld, an expert on humor, adds that "the subject matter of humor often pertains to ticklish situations". The word humor is from the Latin humere, meaning "liquid" or "fluid", and betrays the Aristotelian belief (continued into the Middle Ages) that all emotional states were related to the essential four body fluids that drive us.

One definition of humor is "the mental faculty of discovering, expressing, or appreciating the ludicrous or absurdly incongruous". Visual and verbal jokes often emphasize the exaggeration, absurdity, eccentricity, or inconsistency of a situation, a behavior, or an outcome. This exaggeration becomes the core element provoking laughter: the punch line.

Another key element of humor and laughter is the release after danger and surprise. When we laugh our heads off at someone slipping on a banana peel or getting a pie in the face, we are laughing at situations that involve surprise, incongruence, potential damage to the body, or an unexpected outcome—all stimuli that trigger fight-or-flight in our primitive, jungle-primate selves. Philosopher John Morreall believes that human laughter may have its biological origins as a kind of shared expression of relief at the passing of danger. The relaxation of tension we feel after laughing may help inhibit the fight-or-flight response, making laughter a behavioral sign of trust in one's companions.

This connection between humor and the release of tension makes sense in brain terms. Animal (and human) brains do not like novelty and change; they are hardwired to produce a certain amount of tension when something unexpected occurs, because any environmental change could be a threat. A sudden noise startles us. A playful lunge at our belly by a friend provokes instinctive recoil and a suitably scared expression, then laughter. If the stimulus were a gunshot, however, or a real punch in the gut, we would most assuredly not laugh but seek cover or defend ourselves.

Watch people laughing at an amusement park and you see this connection between release from danger and laughter. A boat swooping down a steep chute into water first evokes expressions of horror and fear. When no danger ensues, laughter erupts. In the same vein, slapstick comedies feature a lot of head banging, falls, and edge-of-the-cliff situations to induce laughter. We enjoy make-believe aggression and danger and we laugh to relieve the tension and signal to our companions that all is well. Weisfeld notes that "lots of humor pertains to aggressive or competitive situations in which someone gets hurt". See how professional comedians or clowns use stooges who are constantly embarrassed, hit, and harassed.

Questions 1−5

Classify the following according to whether they are typical of ______.

A. humans

B. animals

C. both humans and animals

Write the correct letter A, B or C, in boxes 1−5 on your answer sheet.

1. only lower cognition mechanism involved in laughter
2. laughing in response to visual stimuli
3. capable of appreciating humor
4. laughing in response to physical contact
5. self-created trickling is not effective

Keys:

1. B　2. A　3. A　4. C　5. A

Exercise 2

The Qualitative versus Quantitative Debate

In Miles and Huberman's 1994 book *Qualitative Data Analysis*, quantitative researcher Fred Kerlinger is quoted as saying, "There's no such thing as qualitative data. Everything is either 1 or 0" (p. 40). To this, another researcher, D. T. Campbell, asserts "all research ultimately has a qualitative grounding" (p. 40). This back and forth banter among qualitative and quantitative researchers is "essentially unproductive" according to Miles and Huberman. They and many other researchers agree that these two research methods need each other more often than not. However, because typically qualitative data involves words and quantitative data involves numbers, there are some researchers who feel that one is better (or more scientific) than the other. Another major difference between the two is that qualitative research is inductive and quantitative research is deductive. In qualitative research, a hypothesis is not needed to begin research. However, all quantitative research requires a hypothesis before research can begin.

Another major difference between qualitative and quantitative research is the underlying assumptions about the role of the researcher. In quantitative research, the researcher is ideally an objective observer that neither participates in nor influences what is being studied. In qualitative research, however, it is thought that the researcher can learn the most about a situation by participating and/or being immersed in it. These basic underlying assumptions of both methodologies guide and sequence the types of data collection methods employed.

Although there are clear differences between qualitative and quantitative approaches, some researchers maintain that the choice between using qualitative or quantitative approaches actually has less to do with methodologies than it does with positioning oneself within a particular discipline or research tradition. The difficulty of choosing a method is compounded by the fact that research is often affiliated with universities and other institutions. The findings of research projects often guide important decisions about specific practices and policies. The choice of which approach to use may reflect the interests of those conducting or benefitting from the research and the purposes for which the findings will be applied. Decisions about which kind of research method to use may also be based on the researcher's own experience and preference, the population being researched, the proposed audience for findings, time, money, and other resources available.

Some researchers believe that qualitative and quantitative methodologies cannot be combined because the assumptions underlying each tradition are so vastly different. Other researchers think they can be used in combination only by alternating between methods: qualitative research is appropriate to answer certain kinds of questions in certain conditions and quantitative is right for others. And some researchers think that both qualitative and quantitative methods can be used simultaneously to answer a research question.

To a certain extent, researchers on all sides of the debate are correct: each approach has its drawbacks. Quantitative research often "forces" responses or people into categories that might not "fit" in order to make meaning. Qualitative research, on the other hand, sometimes focuses too closely on individual results and fails to make connections to larger situations or possible causes of the results. Rather than discounting either approach for its drawbacks, though, researchers should find the most effective ways to incorporate elements of both to ensure that their studies are as accurate and thorough as possible.

It is important for researchers to realize that qualitative and quantitative methods can be used in conjunction with each other. In a study of computer-assisted writing classrooms, Snyder employed both qualitative and quantitative approaches. The study was constructed according to guidelines for quantitative studies: the computer classroom was the "treatment" group and the traditional pen and paper classroom was the "control" group. Both classes contained subjects with the same characteristics from the population sampled. Both classes followed the same lesson plan and were taught by the same teacher in the same semester. The only variable used was the computers. Although Snyder set this study up as an "experiment", she used many qualitative approaches to supplement her findings. She observed both classrooms on a regular basis as a participant-observer and conducted several interviews with the teacher both during and after the semester. However, there were several problems in using this approach: the strict adherence to the same syllabus and lesson plans for both classes and the restricted access of the control group to the computers may have put some students at a disadvantage. Snyder also notes that in retrospect she should have used case studies of the students to further develop her findings. Although her study had certain flaws, Snyder insists that researchers can simultaneously employ qualitative and quantitative methods if studies are planned carefully and carried out conscientiously.

Questions 1–4

Classify the following researchers according to their different positions.

A. Quantitative method

B. Qualitative method

C. Combination of both

Write the correct letter A, B or C, in boxes 1–4 on your answer sheet.

1. D. T. Campbell
2. Snyder
3. Fred Kerlinger
4. Miles and Huberman

Keys:

1. B　2. C　3. A　4. C

星期三

简答题（short-answer questions）

一 题型描述

题目会以几个问句的形式出现，一般情况下会要求考生从原文中选取一定数目的（比如不得超过两个或三个）单词或数字作答，少数情况是需要考生用自己的话作答。

二 题型透视

这种题目考查考生查找并理解文章细节信息的能力。成功攻克此类题目需要考生能准确判断题目的关键词，学会略读确定相关信息在文中的大致位置，并能通过查读确定相关信息的准确位置，最后还能够识别题目中对原文信息的转述。

三 解题步骤

Step 1：仔细阅读题目说明，看清题目对答案的字数限制。

Step 2：迅速浏览所有题目，划出每题的关键词，并仔细思考关键词的相关词汇（包括同义词、反义词、同根词等），题目中如果有容易辨认的特殊字，优先把它们作为线索词（在多道题目中同时出现的一些特殊词除外）。

Step 3：顺序运用略读和查读来迅速找到每题相关信息所在的大致位置，然后仔细阅读文章相关部分，确定答案。

Step 4：书写答案时，注意拼写正确，并仔细检查确保没有语法错误。

四 技巧点拨

1．简答题的出题顺序与文章信息出现的先后顺序是一致的，也就是某道题的答案一定是出现在它之前的那答题的答案之后和它之后的那道题的答案之前，考生可以利用这个原则缩小答案的查找范围。

2．注意题目是不是有一些特殊的疑问词，如 when，where，how，who，这些特殊的疑问词可以帮助我们预测答案的类型，比如疑问词是 when 的题目，答案在原文中一定是以数字或年代表示的时间，疑问词是 who 的题目则需要我们找一些大写的人名。

五 例题精讲

例 1：选自剑 6 Test1

Questions 12 and 13

Answer the questions below.
Choose ***NO MORE THAN THREE WORDS AND/OR A NUMBER*** *from the passage for each answer.*
Write your answers in boxes 12 and 13 on your answer sheet.

12. What is produced to help an athlete plan their performance in an event?
13. By how much did some cyclists' performance improve at the 1996 Olympic Games?

分析：第一题问什么东西被设计出来帮助运动员设计在赛事中的表现，疑问词是 what，那么答案应该是一个名词或名词词组。第二题问在 1996 年的奥林匹克运动会上，自行车选手的表现提高了多少，疑问词是 by how much，因而答案可能会以数字的形式出现。

策略：由于第一个问题中没有特殊的字词，我们需要找出关键词：plan their performance 和 event。第二题中有一个明显的数字 1996，我们可以把它作为线索词，本题的关键词是 cyclists。

解析：

题目	原文	分析	答案
12	Well before a championship, sports scientists and coaches start to prepare the athlete by developing a "competition model", based on what they expect will be the winning times.	原文中的 championship 是"冠军赛、锦标赛"的意思，照应了题目中的 event，prepare the athlete 照应了题目中的 plan their performance，develop 照应了题目中的 produce，因此答案应该 develop 后面的名词词组。	a "competition model"
13	At the Atlanta Olympic Games in 1996, these sliced as much as two per cent off cyclists' and rowers' times.	这个含有 1996 的句子的意思是，"在 1996 年的奥林匹克大赛上，这些使得自行车选手和划船运动员的时间减少了百分之二"，换句话说也就是自行车选手的表现提高了百分之二。	two per cent

例 2：选自剑 4 Test1

Questions 22−26

Answer the questions below using ***NO MORE THAN TREE WORDS*** *from the passage for each answer.*
Write your answers in boxes 22−26 on your answer sheet.

22. Which of the senses is described here as being involved in mating?
23. Which species swims upside down while eating?
24. What can bottlenose dolphins follow from under the water?
25. Which types of habitat is related to good visual ability?

26. Which of the senses is best developed in cetaceans?

分析： 题目要求从原文中选词回答，且每道题目的答案词数不得超过 3 个。另外迅速浏览过题目之后没有发现容易辨认的特殊词，因此我们需要先找出每道题的关键词。

策略： 22 译文：这里描述的感觉中哪种被用来求偶？关键词：mating

23 译文：哪个种类在吃东西的时候倒游过来？关键词：swim upside down，eating

24 译文：宽吻海豚在水下能够追随什么？关键词：bottlenose dolphins，follow from

25 译文：哪种栖息地跟良好的视力相关？关键词：habitat，good visual ability

26 译文：鲸目动物的那种感觉最发达？关键词：best developed，cetaceans

解析：

。	原　　文	分　　析	答　　案
22	The sense of touch has sometimes been described as weak too, but this view is probably mistaken. ________ This contact may help to maintain order within a group, and stroking or touching are part of the courtship ritual in most species.	文中的这一段落主要讨论了鲸目类动物的触觉。中间的一句提到“这种接触可以帮助维持群体内部的秩序，抚摸和轻触还是大多数种类进行求偶仪式的一部分”。文章中的courtship 与题目中的 mating 相照应。	touch / sense of touch
23	Eye position in freshwater dolphins, which often swim on their side or **upside down while feeding**, suggests that ______.	文章中的 upside down 与题目中的 upside down 一致，while feeding 照应了题目中的 while eating，而这种游泳时的特殊动作是淡水海豚的一种行为特征。	freshwater dolphin(s) / the freshwater dolphin(s)
24	By comparison, the **bottlenose dolphin** has extremely keen vision in water. Judging from the way it watches and **tracks** airborne flying fish, it can apparently see fairly well through the air-water interface as well.	文中的 bottlenose dolphin 和题目中的完全一致，in water 照应了题目中的 under the water，而 track 和题目中的 follow from 是近义表达，因此答案应该是 tracks 后面的名词词组。	airborne flying fish
25	Such variation can no doubt be explained with reference to the **habitats** in which individual species have developed. For example, **vision** is obviously more useful to species **inhabiting** clear open waters than to those living in turbid rivers and flooded plains.	文中出现了题目的关键词 habitats，说明答案就在周围。文中说：“这种（感觉的）差异无疑可以通过不同物种赖以生存的栖息地来解释。例如，与生活在浑浊的河流和洪水泛滥的平原的物种相比，视力对生活在清澈的开放水域中的物种明显更重要”。这两句话暗含的意思是清澈的开放水域使得某些物种具备了良好的视力。	clear open water(s) / clear water(s)
26	Although the senses of taste and smell appear to have deteriorated, and vision in water appears to be uncertain, such weakness are more than compensated for by cetacean's **well-developed** acoustic sense.	文中 well-developed 和题目中的 best developed 相照应，包含这个单词的句子的意思是：“尽管（鲸目类动物）的味觉和嗅觉似乎都退化了，水中的视力也不太稳定，这种缺点却被它们发达的听觉弥补了”。	acoustic sense / the acoustic sense

六 专题演练

Exercise 1

Tracking the Invaders

A new study uses air travel and climate data to predict the riskiest times for invasions by nonnative species.

It's not just ecosystems that feel the effects of invasive species. They're an increasingly obvious threat to economies as well. A 2005 estimate from David Pimentel and his colleagues at Cornell University put the cost of annual environmental damage and losses due to invasive species at nearly $120 billion — and that was just for the United States. But with limited funds and the involvement of many parties, it can be hard to prevent the introduction of potentially harmful species into new locales, and even harder to restore ecosystems once such species have become established.

Andy Tatem, a professor of geography with the Emerging Pathogens Institute at the University of Florida, believes we need better tools for predicting when and where the risk of species invasion is high. In a paper published online in March in the journal Ecography, he demonstrates just such a tool.

"It's really about exploring what barriers there are left in the world to the movement of invasive species," Tatem says. "Up to a hundred years ago, sheer distance would have been the major barrier preventing species movement."

But the worldwide airline network has changed all that. As international travelers know from strict customs warnings, the likelihood of potentially invasive organisms traveling by air to new destinations can be high. Fruit flies, beetles, moths, mollusks, nematodes, mites, mosquitoes — all have been known to hitch an airplane ride, whether it's in a suitcase, inside a mango someone has brought home to eat or buzzing about in the flight cabin.

Another important factor is easier to miss: If the places of origin and destination have similar climates, the risk that a climatically sensitive organism will get established in a new place increases.

In a 2007 study, Tatem and epidemiologist Simon I. Hay detailed a set of indices for measurement of these factors. Tatem has now applied them to create predictions about future risk. "This is the first time more contemporary and future projections have been used," he says. He compiled data on international air-traffic routes, passenger and freight volumes, and yearly and seasonal climatic conditions for each of 3,570 airports and a total of 44,000 flight routes. These current measurements and economic and climate-change projections allowed him to create models for each month from 2007 to 2010.

First, Tatem focused on flight routes. To determine how similar the climatic conditions are at the origin and destination of a given route, he calculated the Euclidean distance between the set of several climatic variables at each location. The climatic Euclidean distance (CED) for a given route and month incorporates data on projected air temperature, total precipitation and relative humidity. A relatively low CED indicates that the regions connected by the route have similar climates during that month; a relatively high CED suggests that the regions will have dissimilar climates. Next, the factor of air-traffic volume was added to produce the CEDt, or traffic-scaled climatic Euclidean distance, for each route.

To identify airports with higher numbers of low-CED routes, the climatic similarity index (CSI) was calculated. For a given airport, this index takes into account the number of other airports from which incoming direct flights arrive. Finally, a traffic-scaled climatic similarity index, CSIt, combines climatic distance, traffic volume and number of low-CED routes to create a relative indicator that identifies airports with high incoming traffic from a greater number of regions with similar climates — and thus higher risk.

For example, according to the indices, June 2010 will have particularly high overall risk. But that's just "within the limits of the study", Tatem cautions, highlighting the need for further work. "If we extrapolate to 2011 or 2012, the summertime may be the most risky."

Stas Burgiel, policy director for the Global Invasive Species Programme, likes the study's real-world relevance: "This type of work offers tools and analysis with direct application for decision-makers and border control staff, whereas a significant portion of the academic literature on invasive species remains two to three degrees removed from policy relevance."

Tatem would like to take this even further. "I'd like to make it available as a free online resource and have data sets on specific species that have invaded in the past," he says. This would allow airport authorities to figure out when their highest-risk times are and even what organisms to watch for.

Even without such a program, though, airport authorities can use inferences from the study to determine when to concentrate staff and resources for the next couple of years. "Governments need good early warning and inspection procedures — ultimately, to save them money," says Tatem.

Speaking of money, what would he do if he had unlimited funding for this work? "I'd probably try to implement standardized data-gathering techniques at all airports, seaports and border crossings for a range of notifiable species," he says, "so that we can get an idea of how different transport techniques, traffic levels, times of year and routes translate to numbers of exotic organisms being moved around the world."

Such extensive study would "give us a solid quantitative base on which to build models". Economists and ecologists can likely agree that this would be a good thing. — Anna Lena Phillips

Questions 1–5

*Answer the questions below using **NO MORE THAN TREE WORDS** from the passage for each answer.*

1. How much loss do the invasive species bring to the environment in the United States?
2. Before the introduction of airplanes, what effectively prevented the movement of species?
3. What factor about the origin and destination can increase the likelihood of new species settling in the destination?
4. Which can help predict how similar the climates of the origin and destination are?
5. What would Tatem use if he were short of financial support for his research?

Keys:

1. Nearly $120 billion.
2. Distance.
3. Similar climates/similar climatic conditions.
4. Climatic Euclidean distance.
5. Standardized data-gathering techniques.

Exercise 2

On the Factory Floor

Perhaps the most thoughtful and knowledgeable of the early writers on automation was John Diebold, a consultant and author. It was Diebold who introduced the word automation in its broad, modern sense. He clearly understood that there was more to it than reducing labor costs in factories. He foresaw applications to many other kinds of work, including clerical tasks, warehousing and even retailing. Nevertheless, when he chose examples for detailed description, they almost always came from manufacturing.

Automatic control first took hold in continuous-process industries such as oil refining. A closed-loop control mechanism could regulate the temperature of a distilling tower, eliminating the need for a worker to monitor a gauge and adjust valve settings. As such instruments proliferated, a refinery became a depopulated industrial landscape. An entire plant could be run by a few technicians, huddled together in a glass-walled control room. This hands-off mode of operation became the model that other industries strove to emulate.

In the automation literature of the 1950s and' 60s, attention focuses mainly on manufacturing, and especially on the machining of metal. A celebrated example was the Ford Motor Company's Cleveland Engine Plant No. 1, built in 1951, where a series of interconnected machines took in raw castings at one end and disgorged finished engine blocks at the other. The various tools within this complex performed several hundred boring and milling operations on each engine, with little manual intervention.

A drawback of the Ford approach to automation was inflexibility. Any change to the product would require an extensive overhaul of the machinery. But this problem was overcome with the introduction of programmable metalworking tools, which eventually became computer-controlled devices.

Other kinds of manufacturing also shifted to automated methods, although the result was not always exactly what had been expected. In the early years, it was easy to imagine a straightforward substitution of machines for labor: shove aside a worker and install a machine in his or her place. The task to be performed would not change, only the agent performing it. The ultimate expression of this idea was the robot — a one-for-one replacement for the factory worker. But automation has seldom gone this way.

Consider the manufacture of electronic devices. At the outset, this was a labor-intensive process of placing components on a chassis, stringing wires between them and soldering the connections one by one. Attempts to build automatic equipment to perform the same operations proved impractical. Instead, the underlying technology was changed by introducing printed circuit boards, with all the connections laid out in advance. Eventually, machines were developed for automatically placing the parts on the boards and for soldering the connections all at once.

The further evolution of this process takes us to the integrated circuit, a technology that was automated from birth. The manufacture of microprocessor chips could not possibly be carried out as a handicraft business; no sharp-eyed artisan could draw the minuscule circuit patterns on silicon wafers. For many other businesses as well, manual methods are simply unthinkable. Google could not operate by hiring thousands of clerks to read Web pages and type out the answers to queries.

The automation of factories has gone very much according to the script written by Diebold and other early advocates. Computer control is all but universal. Whole sections of automobile assembly plants are now walled off to exclude all workers. A computer screen and a keyboard are the main interface to most factory equipment.

Meanwhile, though, manufacturing as a whole has become a smaller part of the U.S. economy — 12 percent of gross domestic product in 2005, down from more than double that in the 1950s. And because of the very success of industrial automation, employment on production lines has fallen even faster than the share of GDP. Thus, for most Americans, the factory automation that was so much the focus of early commentary is all but invisible. Few of us ever get a chance to see it at work.

But automation and computer technology have infiltrated other areas of the economy and daily life — office work, logistics, commerce, finance, household tasks. When you look for the impact of computers on society, barcodes are probably more important than machine tools.

Questions 1–5

Answer the questions below using ***NO MORE THAN TREE WORDS*** *from the passage for each answer.*

1. Which industries first used automatic control process?
2. What is the problem with the Ford Motor company's automated manufacturing process?
3. What helped solve the problem of the Ford approach to automation?
4. What became unpractical with the advent of the era of integrated circuit?
5. By 2005, which industry has dwindled to a minor section of America's economy?

Keys:

1. Continuous-process industries.
2. Inflexibility.

3. Programmable metalworking tools.   4. Manual methods.   5. Manufacturing.

Exercise 3

Building a Better Salt Trap

With cell-specific bioengineering, scientists may have found a way to make plants more salt tolerant.

A strategy to protect crops from salty soils hit plant scientist Mark Tester in a flash ten years ago, while he was delivering a classroom lecture. "I thought, we need to work out how to control gene expression around the roots and suck the salt out before it gets to the shoot," says the University of Adelaide biologist based at the Australian Centre for Plant Functional Genomics.

In July, Tester and collaborators in Australia and England delivered on the vision. In the journal *The Plant Cell*, they showed how they amplified a laboratory plant's natural ability to draw salt out of its xylem, diverting some of it from the plant's water pipes in stems and, ultimately, in leaves, where salt buildup can become toxic.

The better-salt-trap trait is heritable in the *Arabidopsis thaliana* laboratory plants that Tester's team bioengineered. He predicts they will repeat the feat in crop plants. Experiments with rice in his laboratory already show promising results, Tester says.

Soil salinity is one of a growing number of challenges facing agriculture around the world. As the human population continues to swell, so does demand for fertile ground to grow food. As the drive to plant more biofuel feedstock expands, competition for good farmland is expected to increase further.

Lurking in the background are the uncertain impacts of human-induced climate change, which may alter rain patterns, increase temperatures, raise sea levels and otherwise disrupt agriculture. Farmers large and small could be looking for means to plant on less-than-ideal farmland, including land with higher-than-desired salt levels, to cope with it all.

High soil salinity is believed to hinder crop yields in 100 countries. Hardest hit are farms and gardens in arid areas such as Pakistan, India, Egypt, Tunisia, Morocco, Peru and Bolivia, according to a 2008 *Science* report by Jelte Rozema of Vrije Universiteit in the Netherlands and plant physiologist Timothy Flowers of the University of Sussex in England.

But the contamination exists in more economically developed places too, including the United States and Australia. In an odd twist, irrigation is the most common human-induced cause of increased soil salinity. Applying water can double a field's crop yield, but it can also deposit salt. Even more frequently, higher levels of evaporation and transpiration on irrigated fields draw salts closer to the surface. Once there, they are very hard to remove.

High salt concentrations can hurt plants in two ways. The osmotic effect hinders plants' ability to draw water from soil. Second, when salt accumulates in plant tissue, it can cause premature leaf death.

So far, bioengineering has not delivered solutions. Rozema and Flowers in 2008 noted that between 1996 and 2006, 30 scientific reports emerged detailing approaches to genetically altered rice, a cereal highly intolerant of salt, to make it more salt tolerant. But such rice remains a work in progress.

Tester's team focused only on certain cells in roots to rev up systems that already provide varying amounts of salt tolerance, depending on the plant species. Some plants have the ability to reduce the amount of salt that can reach their transpiration stream by diverting some into their roots before it travels up their shoots. "It's a last-ditch defense," Tester said.

Building on research by others, the investigators targeted the Arabidopsis *HKT1; 1* gene in cells near water-transport systems in mature roots. They inserted a second copy of the gene sequence itself, as well as a promoter designed to maintain high expression of the inserted gene. Laboratory plants modified in this way had 37 to 64 percent less salt in their shoots compared with unaltered plants after exposure to high salinity.

Questions remain about the capacity of this approach. Flowers, one of the coauthors of the 2008 *Science* article on the toll of salinated soil on crops, wonders just how much salt plants will be able to store in their roots.

"The limited capacity of the root parenchyma is likely to limit the quantity of sodium and chloride that can be removed from the transpiration stream," says Flowers.

Tester says the approach could make a difference in the field. "We have not yet tested the limits of the technology, but we do know it works at fairly high levels of salinites."

If it does work adequately, Tester hopes his focus on a gene already present in plants, rather than one imported from a very different organism, will make his strategy less disagreeable to people opposed to genetic transplantation because of concerns about potential environmental risks.

Julian Schroeder, Novartis professor in plant sciences at the University of California, San Diego, says that may be possible. "Research in wheat suggests that naturally occurring variation in *HKT* transporter expression can enhance salt tolerance. The difference between molecular breeding and transgenic plants becomes small in this case," Schroeder says.

Questions 1–4

Answer the questions below using **NO MORE THAN FOUR WORDS (NUMBERS)** *from the passage for each answer.*

1. What is thought to affect crop yields in many countries?
2. Which human-induced factor increased the soil salinity?
3. What did Tester's team work on in order to improve the level of salt tolerance of plants?
4. By how much did the modified laboratory plants improve their ability to reduce the amount of salts?

Keys:

1. High soil salinity.　2. Irrigation.　3. Cell in roots.　4. 37 to 64 percent.

星期四

完成句子题（sentence completion）

一 题型描述

这种题目通常有两种形式：填空式和选择式。填空式会给出若干挖空的句子，要求考生从原文中选词把句子补充完整，填入的字数通常都会有限制（如不超过三个单词），题目中会加以强调说明。选择式也会给出一些不完整的句子，但往往是句子的前半部分，句子的后半部分会在一个方框中列出，考生需要根据原文相关信息从方框中为每个句子选出一个正确的选项，为了增加题目难度，给出的选项会大于正确选项的数目，因此需要考生能够排除干扰项。

二 题型透视

这种题型仍然考查考生理解文章细节信息的能力。完成这种题目需要考生较好地掌握略读、研读和理解识别转述的能力。

三 解题步骤

Step 1：仔细阅读题目说明，看清题目对答案词数的限制。

Step 2：迅速浏览所有题目，划出易辨词、关键词，并能根据句子提供的信息预测答案类型。

Step 3：记住关键词并回到文中运用略读和查读等技巧，确定答案的大致位置。

Step 4：当找到信号词、关键词或关键词的相关词时，停下来研读相关句子或段落，找出答案。

四 技巧点拨

1．题目的顺序与文中的信息出现的先后顺序是一致的，下一题的答案一定是在上一题的答案之后。

2．答案必须符合语法规则，如果找到的答案放在句子中却违反语法规则的话，那么说明答案错误。

3．由于字数限制，当需要对答案中的单词进行取舍时，首先去掉修饰词。

三 例题精讲

例 1：选自剑 7 Test1

Questions 10–13

Complete the sentences below.

Choose ***NO MORE THAN TWO WORDS*** *from the passage for each answer.*

Write your answer in boxes 10–13 on your answer sheet.

10．Long before the invention of radar, ______ had resulted in a sophisticated radar-like system in bats.

11．Radar is an inaccurate term when referring to bats because ______ are not used in their navigation system.

12．Radar and sonar are based on similar ______.

13．The word “echolocation” was first used by someone working as a ______.

分析：本题是填空式完成句子，迅速浏览这四个小题，可以发现除了 13 题有一个加引号的特殊词外，其他题都没有易辨词，因此我们需要先找出其他三道题目的关键词。

策略：10. 译文：在雷达被发明之前，______ 就已经造就了蝙蝠身上复杂的像雷达一样的系统。关键词：sophisticated

11. 译文：提到蝙蝠时，雷达不是个准确的词，因为 ______ 没有被用在它们的导航系统中。关键词：radar，inaccurate，navigation system

12. 译文：雷达和声纳都建立在相似的 ______ 之上。关键词：sonar，similar

13. 译文：“echolocation” 首先被作为 ______ 的某人使用。线索词：echolocation；关键词：first used，working as

解析：

题号	原　文	分　析	答　案
10	The Sonar and Radar pioneers didn’t know it then, but all the world now know that bats, or rather natural selection **working on** bats, had perfected the **system** tens of millions of years earlier, and their**radar** achieves feats of detection and navigation that would strike an engineer dumb with admiration.	文中此处多次出现题目中的字眼：system，radar。tens of millions of years earlier 与题目中的 long before the invention of radar 相照应，achieves feats of detection and navigation that would strike an engineer dumb with admiration 说明了蝙蝠的雷达系统多么的复杂。working on 与题目中的 result in 近义，因此答案应该是这个短语前面的名词词组。	natural selection
11	It is technically **incorrect** to talk about bat “radar”, since they do not**use** radio waves.	文中的 incorrect 和题目中的 inaccurate 是近义词，而且题目中的 radar 在此处也出现。题目中问什么没有被使用，因此答案应该是 use 的宾语。该句的意思是：“严格来讲，谈论蝙蝠‘雷达’是不准确的，因为它们不使用无线电波”。	radio waves

（续）

题目	原　文	解　析	答　案
12	But the underlying mathematical theories of radar and sonar are very similar.	题目和原文的对应的地方有：radar and sonar，similar。文中这句话说“雷达和声纳的内在数学原理十分相似”，因此答案应该是这句话的主语。	mathematical theories
13	The American zoologist Donald Griffin, who was largely responsible for the discovery of sonar in bats, coined the term “echolocation” to cover both radar and sonar, whether used by animals or human instruments.	文中的“echolocation”说明答案就在周围。文中的coin在这里是个动词，是发明或创造出的意思，与题目中的first used是近义表达。题目中问首次使用这个术语的人是做什么的，因此我们只需要找到这个人的职业即可。Donald Griffin发明了“echolocation”这个名词，前面的zoologist正是他的职业。	zoologist

例2：选自剑6 Test2

Questions 23–26

Complete each sentence with the correct ending, ***A–H****, below.*

Write the correct letter, ***A–H****, in boxes 23–26 on your answer sheet.*

23. Home medical aids
24. Regular amounts of exercise
25. Feelings of control over life
26. Feelings of loneliness

List of Headings

A may cause heart disease.

B can be helped by hormone treatment.

C may cause rises in levels of stress hormones.

D have cost the United States government more than $200 billion.

E may help prevent mental decline.

F may get stronger at night.

G allow old people to be more independent.

H can reduce stress in difficult situations.

分析：4个小题都是以名词短语的形式出现，给出的选项有9个，说明有些是多余的干扰项，对于这样的选择式完成句子，我们只能从题目给出的已知信息入手，并思考一下这些名词词组在文中可能的近义表达。

策略：23. 译文：家庭医疗设备；由于单词并不长，我们可以把整个名词词组记下来。

24. 译文：定量活动；关键词：regular，exercise

25. 译文：对生活的控制感；关键词：control

26. 译文：孤独感；关键词：loneliness

解析：

题号	原　文	分　析	答　案
23	The increasing self-reliance of many elderly people is probably linked to a massive increase in the use of simple home medical aids. ______ The group found that those elderly people who were able to retain a sense of independence were more likely to stay healthy in old age.	文中出现了与题目完全一致的 home medical aids。文中说"许多老年人越来越多地依靠自己可能与他们越来越多地使用简单的家庭医疗设备有关"。这一段的最后一句又强调："这些能够使独立的老人在年老时更加健康"。因此这二者的关系是：home medical aids 使老人更加独立，而独立又可能使老人更加健康。	G. 译文：使得老年人更加独立。
24	Maintaining a level of daily physical activity may help mental functioning, ______ Cotman believes this hormone, which keeps neurons functioning, may prevent the brains of active humans from deteriorating.	maintain a level of daily physical activity (每天保持一定水平的体力活动)与题目中的 regular amounts of exercise 是同义表达。help mental functioning："能帮助大脑正常活动"。接下来本段具体解释原因，说"活动能产生一种维持神经原活动的荷尔蒙，它能防止人的大脑老化"。	E. 译文：可以帮助防止大脑老化。decline 和 deteriorating 是同义词。
25	In laboratory simulations of challenging activities such as driving, those who felt in control of their lives pumped out lower levels of stress hormones such as cortisol.	felt in control of their lives 是题目中的 feelings of control over life 的转述。文中说："在实验室对某些挑战性的活动如开车的模拟环境中，那些感觉能够控制他们生活的人产生了较低水平的压力荷尔蒙，比如考的素，换句话说也就是对生活的控制感可以带来较低的压力"。	H. 译文：可以在困难的情况下降低压力。
26	Seeman found that elderly people who felt emotionally isolated maintained higher levels of stress hormones even when asleep.	felt emotionally isolated 和题目中的 feeling of loneliness 是同义表达。文中说："感觉孤独的老年人即便是在睡觉时也保持了较高的压力荷尔蒙水平"，说明孤独感与较高的压力荷尔蒙水平有关。	C. 译文：导致了压力荷尔蒙的上升。

六 专题演练

Exercise 1

Routes of Resistance

Our focus on using antibiotics to kill bacteria has blinded us to their diverse functions in the organisms that make these chemicals.

Last year, some 50 million pounds of antibiotics were used in the United States, an amount that would correspond to roughly 5 tablespoons — or 75 doses — of antibiotics per person. In fact, much of this antibiotic — as much as 70 percent by some estimates — is being used not to treat infections, but instead to promote food production, as antibiotics have become a key ingredient in the American food chain. We are, in short, marinating the living world in antibiotics.

Against this backdrop, the emergence of antibiotic-resistant pathogenic bacteria can hardly come as a surprise. Antibiotics, after all, are used to suppress and kill bacteria, and bacteria, like every other living thing, have no greater evolutionary imperative than to stay alive. Our overuse of antibiotics methodically rewards any bacterium fortunate enough to carry a mutation that confers even slight resistance to the substance in its environment. The less-fortunate bacteria die, leaving behind empty ecological space for resistant strains to fill. Slowly and inexorably, we thus enrich the world with bacteria that now scoff at our attempts to control them.

It did not take long for antibiotic resistance to emerge once the drugs entered the arsenal of modern medicine. Penicillin, discovered in 1929, came into widespread use on the battlefield during World War II: Some 100 million doses were produced between 1943 and 1945. But even before the end of the war, the first penicillin-resistant strains of bacteria appeared. Over the next five decades, the pattern repeated numerous times. The discovery of every new antibiotic class created excitement by promising to bring bacterial infections to heel. Inevitably, however, the edge of this new tool for the treatment of infections became blunt with overuse as resistant strains grew common. The useful clinical life of new antibiotics, defined as the time between clinical introduction and the rise of resistant strains, is often no more than a matter of three to five years. Over the past decade, moreover, antibiotic resistance, once only a public-health concern, has morphed into a measurable cause of death. Conservatively, untreatable bacterial infections result in some 100,000 deaths per year in the United States. The early promise of the age of antibiotics — an end to infectious diseases — now seems absurdly naive.

But every day, in clinics and hospitals around the world, doctors are forced to administer antibiotics to clear up bacterial infections that threaten the lives of patients. And every day, the bacteria — both the pathogens we are targeting and the innocent bystanders that end up as collateral damage — respond by evolving mechanisms to resist the antibiotics. Each dose is a skirmish in a larger war. Yet, focused as we are on what we see as an epic battle between humans and pathogens, we forget that both antibiotics and antibiotic resistance have been part of the microbial world for the past 3 billion years. Yes, the widespread use of antibiotics to combat infections has had profound implications for the evolution of infectious disease, but it is a mere blip in the history of the microbial world.

Four out of five antibiotics in use today are based on naturally occurring compounds produced by bacteria and fungi. The organisms that produce antibiotics have not, of course, been doing so over billions of years just so that we might discover them and put them to therapeutic use in the 21st century. So what are antibiotics doing for the organisms that produce them? The explanation most obvious to us, of course, is to see these compounds as part of the competitive arsenal of the bacteria that produce them. In this model, antibiotic-producing bacteria kill their competitors and make ecological space available for themselves and their genetic kin. Seen this way, antibiotics in microbial ecosystems and antibiotics in the clinic do one and the same thing: kill bacteria.

To be sure, naturally produced antibiotics in intact microbial ecosystems enable producing strains to kill other bacteria. Some antibiotics, such as a class of proteins called the bacteriocins, are not subtle: A single molecule entering a target cell will kill it. These molecules are designed to kill and nothing more. But the concentrations of many other antibiotics in natural ecosystems seem consistently too low to kill surrounding organisms effectively. Why would bacteria bother to produce antibiotics—which are expensive molecules to synthesize—at concentrations too low to reap the benefits? It now appears that at lower concentrations, antibiotics may well, to the bacteria, mean something utterly different than they do at the massive concentrations encountered in the clinic. In their original context, antibiotics may not be killers at all, but instead messengers enabling cell-to-cell communication both within and across bacterial species boundaries.

Questions 1–6

Complete the sentences below.

Choose ***NO MORE THAN TWO WORDS*** *from the passage for each answer.*

1. It is estimated that a large part of antibiotics in the United States is used to increase ______.
2. The overuse of antibiotics leads to the appearance of ______ bacteria.
3. The increasing use of antibiotics caused them to have a shortened clinical life span of only ______ years.
4. Despite the risk of overusing antibiotics, doctors around the world are still using antibiotics to combat ______.
5. Most antibiotics today are made from ______.
6. Naturally produced antibiotics make ______ possible within the bacterial world.

Keys:

1. food production 2. antibiotic-resistant 3. three to five 4. bacterial infections
5. bacteria and fungi 6. cell-to-cell communication

Exercise 2

European immigrants to Colonial America brought with them their culture, traditions and philosophy about education. Much of the formal educational system in the United States is rooted in the European or Western belief system. Though an indigenous population of Native Americans lived on the North American continent, their influence on the development of formal educational practice in America was minimal. Many tribes had not yet developed writing or a system of formal educational practice. Additionally, there was a systematic effort to eradicate this population as opposed to assimilating them.

Among the tribes that had developed written languages, the Cherokee tribe who originally lived in the Southern portion of the United States had developed a system of formal education to pass knowledge from one generation to the next. They, however, were methodically pushed out of their native territory in the early 1800's and forced to move to the Oklahoma territory, which limited their ability to influence educational practice in early America.

The English were the predominant settlers in the New World and as a result education in colonial America was patterned on the English model. It originally developed as a two-track system with people from the lower classes receiving minimal instruction and only learning to read and write, calculate and receive religious instruction. The upper classes were allowed to pursue an education beyond the basics and oftentimes attended Latin grammar or secondary schools where they learned Greek and Latin and studied the classics in preparation for a college education.

Religion played an important rule in developing an educational system in the United States. The Puritans, a strict fundamentalist Protestant sect who immigrated to the New World for religious freedom beginning in 1609, believed that education was necessary in order to read the Bible to receive salvation. This was in line with the beliefs of the Protestant Reformers. Their schools made no distinction between religious and secular life and were also used to inspire children to endure the hardships of a life in the New World through religious devotion.

Teachers had some status in the community because they, along with the clergy, had more education than most of the population. However, their position was secondary to that of the clergy. Additionally, teachers had to be of high moral character, which came under intense scrutiny by the rest of the community. They also had many other duties besides teaching, such as cleaning the school, substituting for the minister, and ring the church bell.

The settlers in a particular area heavily influenced the development of schools and formal education in the American colonies. For example in the New England Colonies, which was primarily Puritan, religious instruction was of paramount importance. Puritans believed that people (children in particular) were inherently bad (sinners) and had to learn to behave. Salvation lay in learning to check one's natural instincts and behave as an adult.

The Mid-Atlantic colonies had a more diverse population consisting of the Dutch, English, Irish, Scottish, German, etc. They were also more varied in their religious beliefs and therefore did not develop a common school system such as the one that prevailed in the New England colonies. Instead each group often developed their own schools which promoted their culture, religion and traditions. The Quakers who settled in the Philadelphia area in the 1680's believed in educating the populace. They were also tolerant of others' beliefs and ways of life. They had a strong influence on the development of education and established the first public school.

In the Southern Colonies, where society was more structured and stratified according to socioeconomic classes, the wealthy plantation owners developed their own system to prepare their sons for further education. Children from poorer households received a minimal education and slaves from Africa only learned what was necessary to attend their masters.

Here, religious instruction had an important role, but so too did the more rigorous education of secondary schools, where the sons of the wealthy learned the necessary subject matter to prepare them for college on the European continent. In 1636 Harvard College, the first post-secondary school on the North American continent, was established in the Boston, Massachusetts area and in 1693 the College of William and Mary in Williamsburg, Virginia was founded.

Dame Schools were one of the more common types of schools found in the colonies. They were often established by women, and more often than not run from the home of the person in charge. Students were charged a modest fee to attend. Education was basic, concentrating on reading, writing, and calculation. Attendance was often erratic and dependent on the season and work at home that needed to be done. For most females the dame school provided their only education and homemaking skills such as sewing were also included in the instructional process.

Questions 1–5

*Complete each sentence with the correct ending, **A–K**, below.*

*Write the correct letter, **A–K**, in boxes 1–5 on your answer sheet.*

1. Native Americans
2. The English settlers
3. The puritans' schools
4. The Mid-Atlantic colonies
5. Dame schools

List of Headings

A	was the most populous region in colonial America.
B	generated little influence upon America's formal education system.
C	established the first public school in America.
D	had a population of diverse origins.
E	provided post-secondary education to their students.
F	taught the Bible to students.
G	did not have a formal educational system.
H	originally had a two-track educational system.
I	established a school system modeled on that of English settlers.
J	focused on religion-related instruction.
K	only admitted female students.

Keys:

1. B 2. H 3. J 4. D 5. K

Exercise 3

Hearing Problems

The old adage extols the virtue of silence by claiming it is golden, yet experience tells us that silence is as hard to come by as the precious metal itself. The benefit of silence to the human ear is scientifically demonstrable. Less superfluous noise; less impairment to the hearing. Yet this precious commodity is no longer valued. Noise is ever present in modern life and is an accumulative experience. The ill effects of noise pollution are of two kinds: acute exposure to an individual instance of a very loud noise, such as a gunshot or explosion; and chronic—the experience of too much noise over an extended period of time.

City and urban dwellers exist in an increasingly noise-ridden environment, and it is now almost impossible to escape exposure to high noise levels. Even if we exclude the more obvious sources of noise pollution such as jet plane engines, road works, power tools, loud music at dance parties and so on, it is clear that noise is a constant and often unwelcome companion. We have only to walk through a suburban shopping mall or department store, or catch a bus or train to be subjected to noise levels that a few decades ago would have been considered beyond human endurance. The popular practice of "layering" sound, by adding a louder source of noise to that which already exists in order to mask it, merely compounds the problem. Because of the accumulative nature of noise abuse, constant noise is worse than noisy periods interspersed with silence.

Our noise level acceptance threshold is rising in step with the number of persons developing hearing problems. Data available from a recent survey conducted by the Australian Bureau of Statistics show that 7.4% of people over 14 years of age have some discernible hearing problem. According to the survey, 24.6% of the 7.4% of persons with affected hearing have problems caused by subjection to a constant barrage of noise, either at work, in the everyday living environment, or as the result of a particular choice of leisure activity. The problem is most severe for males aged between 25 and 64 years of age, 9.1% of whom have a hearing disability, and for which the cause inconstant noise in 44.4% of cases.

Of current concern to acoustical engineers and psychologists at the National Acoustics Laboratories in Sydney, Australia, is the potential for damage to the eardrum caused by the transmission of loud sound through earphones placed directly into the ear canal. An almost universal fad among young people, the pocket-sized radio-cassette player (commonly known by the brand name "Walkman") may be exposing its owner to greater than the maximum safe dosage of noise recommended for industrial workers—90 decibels* over a period of 8 hours. This dosage, called Dose 1, can be achieved much sooner by exposing the ear to only slightly more than 90 decibels. Increases to the decibel level logarithmically shorten the exposure time required to reach a given dose. For instance, to achieve Dose 1 in 4 hours, it is necessary to raise the decibel exposure level by a mere 3 decibels.

One danger posed to young ears is that the peak sound level from these radio-cassette players is often far too great; at high volume it is all too easy to receive Dose 1 in a short period of time. Any further noise heard above 90 decibels that day and the recipient is causing measurable damage to his or her ears. Another danger is the likelihood of a change in the pain threshold of noise resulting in users compensating by increasing the volume to levels way above what is considered safe. Finally, insertable earphones block the ear canal, thereby further increasing the noise level absorbed.

But perhaps the most alarming potential for danger caused by insertable earphones is the ease with which the listener can exceed the safe time length of exposure to noise. The small earphones can be comfortably worn for extended periods of time. What is more, there is the danger of falling asleep with the earphones inserted, leading to an accumulation of excess noise while unconscious.

Noise abuse soon leads to varying degrees of hearing loss. What may begin as an acute temporary condition, in time becomes a chronic and irreversible disability. A common complaint is "tinnitus", or a "ringing in the ears" which fails to subside after the ears are subjected to a short but extreme dose of noise. It is an exhausting condition that can seriously threaten the composure of the sufferer who can be driven to near madness. It is believed the composer Beethoven was particularly aggravated by this malady. At present, there is little that can be done in the majority of cases, although the victim might be able to obtain some temporary relief by using a masking device which blocks out the offending frequencies of sound with other, less annoying frequencies.

Inevitably, though, years of excessive noise accumulation take their toll and partial or complete deafness results. If silence is the cure for ailing ears (or, at least, the best way to prevent further deterioration of one's hearing), it is sobering to realize that it is also the unfortunate and permanent curse of a lifetime of noise abuse caused by ignoring the warnings.

* decibel: standard unit of sound measurement

Questions 1-6

Complete the sentences below.

Choose ***NO MORE THAN THREE WORDS*** *from the passage for each answer.*

1. In the modern society where noise is almost everywhere, ______ has become a rare, precious, yet not valued commodity.
2. With more people having hearing problems, our noise level ______ is also increasing.
3. The loud noise transmitted by the insertable earphones is likely to hurt ______.
4. One of the dangers caused by insertable earphones is that the listener can easily exceed the ______ of exposure to noise.
5. Beethoven is believed to have been suffered from a common hearing problem called ______.
6. A lengthy period of too much noise accumulation can lead to partial or complete ______.

Keys:

1. silence	2. acceptance threshold	3. the eardrum
4. same time length	5. tinnitus	6. deafness

星期五

完成表格、流程图、示意图(Complete Tables, Flow-chart, diagram)

一 题型描述

题目给出一个表格、流程图或示意图，然后设置一些空白处，要求考生根据原文信息，从原文选词把它们补充完整，通常题目会对答案的词数进行限制。

二 题型透视

这种题型仍然属于细节题，目的是综合考查识别转述、略读和查读的能力。

三 解题步骤

Step 1：看一下给出的表格、流程图或示意图是否有标题，如果有的话，借助标题定位答案在文章中的大致位置。

Step 2：如果没有标题，查看是否有易辨字词，根据易辨词确定答案在文中的大致位置。

Step 3：顺序阅读每题，注意空格前后的词，划出关键词（注意是否有易辨字词），并回到原文查读。

Step 4：当在文中发现关键词的相关词汇后，停下来仔细阅读关键词所在的句子以及前后的句子，找出答案。

四 技巧点拨

1. 通常表格、流程图或示意图的答案会集中出现在文中的某个或若干连续的自然段，且答案都是顺序出现，因此只要找到其中某一个问题的答案，其他答案就比较容易在附近找到。

2. 我们可以利用表格中的横标题和纵标题来定位某个问题的答案在原文中的位置。

五 例题精讲

例 1：选自剑 4 Test1

Questions 15-21

Complete the table below.

*Choose **NO MORE THAN THREE WORDS** from Reading Passage 2 for each answer.*

Write your answers in boxes 15-21 on your answer sheet.

SENSE	SPECIES	ABILITY	COMMENTS
Smell	toothed	no	evidence from brain structure
	baleen	Not certain	related brain structures are present
Taste	some types	poor	nerves linked to their __15__ are underdeveloped
Touch	all	yes	region around the blowhole very sensitive
Vision	__16__	yes	probably do not have stereoscopic vision
	dolphins, porpoises	yes	probably have stereoscopic vision __17__ and ______
	__18__	yes	probably have stereoscopic vision forward and upward
	bottlenose	yes	exceptional in __19__ and good in air-water interface
	Boutu and beiji	poor	have limited vision
	Indian susu	no	probably only sense direction and intensity of light
Hearing	most large baleen	yes	usually use __20__; repertoire limited
	__21__ whales and whales	yes	song-like
	toothed	yes	use more of frequency spectrum; have wider repertoire

分析：本题给出了一个比较复杂的表格，一共有7道小题。表格没有标题，但是我们可以通过表格横标题和纵标题来确定每道小题的答案在文中的大致位置，空格前后的词则可以告诉答案在文中的准确位置。

策略：15．线索词：taste，some types；关键词：nerves，linked，underdeveloped

16．线索词：vision，species；关键词：stereoscopic

17．线索词：dolphins，porpoises；关键词：stereoscopic

18．线索词：vision，species；关键词：forward and upward

19．线索词：bottlenose；关键词：exceptional，air-water interface

20．线索词：hearing，large baleen；关键词：usually use，repertoire limited

21．线索词：hearing；关键词：song-like

解析：

题目	原　文	分　析	答　案
15	Similarly, although at least some cetaceans have **taste** buds, the **nerves** serving these have **degenerated** or are **rudimentary**.	原文与题目完全对应的地方有 taste 和 nerves，degenerated 和 rudimentary 和题目中的 underdeveloped 同义，serving 和 linked 同义，因此答案为 these 指代的事物：taste buds。	taste buds

（续）

题目	原　　文	解　　析	答　　案
16	However, the position of the eyes so restricts the field of vision in baleen whales that they **probably do not have stereoscopic vision**.	probably do not have stereoscopic vision与题目中已给出的信息完全一致，题目要求填写一个物种名称，因此是 they 指代的事物。	baleen whales
17	On the other hand, the position of the eyes in most **dolphins and porpoises** suggests that they **have stereoscopic vision** forward and downward.	原文与题目完全一致的地方：dolphins and porpoises，have stereoscopic vision，答案很明显是这之后用 and 连接的两个单词	forward, downward
18	Eve position in freshwater dolphins, which often swim on their side or upside down while feeding, suggests that what **vision** they have is stereoscopic **forward and upward**.	关键词 forward and upward 在原文中出现，且讨论的是 stereoscopic vision，我们只需要找到 they 指代的事物即可，而句子的前半句的主语 freshwater dolphins 正是they指代的事物。	freshwater dolphins
19	By comparison, the **bottlenose dolphin** has **extremely keen** vision in water. Judging from the way it watches and tracks airborne flying fish, it can apparently see fairly well through the **air-water interface** as well.	题目与原文完全一致的地方有 bottlenose 和 air-water interface，fairly well 和 good 同义，extremely keen 与 exceptional 是同义，因此答案应该是 extremely keen 之后的名词。	vision
20	**Large baleen** whales **primarily use** the lower frequencies and are often **limited in their repertoire**.	Large baleen 在原文中再现，primarily use 相当于 mainly use，limited repertoire 和 limited in their repertoire 是同义表达，答案应为 use 之后的宾语。	the lower frequencies
21	Notable exceptions are the nearly **song-like** choruses of bowhead whales in summer and the complex, haunting utterances of the humpback whales.	文中出现题目中的关键词 song-like，答案应为文中 whales 前面的名词。	bowhead

例 2：流程图，题目选自剑 6 Test 3

Questions 38–40

Complete the flow-chart below.

*Choose **NO MORE THAN TWO WORDS** from the passage for each answer.*

Write your answers in boxes 38–40 on our answer sheet.

How a caloric-restriction mimetic works

CR mimetic

↓

Less……38……….is processed

↓

production of ATP is decreased

↙ ↘

Theory 1:

cells less damaged by disease because fewer ……39………..are emitted.

Theory 2:

cells focus on……40………..

because food is in short supply.

分析：题目中的流程图有一个小标题，我们可以利用标题寻找答案在文中的大致位置，三道小题可以利用流程图中已给出的信息和空格前后的单词来确定答案的准确位置。

策略：38．线索词：CR mimetic；关键词：processed

39．线索词：ATP；关键词：damage，disease，fewer，emitter

40．关键词：focus on，food in short，supply

解析：

题号	原　文	分　析	答　案
38	The best-studied candidate for a caloric-restriction mimetic, 2DG (2-deoxy-D-glucose), works by interfering with the way cells **process** glucose.	文中出现了题目中的关键词 process，题目中用的被动时态，那么答案应该是原文中 process 的宾语。这句话的意思是："在模仿热量制约的研究中被研究最多的是 2DG，它的主要功能是干扰细胞处理葡萄糖"。	glucose
39	One possibility relates to the ATP-making machinery's **emission** of free radicals, which are thought to contribute to aging and to such age-related diseases as cancer by damaging cells.	文中的 emission 是题目中的关键词 emitted 的名词形式。其他照应的地方有：disease，damaging cells。题目中要求填入什么被释放出来，因此答案为 emission 后面的名词短语 free radicals。	free radicals
40	Another hypothesis suggests that decreased processing of glucose could indicate to cells that **food is scarce** (even if it isn't) and induce them to shift into an anti-aging mode that **emphasizes** preservation of the organism over such "luxuries" as growth and reproduction.	文中的 emphasizes 和题目中的 focus on 是同义，food in short supply 与文中的 food is scarce 相照应，且主语都是 cells。答案应为 emphasizes 后面的单词 preservation。	preservation

六 专题演练

Exercise 1

Four General or World Philosophies

The term metaphysics literally means "beyond the physical". This area of philosophy focuses on the nature of reality. Metaphysics attempts to find unity across the domains of experience and thought. At the metaphysical level, there are four broad philosophical schools of thought that apply to education today. They are idealism, realism, pragmatism (sometimes called experientialism), and existentialism. Each will be explained shortly. These four general frameworks provide the root or base from which the various educational philosophies are derived.

A fifth metaphysical school of thought, called Scholasticism, is largely applied in Roman Catholic schools in the educational philosophy called "Thomism". It combines idealist and realist philosophies in a framework that harmonized the ideas of Aristotle, the realist, with idealist notions of truth. Thomas Aquinas, 1255-127, was the theologian who wrote "Summa Theologica", formalizing church doctrine. The Scholasticism movement encouraged the logical and philosophical study of the beliefs of the church, legitimizing scientific inquiry within a religious framework.

Two of these general or world philosophies, idealism and realism, are derived from the ancient Greek philosophers, Plato and Aristotle. Two are more contemporary, pragmatism and existentialism. However, educators who share one of these distinct sets of beliefs about the nature of reality presently apply each of these world philosophies in successful classrooms. Let us explore each of these metaphysical schools of thought.

Idealism

Idealism is a philosophical approach that has as its central tenet that ideas are the only true reality, the only thing worth knowing. In a search for truth, beauty, and justice that is enduring and everlasting, the focus is on conscious reasoning in the mind. Plato, father of Idealism, espoused this view about 400 years BC, in his famous book, *The Republic*. Plato believed that there are two worlds. The first is the spiritual or mental world, which is eternal, permanent, orderly, regular, and universal. There is also the world of appearance, the world experienced through sight, touch, smell, taste, and sound, that is changing, imperfect, and disorderly. This division is often referred to as the duality of mind and body. Reacting against what he perceived as too much of a focus on the immediacy of the physical and sensory world, Plato described a utopian society in which "education to body and soul all the beauty and perfection of which they are capable" as an ideal. In his allegory of the cave, the shadows of the sensory world must be overcome with the light of reason or universal truth. To understand truth, one must pursue knowledge and identify with the Absolute Mind. Plato also believed that the soul is fully formed prior to birth and is perfect and at one with the Universal Being. The birth process checks this perfection, so education requires bringing latent ideas (fully formed concepts) to consciousness.

In idealism, the aim of education is to discover and develop each individual's abilities and full moral excellence in order to better serve society. The curricular emphasis is subject matter of mind: literature, history, philosophy, and religion. Teaching methods focus on handling ideas through lecture, discussion, and Socratic dialogue (a method of teaching that uses questioning to help students discover and clarify knowledge). Introspection, intuition, insight, and whole-part logic are used to bring to consciousness the forms or concepts which are latent in the mind. Character is developed through imitating examples and heroes.

Realism

Realists believe that reality exists independent of the human mind. The ultimate reality is the world of physical objects. The focus is on the body/objects. Truth is objective-what can be observed. Aristotle, a student of Plato who broke with his mentor's idealist philosophy, is called the father of both Realism and the scientific method. In this metaphysical view, the aim is to understand objective reality through "the diligent and unsparing scrutiny of all observable data".

Aristotle believed that to understand an object, its ultimate form had to be understood, which does not change. For example, a rose exists whether or not a person is aware of it. A rose can exist in the mind without being physically present, but ultimately, the rose shares properties with all other roses and flowers (its form), although one rose may be red and another peach colored. Aristotle also was the first to teach logic as a formal discipline in order to be able to reason about physical events and aspects. The exercise of rational thought is viewed as the ultimate purpose for humankind. The Realist curriculum emphasizes the subject matter of the physical world, particularly science and mathematics. The teacher organizes and presents content systematically within a discipline, demonstrating use of criteria in making decisions. Teaching methods focus on mastery of facts and basic skills through demonstration and recitation. Students must also demonstrate the ability to think critically and scientifically, using observation and experimentation. Curriculum should be scientifically approached, standardized, and distinct-discipline based. Character is developed through training in the rules of conduct.

Pragmatism (Experientialism)

For pragmatists, only those things that are experienced or observed are real. In this late 19th century American philosophy, the focus is on the reality of experience. Unlike the Realists and Rationalists, Pragmatists believe that reality is constantly changing and that we learn best through applying our experiences and thoughts to problems, as they arise. The universe is dynamic and evolving, a "becoming" view of the world. There is no absolute and unchanging truth, but rather, truth is what works. Pragmatism is derived from the teaching of Charles Sanders Peirce (1839-1914), who believed that thought must produce action, rather than linger in the mind and lead to indecisiveness.

John Dewey (1859-1952) applied pragmatist philosophy in his progressive approaches. He believed that learners must adapt to each other and to their environment. Schools should emphasize the subject matter of social experience. All learning is dependent on the context of place, time, and circumstance. Different cultural and ethnic groups learn to work cooperatively and contribute to a democratic society. The ultimate purpose is the creation of a new social order. Character development is based on making group decisions in light of consequences.

For Pragmatists, teaching methods focus on hands-on problem solving, experimenting, and projects, often having students work in groups. Curriculum should bring the disciplines together to focus on solving problems in an interdisciplinary way. Rather than passing down organized bodies of knowledge to new learners, Pragmatists believe that learners should apply their knowledge to real situations through experimental inquiry. This prepares students for citizenship, daily living, and future careers.

Existentialism

The nature of reality for Existentialists is subjective, and lies within the individual. The physical world has no inherent meaning outside of human existence. Individual choice and individual standards rather than external standards are central. Existence comes before any definition of what we are. We define ourselves in relationship to that existence by the choices we make. We should not accept anyone else's predetermined philosophical system; rather, we must take responsibility for deciding who we are. The focus is on freedom, the development of authentic individuals, as we make meaning of our lives.

There are several different orientations within the existentialist philosophy. Soren Kierkegaard (1813-1855), a Danish minister and philosopher, is considered to be the founder of existentialism. His was a Christian orientation. Another group of existentialists, largely European, believes that we must recognize the finiteness of our lives on this small and fragile planet, rather than believing in salvation through God. Our existence is not guaranteed in an after life, so there is tension about life and the certainty of death, of hope or despair. Unlike the more austere European approaches where the universe is seen as meaningless when faced with the certainty of the end of existence, American existentialists have focused more on human potential and the quest for personal meaning. Values clarification is an outgrowth of this movement. Following the bleak period of World War II, the French philosopher, Jean Paul Sartre, suggested that for youth, the existential moment arises when young persons realize for the first time that choice is theirs, that they are responsible for themselves. Their question becomes "Who am I and what should I do?"

Related to education, the subject matter of existentialist classrooms should be a matter of personal choice. Teachers view the individual as an entity within a social context in which the learner must confront others' views to clarify his or her own. Character development emphasizes individual responsibility for decisions. Real answers come from within the individual, not from outside authority. Examining life through authentic thinking involves students in genuine learning experiences. Existentialists are opposed to thinking about students as objects to be measured, tracked, or standardized. Such educators want the educational experience to focus on creating opportunities for self-direction and self actualization. They start with the student, rather than on curriculum content.

Questions 1–10

Complete the table below.

Choose ***NO MORE THAN THREE WORDS*** *from Reading Passage above for each answer.*

School	Tenet	Founder(s)	Educational beliefs	Focus of curriculum	Teaching methods
Idealism	Ideas are the only true reality. Focus: __1__ in the mind	Plato	Bringing __2__ to consciousness.	subject matter of mind	handling ideas through lecture, discussion, and Socratic dialogue
Realism	Reality exists independent of __3__. Focus: body/objects	Aristotle	The exercise of rational thought is the ultimate purpose for humankind.	the subject matter of the __4__	mastery of facts and basic skills through __5__

（续）

School	Tenet	Founder(s)	Educational beliefs	Focus of curriculum	Teaching methods
Pragmatism	Things that are experienced or observed are real. Focus: the reality of __6__	__7__	Learners must adapt to each other and to their environment.	solving problems in an __8__ way	hands-on problem solving, experimenting, and projects
Existentialism	The nature of reality is subjective and lies within the individual. Focus: freedom	Soren Kierkegaard	Individual is an entity within a social context in which the learner must confront others' views to clarify his or her own.	subject to __9__	creating opportunities for __10__

Keys:

1. conscious reasoning　2. latent ideas　3. the human mind　4. physical world
5. demonstration and recitation　6. demonstration and recitation
7. Charles Sanders Peirce　8. interdisciplinary
9. personal choice　10. self-direction and self actualization

Exercise 2

A Nuke on the Yukon?

Galena, Alaska, could be the type specimen for remoteness. A tiny town of about 700 on a bend of the Yukon River, it has no roads in and depends on the river for food, fuel and supplies. The river is frozen eight to nine months of the year. Galena residents pay three times the national average per kilowatt hour for diesel-generated electricity. Alternative energy would have special appeal for Galena, but with an evening that stretches 20 hours in the winter, solar is out. With the help of Toshiba and its American holding, Westinghouse, Galena is thinking nuclear.

Will a swaggering nuclear policy in Galena be the next big headache for nearby Tanana and McGrath? The key to Galena's ambitions is the Toshiba 4S — the Super-Safe, Small and Simple reactor, a torpedo-shaped unit that surrounds a core about 2 meters long and 0.6 meters across. The entire unit, core and casing, is to be manufactured off-site by Toshiba, delivered to the customer, and then lowered into a cylindrical concrete vault 30 meters underground. Expected to run for 30 years with minimal operator intervention, the 4S is designed to pump out 10 megawatts of electric power, just 1 percent of the output of conventional nuclear power plants. When the nuclear fuel is exhausted after three decades, Toshiba will extract the 4S and take it away, presumably leaving behind a replacement (which for all we know will be the size of a beachball by then). Tony Grenci, principal engineer at Westinghouse and lead for the licensing process, reports that the remote-community application is likely to be the first use for the 4S, but that other roles will probably be more important overall, such as supplying power for mining, desalinization, oil-sands operations and remote research facilities.

Discussions about the Galena-Toshiba project began in 2005 and have been proceeding at regulatory speed — which is to say, slowly. Initially, Toshiba offered to install the unit for free as a pilot project, with Galena arranging to finance the operating costs and Toshiba leading the effort to acquire regulatory approval. The Nuclear Regulatory Commission (NRC) is widely regarded as a government entity that does well what it is supposed to do. It offers consultation at the pre-design and pre-application stage, and imposes a notoriously arduous review of applications that seems to generate little complaint. Everyone understands how high the stakes are. Toshiba/Westinghouse initiated discussions with the NRC in 2007 and had its fourth pre-application meeting in late 2008. The current plan is to file for design approval in 2009. After that comes filing for a site permit, which takes into account environmental information specific to the operating site, and a Combined Construction and Operating License, allowing the plant to be built and fired up. Grenci is unwilling to project a date for first steam — original estimates of 2012 now seem implausible — "but we're going great guns on this."

Technologically, the 4S is a captivating item. Cylindrical fuel rods 2 meters long surround an inner neutron absorber, and the fuel rods are surrounded by a neutron-reflecting collar. Operation begins with the collar covering just the bottom portion of the fuel rods, reflecting scattered neutrons back into the fuel. Slowly the collar creeps up the length of the fuel-rod assembly, exhausting the fuel it surrounds until it reaches the top of the fuel rods 30 years later. The reactor is cooled by liquid sodium, and the heat generated is transferred to steam turbines in a separate structure. Among the designed-in safety features are the mechanisms for cycling the liquid-metal coolant through the reactor: electromagnetic pumps, which have no moving parts to fail, and the routing of the coolant, which is designed to transport the sodium by convection alone if the pumps fail. The choice of sodium instead of water for the coolant is itself a safety consideration, because the sodium channels aren't pressurized. A leak would be a serious problem, but in a crisis, molten sodium seeps. The high-temperature, high-pressure water-cooling systems of conventional reactors explode.

A recent rise of commercial interest in nuclear power has been called the nuclear renaissance. The technology for big plants is becoming more robust, the regulatory process is being streamlined as the heritage of experience gets deeper, new-plant costs are coming down just as the prices of conventional energy sources such as oil and gas become increasingly volatile, and climate change has many players taking a fresh look at nuclear. Ironically, the renaissance may work against Galena and Toshiba/Westinghouse. At least 29 new big reactors are at various stages of planning, and the NRC is staffing up for an anticipated burst in the number of filings for approval. (There are 104 nuclear plants currently operating in the U.S.) The Office of New Reactors at the NRC has advised Toshiba that only limited attention will be given through 2010 to "grid-appropriate" (their term for *small*) reactor designs. It remains to be seen whether the incoming Obama administration will take a more enthusiastic view of small nukes, or a more sympathetic view of citizens in the outlands. In the NRC's 4S file, a letter from the licensing lead for a competing "grid-appropriate" reactor, the Hyperion Power Module (the size of a hot tub, at least on the drawing board), reads "These are areas that are paying through the nose for diesel fuel to keep the lights on. Some are charging 47 cents per kWh, and a lot of people are sitting in the dark."

Questions 1–4

*Complete the following diagram below. Choose **NO MORE THAN TWO WORDS** from the passage above for each blank.*

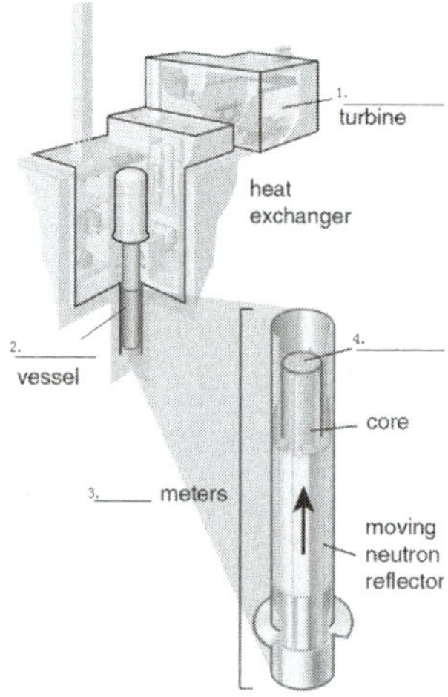

Keys:

1. steam 2. reactor 3. 2 4. fuel rods

Exercise 3

The Origin of Life

A case is made for the descent of electrons

As the frontiers of knowledge have advanced, scientists have resolved one creation question after another. We now have a pretty good understanding of the origin of the Sun and the Earth, and cosmologists can take us to within a fraction of a second of the beginning of the universe itself. We know how life, once it began, was able to proliferate and diversify until it filled (and in many cases created) every niche on the planet. Yet one of the most obvious big questions—how did life arise from inorganic matter?—remains a great unknown.

Our progress on this question has been impeded by a formidable cognitive barrier. Because we perceive a deep gap when we think about the difference between inorganic matter and life, we feel that nature must have made a big leap to cross that gap. This point of view has led to searches for ways large and complex molecules could have formed early in Earth's history, a daunting task. The essential problem is that in modern living systems, chemical reactions in cells are mediated by protein catalysts called enzymes. The information encoded in the nucleic acids DNA and RNA is required to make the proteins; yet the proteins are required to make the nucleic acids. Furthermore, both proteins and nucleic acids are large molecules consisting of strings of small component molecules whose synthesis is supervised by proteins and nucleic acids. We have two chickens, two eggs, and no answer to the old problem of which came first.

In this article we present a view gaining attention in the origin-of-life community that takes the question out of the hatchery and places it squarely in the realm of accessible, plausible chemistry. As we see it, the early steps on the way to life are an inevitable, incremental result of the operation of the laws of chemistry and physics operating under the conditions that existed on the early Earth, a result that can be understood in terms of known (or at least knowable) laws of nature. As such, the early stages in the emergence of life are no more surprising, no more accidental, than water flowing downhill.

The new approach requires that we adopt new ways of looking at two important fields of science. As we will see below, we will have to adjust our view of both cellular biochemistry and thermodynamics. Before we talk about these new ideas, however, it will be useful to place them in context by outlining a little of the history of research on the origin of life.

Most historians would say that the modern era of experimental research in origin-of-life studies began in a basement laboratory in the chemistry department of the University of Chicago in 1953. Harold Urey, a Nobel laureate in chemistry, and Stanley Miller, then a graduate student, put together a tabletop apparatus designed to look at the kinds of chemical processes that might have occurred on the planet soon after its birth. They showed that organic molecules (in this case amino acids) could be created from inorganic materials by natural environmental conditions such as acidic solution, heat and electrical discharge (lightning), without the mediation of enzymes. This finding triggered a wave of new thinking about both the origin and nature of life. (Today, the consensus is that Miller and Urey had the wrong atmospheric components in their apparatus, so the process they discovered was probably not representative of the emergence of life on Earth. It nevertheless pointed to the potential fecundity and diversity of nonenzymatic primordial chemistry.)

Since 1953, we have found many of the same simple organic molecules in meteorites, comets and even interstellar gas clouds. Far from being special, then, the simplest of the molecules we find in living systems — life's building blocks — seem to be quite common in nature. To many, the real question was how these basic building blocks got put together into living systems, and, equally important, how the molecules that led to modern life were selected out of the messy molecular milieu in which they arose.

The ubiquity of simple molecules suggested an appealing scenario that had a profound effect on the way investigators approached the origin of life throughout the last half of the 20th century. The scenario went like this: After the Earth cooled enough to allow oceans to form, the Miller-Urey process or something like it produced a rain of organic matter. In a relatively short time, the ocean became a broth of these molecules, and given enough time, the right combination of molecules came together by pure chance to form a replicating entity of some kind that evolved into modern life.

Scientists called this scenario the Oparin-Haldane conjecture, but it was given a provocative nickname that endures in the popular consciousness — Primordial Soup.

The essential legacy of the Primordial Soup was twofold: It simplified the notion of the origin of life to a single pivotal event, and then it proposed that that event — the step that occurred after the molecules were made — was a result of chance. In the standard language, life is to be seen, in the end, as a "frozen accident". In this view, many fundamental details about the structure of life are not amenable to explanation. The architecture of life is just one of those things. Although many modern theories are less extreme than this, frozen-accident thinking still influences what some of us ask about the origin of life and how we prioritize our experiments.

Questions 1–5

Complete the following chart.
*Choose **NO MORE THAN TWO WORDS** from the passage above for each answer.*

Oparin-Haldane Conjecture

The temperature on the __1__ dropped

↓

a __2__ of organic matter produced

↓

oceans full of __3__ formed

↓

molecules __4__

↓

modern __5__ came to birth

Keys:

1. earth　　2. rain　　3. organic molecules
4. combined/come together　　5. living things

星期六

综合训练（一）

READING PASSAGE 1

*You should spend about 20 minutes on **Questions 1–13**, which are based on Reading Passage 1 below.*

Fish and no chips

To pin one big evolutionary shift on a particular molecule is ambitious. To pin two on it is truly audacious. Yet doing so was just one of the ideas floating around at "A Celebration of DHA" in London this week. The celebration in question was a scientific meeting, rather than a festival. It was definitely, however, a love-in. It was held on May 26th and 27th at the Royal Society of Medicine to discuss the many virtues of docosahexaenoic acid, the most important of that fashionable class of dietary chemicals, the omega-3 fatty acids.

DHA is a component of brains, particularly the synaptic junctions between nerve cells, and its displacement from modern diets by the omega-6 acids in cooking oils such as soya, maize and rape is a cause of worry. Many researchers think this shift — and the change in brain chemistry that it causes — explains the growth in recent times of depression, manic-depression, memory loss, schizophrenia and attention-deficit disorder. It may also be responsible for rising levels of obesity and thus the heart disease which often accompanies being overweight.

Michael Crawford, a researcher at the Institute of Brain Chemistry and Human Nutrition in London, believes, however, that DHA is even more important than that. He suggests that it was responsible for the existence of nervous systems in the first place, and that access to large quantities of the stuff was what permitted the evolution of big brains in mankind's more recent ancestors.

According to Dr Crawford, DHA's first job was to convert light into electricity in single-celled organisms. This gave them a crude form of vision, allowing them to move in response to light and shade, but also brought into biology a way of controlling electrical potential. If organisms are to be multicellular, cells must be able to talk to each other. Electrical potentials, the basis of every nervous system, are one way of doing this. And DHA was the enabler.

The molecule is certainly ubiquitous. Some 600m years after animals became multicellular, more than half of the fatty-acid molecules in the light-sensitive cells of the human eye are still

DHA, and the proportion of DHA in the synapses of the brain is not far short of that, despite the fact that similar molecules are far more readily available. Indeed, Dr Crawford thinks that a shortage of DHA is a long-term evolutionary theme. The molecule is most famously found in fatty fish. He suggests this might explain why, for example, dolphins have brains that weigh 1.8kg whereas zebra brains weigh only 350g, even though the two species have similar body sizes. Furthermore, he argues that the dramatic increase of the size of the brains of humanity's ancestors that happened about 6m years ago was not because apes came out of the trees to hunt on the savannahs, but becausc they arrived at the coast and found a ready supply of DHA in fish.

Not everyone, it must be said, agrees with this interpretation of history. For one thing, humanity's ancestors do not seem to have been exclusively coastal. What they do agree about, though, is that substituting DHA with other, superficially similar molecules is a bad idea.

Joseph Hibbeln, a researcher at America's National Institutes of Health, has been looking at the supply to babies of DHA from breast milk and at genetic variation in the ability to produce this molecule from other omega-3s. A study that began in the early 1990s has shown that children who are breastfed have the same range of IQs, regardless of whether they have the ability to make their own DHA. In the case of those fed on formula milk low in DHA, though, children without the DHA-making ability had an average IQ 7.8 points lower than those with it.

Nor is intelligence the only thing affected by a lack of DHA. There is also a body of data linking omega-3 deficiencies to violent behaviour. Countries whose citizens eat more fish (which is rich in DHA) are less prone to depression, suicide and murder. And new research by Dr Hibbeln shows that low levels of DHA are a risk factor for suicide among American servicemen and women. Actual suicides had significantly lower levels of DHA in the most recent routine blood sample taken before they killed themselves than did comparable personnel who remained alive. More worryingly, 95% of American troops have DHA levels that these results suggest put them at risk of suicide.

America's department of defence has taken note. It will soon unveil a programme to supplement the diets of soldiers with omega-3s. The country's Food and Drug Administration may change one of its policies, too. Thomas Brenna, a professor of nutrition at Cornell University, has written a letter (co-signed by many of the scientists at the meeting) urging the agency to revise its advice to pregnant and fertile women that they limit their consumption of fish. This advice, promulgated in 2004, was intended to protect fetuses from the malign effects of methyl mercury, which accumulates in fish such as tuna. The signatories argue that this effect is greatly outweighed by the DHA-related benefits of eating fatty fish.

They may, however, be swimming against the tide. The popularity of omega-6-rich foods based on cheap vegetable oils will be difficult to reverse. Indeed, if another of Dr Hibbeln's studies proves true of people as well as rodents, it may be self-fulfilling.

In this experiment he fed rats diets that were identical except that in one case 8% of the calories came from linoleic acid (an omega-6 fatty acid) while in the other that value was 1%. These percentages reflect the shift in the proportion of omega-6s in the American diet between 1909 and the early 21st century.

In the 8% diet, levels of rat obesity doubled. It turns out that in rats (and also in humans) linoleic acid is converted into molecules called endocannabinoids that trigger appetite. Those who eat omega-6s, in other words, want to eat more food. And since, in the human case, omega-6-rich food is much cheaper than omega-3-rich food, that is what they are likely to consume.

The way out of this vicious circle is not obvious. Eating fish is all very well, but the oceans are under enough pressure as it is. Biotechnology might be brought to bear — creating genetically modified crops such as soyabeans with higher levels of DHA. Until that day, though, the best advice is probably that which was posted over the oracle at Delphi: "Nothing in excess".

Questions 1–7

Do the following statements agree with information given in Reading Passage 1?

In boxes 1–7 on your answer sheet, write

YES	*if the statement agrees with the writer*
NO	*if the statement contradicts the writer*
NOT GIVEN	*if there is no information about this in the passage.*

1. People at "A Celebration of DHA" mainly discussed the merits of DHA.
2. The omega-6 acids in cooking oils can generate the same effects to our brains as DHA.
3. The rise in the mental and psychological problems is related to the rising levels of obesity.
4. DHA plays an important role in driving the evolution of human brains.
5. Multi-celled organisms need more DHA than single-celled organisms.
6. The proportion of DHA contained in the human eye is larger than that in human brain.
7. According to Dr Crawford, the dolphin's brains weigh heavier than that of the zebra simply because dolphins eat more fish.

Questions 8–10

*Choose the correct letter, **A**, **B**, **C** or **D**.*

Write the correct letter in boxes 8–10 on your answer sheet.

8. What did the study on breast milk and formula milk find out?
   A. Breast milk affects baby's ability of making their own DHA.
   B. Babies fed on formula milk have lower IQ than those fed on breast milk on average.
   C. Formula milk affected the intelligence of those babies who could not make their own DHA.
   D. The amount of DHA in formula milk is less than that in breast milk.
9. What did the scientists at the meeting want the agency to do?

A. Limit the amount of fish consumed by pregnant women.

B. Encourage pregnant women to eat more fish.

C. Ban the sale of tuna in the country.

D. Advising pregnant women to eat less tuna.

10. The best title for the passage is ______.

A. Fish and No Chips

B. Unhealthy Diet Habit

C. DHA and Health

D. Benefits of DHA

Questions 11–13

Complete the sentences below.

Choose ***NO MORE THAN TWO WORDS*** *from the passage for each answer.*

Write your answer in boxes 11–13 on your answer sheet.

11. Studies found that lower levels of DHA could also make people more likely to do ______.

12. People in America prefer omega-6-rich foods because they are ______ than omega-3-rich foods.

13. The best solution to the problem of lack of DHA is to depend on ______.

READING PASSAGE 2

You should spend about 20 minutes on ***Questions 14–27****, which are based on Reading Passage 2 below.*

Investigating a Mega-Mystery

When, at least 12,000 years ago, human beings first crossed into North America from Siberia, the continent teemed with large animals. Today, of course, our only encounters with giant short-faced bears, enormous sloths and dozens of other such extinct species come in museums. On this much, archaeologists and paleontologists agree. The causes of this mass extinction, however, remain clouded by conflicting findings and holes in the archaeological record.

The mystery extends far beyond North America. Between about 50,000 and 10,000 years ago, near the end of the Pleistocene, much of the world's megafauna (usually defined as animals weighing at least 100 pounds) disappeared. At the same time, Homo sapiens was expanding from Africa into Eurasia, Australia and the Americas. The late Pleistocene also witnessed dramatic climate change, especially during the period of warming and deglaciation that followed the Last Glacial Maximum some 20,000 years ago.

This convergence of events makes for exciting — and sometimes contentious — science. High-impact human hunting, referred to by archaeologists as "overkill", and climate change are the two most cited possible causes of the extinctions, but the role of each remains contested.

The debate began to heat up in the late 1960s after Paul S. Martin, a professor of geosciences at the University of Arizona, first proposed a "blitzkrieg" model of human overkill for North America — basically, overkill on fast forward. In this scenario, humans moved rapidly through the continent, slaughtering mammoths, mastodons and other large prey as they went. Within about 1,000 years, most North American endemic megafauna were gone.

The blitzkrieg hypothesis has since been applied elsewhere, but it remains controversial. Criticism has focused on the lack of archaeological evidence, a charge Martin has responded to by arguing that, if the extinctions occurred quickly, there would be little trace of the massacre in the fossil record. Archaeologists Donald Grayson of the University of Washington and David Meltzer of Southern Methodist University have been particularly critical of Martin's response, calling it "faith-based" science.

Surovell, Waguespack and Brantingham outlined two possible extinction scenarios, one based on human overkill and the other on climate change. They then plugged into their models data from 41 archaeological sites in Africa, Europe, Asia and the Americas that contain remains of proboscideans hunted or scavenged by humans. If people hunted these animals to extinction, the authors argue, the kill sites should appear along the border between proboscidean and human ranges. So, as humans expanded south across North America, for example, the sites would also be located farther and farther south. If climate was the culprit, then people and proboscideans should have shared some of the same territory, at least until climate change shrunk proboscidean habitat. Thus, kill sites would be found both along and behind the frontier of human expansion.

The authors concluded that the location and age of the sites correlate closely with an overkill model. As humans moved north into Eurasia from Africa and, later, south from Alaska across the Americas, proboscidean range contracted correspondingly. Climate change, then, cannot account for proboscidean extinction "unless one were to invoke serial climatic change that perfectly tracks human global colonization". The odds, they're saying, aren't good.

Although the authors do not claim to have proved that humans drove other species to extinction, Surovell is skeptical of arguments for climate change. "I would like to see somebody explain how climate change could cause mass extinction on such a large geographical scale," he says. "Climate is constantly changing."

In Australia, much of the evidence for overkill relies on proving that many large animals became extinct within several millennia of the first appearance of humans, usually estimated at about 50,000 years ago. Unlike other parts of the world, nothing in Australia's fossil record proves that humans hunted megafauna. As Trueman and Field note in their paper, there aren't even any sites with evidence that early inhabitants had the tools to kill large animals.

Trueman and Field discuss the dates of a controversial archaeological site, Cuddie Springs, that might prove that at least some Australian megafauna survived much longer than previously thought, dealing a blow to arguments for overkill. The site includes remains of several extinct animals, including Diprotodon, a two-ton marsupial, and Genyornis, a large, flightless bird. Previous efforts, made using radiocarbon dating and other methods, have concluded that some megafauna remains found there are 36,000 to 30,000 years old, but the findings have been disputed. Trueman and Field used a newer technique in their recent work, an analysis of rare earth elements (REEs) in bone fragments, and confirmed these dates. As they're buried, bones adsorb REEs, leaving a "fingerprint" that links the bones to their original layer of deposition.

Proving that people coexisted with large animals for 10,000 years or more would not necessarily remove humans from the extinction equation, but it would make it more likely that other factors, such as climate, also played a key part. Field, for one, is convinced that the findings at Cuddie Springs disprove the possibility of blitzkrieg in Australia and cast doubt on the overkill hypothesis. It's about time, she says, "to start entertaining other ideas about the extinction process."

If Pleistocene humans hunted some large animals to extinction but blitzkrieg is ruled out as a possibility in Australia, as the recent findings suggest, the search for an overarching theory may be futile. In a review of recent research on the extinctions, published in the October 1, 2004, issue of Science, coauthors Anthony D. Barnosky, Paul L. Koch, Robert S. Feranec, Scott L. Wing and Alan B. Shabel argued that it will be more productive to look for localized, species-by-species explanations than a single cause. Some combination of climate change and human activity, they think, probably determined the fate of much of the world's megafauna.

Implicating multiple factors might not be as satisfying as convicting a single perpetrator, but it may better explain the evidence at hand. And as the Science authors point out, the combination of climate change and human action can have a much greater effect on the world's animal species than either factor alone. There's no debate that both are today affecting the viability of the remaining megafauna.

Questions 14–17

Do the following statements agree with information given in Reading Passage 2?

In boxes 14–17 on your answer sheet, write

TRUE	*if the statement agrees with the information*
FALSE	*if the statement contradicts the information*
NOT GIVEN	*if there is no information on this*

14. Climate change drove early human beings to walk out of Africa to other parts of the world.
15. The people in North America far outnumber the megafauna there.
16. The blitzkrieg hypothesis won wide popularity in the circle of archaeology.

17. Surovell, Waguespack and Brantingham's found convincing evidence for overkill model.

Questions 18–27

Complete the summary below.
Choose ***NO MORE THAN TWO WORDS*** *form the passage for each answer.*
Write your answers in boxes 18–27 on your answer sheet.

The mass disappearance of __18__ in North America and other parts of the world around 10,000 years ago remained a __19__ to archaeologists and paleontologists. Human overkill and __20__ were proposed as two factors causing the extinction, but the role of each remains __21__. Professor Paul S. Martin first put forward his __22__ model for North America but was criticized of lacking __23__. Later, some researchers gave two pictures of the extinction based on evidence found in __24__ around the world and they concluded that overkill model was more reasonable. However, __25__ in Australia did not provide any evidence showing that humans killed large animals. Instead, it was found that these larger animals actually __26__ with humans for quite a long time. These conflicting findings suggest that a __27__ of more than one factor might be the better explanation.

READING PASSAGE 3

You should spend about 20 minutes on ***Questions 28–40****, which are based on Reading Passage 3 below.*

Addicts Bet on the Present

Smokers don't put stock in "what might have been" when making choices

A It's pretty obvious that choosing to smoke is a poor decision, considering how much is known about its adverse health effects. But the fact that addicts pursue their habits, even in light of an understanding of the potential rewards of stopping, has long been a topic of research in the neurology of addiction.

B "Humans can use abstract ideas to veto their biological instincts. You can go on a hunger strike until literally you die in pursuit of an idea. There's no other animal on the planet that can do that," explains Read Montague, a neuroscientist at the Baylor College of Medicine in Houston. Addicts seem to lose some of this capacity, he says: "What it means to be an addict is that consequences that might happen in the future—good things that you may forgo, or bad things that you may not be able to avoid—can no longer stop you from chasing your habit."

C Montague has demonstrated that people learn and make value judgments based not only on what they have experienced (called an experiential signal), but also on understanding what they might have gained if they had made other choices (called a fictive signal). Seeing the difference between both an expected outcome and an actual one is called an experiential error, whereas that for an actual outcome versus a better one that might have been possible is called a fictive error. Both of these signals change the activity of dopamine-activated neurons in the brain. Could it be that this change doesn't happen in addicts? Is it that chronic smokers don't experience these nervous system changes, or do such signals just not influence their behavior and choices?

D Montague, along with his colleagues Pearl H. Chiu and Terry M. Lohrenz, decided to explore this question. "We're interested in the general process by which addiction hijacks learning mechanisms in your brain," he says, "and smoking is a gateway drug for lots of other things." The research group tested both chronic smokers and nonsmokers on a mock stock-market investment game. Smokers performed the trial twice, once deprived of nicotine and again when fully sated. During the test, participants underwent functional magnetic-resonance imaging (FMRI) to record changes in blood flow in their brains, a measure of neuronal activity.

E The participants were each allotted $100 to invest in a model stock market, so the participants stood to make real financial gains from their activities. There were 20 investment rounds, and after each step the participants were shown the fluctuation in the market, how much their allotment had changed and the maximum amount they could have gained by investing a different amount. At the end of the trial, participants left with the actual amount of funds they had won — an average of $120. ("Somebody walked out with $400," notes Montague.)

F The investigators focused on data from rounds where participants gained money in the market. They found that it was possible to predict how nonsmokers would alter their investment behavior in the next step, based on how much more they could have gained in the previous round had they allotted their funds differently. "It accounts for 60 percent of the variance in nonsmokers' next choice," Montague says. "In smokers, whether sated or not, it had no influence whatsoever, none."

G "Say you bet 40 percent of your $100, and then the market fluctuates. When it goes up, every bet bigger than 40 percent would have made more money. That drives nonsmokers to really increase their bet next time. But in smokers, it has no impact on what they do next; they are only driven by their actual gains," Montague says. Smokers are only influenced by rewards they directly experience as the result of an action they have taken. They choose smaller, more immediate outcomes over those that are larger but more delayed.

H However, nonsmokers and both sated and nicotine-deprived smokers all had the same neural response on the fMRI scan to the revelation of the largest possible investment return. Thus it appears that smokers' brains do in fact compute and understand that a different outcome might have been possible, but this does not translate into a control signal that affects their next behavioral choice.

I "Another interesting case is, suppose you put in a lot, say 85 percent, and the market fluctuates positively, so now you've won a whole lot. You couldn't have won that much more, just 15 percent in this case. People back down from big wins like that, and there's never been a good explanation for why. We didn't see that effect at all in the smokers." Montague thinks this research may provide an underlying neurological explanation for this phenomenon: There wasn't a big enough fictive-error signal from the experience for nonsmoking participants to decide they should be risking as much in the next round.

J Montague plans to tease out more details by next studying a large group of adolescents, before any have started smoking, over a number of years. Such quantitative results may make it possible for him to develop a risk index for addiction. His work could also be a step toward deciphering any biological explanation, such as an anomalous number of dopamine receptors, that may underlie the breakdown of this behavioral pathway, and help in determining whether there's any chemical way to restore the process.

K So, are people with impaired control signals more likely to take up smoking, or does smoking itself somehow interrupt this neural behavioral-response pathway? Montague's working hypothesis is that it's both: Some people may be predisposed to a weakly coupled behavioral response to the neural signal, but smoking further breaks down the pathway. "I think that it's tending to select people for whom this is already a weak coupling," he says. "Because in a sense, if you've got a really strong capacity to use what might happen to you tomorrow to put a drink or a cigarette down, it's just going to be harder to get you addicted."

Questions 28–31

Reading passage 3 has eleven paragraphs, **A–K**.

Which paragraph contains the following information?

Write the correct letter, ***A–K****, in boxes 28–31 on your answer sheet.*

NB *You may use any letter more than once.*

28. A further study using subjects of different age groups
29. The bases for people make reasonable judgments
30. The neurological reason for explaining nonsmoker's behavior in the test
31. The possible neural reason why addicts are unable to control their biological instincts

Questions 32–35

Do the following statements agree with information given in Reading Passage 3?

In boxes 32–35 on your answer sheet, write

TRUE	*if the statement agrees with the information*
FALSE	*if the statement contradicts the information*
NOT GIVEN	*if there is no information on this*

32. Smokers could not quit smoking simply because they could not foresee the potential health problems brought by smoking.

33. The ability to overcome their biological impulse by reasoning is only human-specific.
34. Smokers won more money than non-smokers in the model stock market.
35. Smokers and non-smoker responded differently on the fMRI scan.

Questions 36–40

Classify the following as typical of

A. both chronic smokers and non-smokers
B. only chronic smokers
C. only non-smokers

*Write the correct letter, **A**, **B** or **C**, in boxes 36–40 on your answer sheet.*

36. take smaller risks in gambling
37. be aware of the possible different outcomes
38. bigger return cause them to give bigger bet
39. have their neuronal activity measured
40. the invest behavior could be predictable to certain degree

Keys:

1. T	2. F	3. NG
4. T	5. NG	6. F
7. F	8. C	9. B
10. A	11. violent behavior	12. cheaper
13. biotechnology	14. F	15. NG
16. F	17. T	18. large animals
19. mystery	20. climate change	21. controversial
22. "blitzkrieg"	23. archaeological evidence	24. archaeological sites
25. fossil record	26. coexisted	27. combination
28. J	29. C	30. I
31. C	32. F	33. T
34. NG	35. F	36. B
37. A	38. C	39. A
40. C		

星期日

综合训练（二）

READING PASSAGE 1

You should spend about 20 minutes on ***Questions 1–13****, which are based on Reading Passage 1 below.*

Study: Parasites and Pathogens Affect Human Intelligence

A Human intelligence is puzzling. It is higher, on average, in some places than in others. And it seems to have been rising in recent decades. Why these two things should be true is controversial. This week, though, a group of researchers at the University of New Mexico propose the same explanation for both: the effect of infectious disease. If they are right, it suggests that the control of such diseases is crucial to a country's development in a way that had not been appreciated before. Places that harbour a lot of parasites and pathogens not only suffer the debilitating effects of disease on their workforces, but also have their human capital eroded, child by child, from birth.

B Christopher Eppig and his colleagues make their suggestion in the Proceedings of the Royal Society. They note that the brains of newly born children require 87% of those children's metabolic energy. In five-year-olds the figure is still 44% and even in adults the brain — a mere 2% of the body's weight — consumes about a quarter of the body's energy. Any competition for this energy is likely to damage the brain's development, and parasites and pathogens compete for it in several ways. Some feed on the host's tissue directly, or hijack its molecular machinery to reproduce. Some, particularly those that live in the gut, stop their host absorbing food. And all provoke the host's immune system into activity, which diverts resources from other things.

C The inverse correlation that the group calculated between a country's disease burden and the average intelligence of its people is impressive. They estimated the disease burden from World Health Organisation data on DALYs (disability-adjusted life years) lost caused by 28 infectious diseases. These data exist for 192 countries. The intelligence scores came from work carried out earlier this decade by Richard Lynn, a British psychologist, and Tatu Vanhanen, a Finnish political scientist, who analysed IQ studies from 113 countries, and from subsequent work by Jelte Wicherts, a Dutch psychologist.

D At the bottom of the average-intelligence list is Equatorial Guinea, followed by St Lucia. Cameroon, Mozambique and Gabon tie at third from bottom. These countries also have among the highest burden of infectious diseases. At the top of the list of countries with the highest average intelligence is Singapore, followed by South Korea. China and Japan tie in third place. These countries all have relatively low levels of disease. America, Britain and a number of European countries, follow behind the leaders. A list of the countries included in the study can be found here.

E The correlation is about 67%, and the chance that it might have come about at random is less than one in 10,000. But correlation is not causation, so Mr Eppig and his colleagues tried to eliminate other possible explanations. Previous work has offered income, education, low levels of agricultural labour (which is replaced by more mentally stimulating jobs), climate (the challenge of surviving cold weather might provoke the evolution of intelligence) and even distance from humanity's African homeland (novel environments could encourage greater intelligence) as explanations for national differences in IQ. However, all of these, except perhaps the last, are also likely to be linked to disease and, by careful statistical analysis, Mr Eppig and his colleagues show that all of them either disappear or are reduced to a small effect when the consequences of disease are taken into account.

F There is, moreover, direct evidence that infections and parasites affect cognition. Intestinal worms have been shown to do so on many occasions. Malaria, too, is bad for the brain. A study of children in Kenya who survived the cerebral version of the disease suggests that an eighth of them suffer long-term cognitive damage. In the view of Mr Eppig and his colleagues, however, it is the various bugs that cause diarrhoea which are the biggest threat. Diarrhoea strikes children hard. It accounts for a sixth of infant deaths, and even in those it does not kill it prevents the absorption of food at a time when the brain is growing and developing rapidly.

G The researchers predict that one type of health problem will increase with rising intelligence. Asthma and other allergies are thought by many experts to be rising in frequency because infantile immune systems, unchallenged by infection, are turning against the cells of the body they are supposed to protect. Some studies already suggest a correlation between a country's allergy levels and its average IQ. Mr Eppig and his colleagues predict that future work will confirm this relationship.

H The other prediction, of course, is that as countries conquer disease, the intelligence of their citizens will rise. A rise in intelligence over the decades has already been noticed in rich countries. It is called the Flynn effect after James Flynn, who discovered it. Its cause, however, has been mysterious—until now. If Mr Eppig is right, the near-abolition of serious infections in these countries, by vaccination, clean water and proper sewerage, may explain much if not all of the Flynn effect.

I When Dr Lynn and Dr Vanhanen originally published their IQ data, they used them to advance the theory that national differences in intelligence were the main reason for different levels of economic development. This study turns that reasoning on its head. It is lack of development, and the many health problems this brings, which explains the difference in levels of intelligence. No doubt, in a vicious circle, those differences help keep poor countries poor. But the new theory offers a way to break the circle. If further work by researchers supports the ideas of Mr Eppig and his colleagues, they will have done the world a good turn by providing policymakers with yet another reason why the elimination of disease should be one of the main aims of development, rather than a desirable afterthought.

Questions 1–7

Reading passage 1 has nine paragraphs, **A–I**.

Which paragraph contains the following information?

*Write the correct letter, **A–I**, in boxes 1–7 on your answer sheet.*

1. The possible factors explaining Flynn effect.
2. Evidence of the effects of infections on human cognition.
3. The possible link between infectious disease and human intelligence
4. Other factors that might cause national differences in intelligence.
5. The way parasites and pathogens compete with the brain for energy.
6. The association between some disease and rising intelligence.
7. The list of countries with the highest average intelligence.

Questions 8–13

Do the following statements agree with information given in Reading Passage 1?

In boxes 8–13 on your answer sheet, write

TRUE	*if the statement agrees with the information*
FALSE	*if the statement contradicts the information*
NOT GIVEN	*if there is no information on this*

8. Brain consumes most of metabolic energy of newly born babies.
9. World Health Organization collected data from all developing countries.
10. Singapore has a higher burden of infectious disease than Mozambique.
11. Other factors play the same role in causing national differences in IQ as disease.
12. Diarrhoea threatens children's health as well as their intelligence.
13. Poor countries are unable to improve their national intelligence because their poor economy.

READING PASSAGE 2

*You should spend about 20 minutes on **Questions 14–26**, which are based on Reading Passage 2 below.*

Questions 14–18

Reading Passage 2 has five sections, **A–E**.

*Choose the correct heading for section **A** to **E** from the list of headings below.*

*Write the correct number, **i-x**, in boxes 14–18 on your answer sheet.*

List of Headings

i	Why do we need laughing
ii	When laughter is not funny
iii	Childish and violent laughter
iv	Good things laughing does to our body
v	Laughter's social power
vi	The risks of not playing
vii	Social origin of teenager problems
viii	Why laughing is good medicine
ix	A better world of laughter
x	The benefits of play

14. Section **A**
15. Section **B**
16. Section **C**
17. Section **D**
18. Section **E**

Section A

Laughter is not only associated with release of tension induced by danger and signaling nonaggression but also with expressing good, positive emotions. It is a social glue that facilitates approach, contact, and intimacy between people and decreases stress from potential conflict. This could be the basis for the intuitive notion that "laughter is the best medicine".

Serious research is showing that this notion is true. Laughter and humor decrease stress and anxiety, reinforce immunity, relax muscle tension, and decrease blood pressure and pain. Modern medicine is beginning to take advantage of these positive effects; hospitalized children who see clown shows have shorter hospital stays than those who do not.

Laughter initiates a chain of physiological reactions. First, it activates the cardiovascular system, so heart rate and blood pressure increase. The arteries then dilate, however, causing blood pressure to fall. Repeated short, strong contractions of the muscles of the thoracic wall, abdomen, and diaphragm increase blood flow into our internal organs. Forced respiration (the ha! ha! of laughter) elevates the flow of oxygen into the blood. Muscle tension decreases, and we may temporarily lose control of our limbs, as in the expression "weak with laughter".

Laughter may also produce beneficial hormonal changes. Scientists speculate that laughter releases neurochemical transmitters called "endorphins", which reduce sensitivity to pain and boost endurance and pleasurable sensations.

Section B

Why does laughter have such pervasive power in our lives? Beyond its physical effects, the answer may lie in our social nature. Laughter appears to be a basic aspect of bonding. We are creatures who need to build stable social structures to live well. Thus we need to enjoy peaceful relations with the people around us. Laughter is a kind of message we send to communicate this joyful disposition and a willingness to play. We rarely laugh when we are alone. We even feel that someone laughing alone may be crazy.

Laughter has many subtle effects on our social companions. It breaks the ice, achieves closeness, bonds us, generates goodwill, and dampens hostility and aggression. Observe how we laugh when we want to deflate tension between strangers or need to say no to someone. We often laugh when we apologize. Laughter disarms people, creates a bridge between them, and facilitates amicable behavior. Even babies laugh. Since they are too young to have a sense of humor, smiling and laughing must reinforce their connections with their parents and others close to them.

Age differences in laughter have also been noted. Adolescents use it more when they are playing or flirting; executives use it more in a professional context, to increase rapport with someone or win a negotiation. On the other hand, laughter may have a negative connotation, even in our own culture. There is a widely appreciated difference between "laughing with" and "laughing at" someone.

Section C

Some people have fits of abnormal laughter, producing an inappropriate, unrestrained, uncontrollable laughter dissociated from any stimulus. To observers, the laughter often appears childish or violent. Clinical researchers report pathological laughter in three main conditions: psychiatric illnesses such as hysteria and schizophrenia; pseudobulbar palsy (a disorder affecting the muscles that control the tongue, throat, and parts of the face); and gelastic epilepsy (a form of temporal lobe epilepsy with fits of mirthless laughter). Scientists believe all these conditions involve disinhibition of impulses in the higher brain stem.

Although the neuroanatomy of pathological laughter is not fully known, three levels of the brain are probably involved: the cortical level, the bulbar level, and an integrative level probably at or near the hypothalamus. Patients with pathological laughter almost invariably have brain damage. Laughter may also cause neural pathology, however, leading to or aggravating some key symptom. For example, in a disease called cataplexy, characterized by sudden lack of muscle tone that leads to falls, laughter is a potent triggering stimuli.

Section D

Given the importance of laughter, the trend in modern Western societies to restrict the play of children is worrying. What will be the consequences, if, indeed, play is important in developing personality and social behavior?

Watching television and engaging in socially isolated, individual play with video games and electronic toys has increasingly displaced social interaction and group play. Fear of crime, illegal drugs, and automobile traffic makes many parents curtail the custom of sending children outdoors to play freely. Parents who arrive home late from work have little time to play with their children in the evenings. Schools cut into playtime to cram more classes and topics into the day; they use detention or suspension of playtime to punish pupils for misbehaving or for getting poor grades. Teaching children to compete seems to have overtaken teaching them to relax, play, and socialize.

Where will all this lead? There are indications that these shifts may have some bearing on many of today's social ills: increasing violence in schools, very young children using weapons and drugs, and social and racial intolerance. Scientists such as Panksepp speculate that the recent astounding increase in the prevalence of attention deficit hyperactivity disorder may be fueled by restrictions on play in American schools. Deprived of exercise and time to play, normal young children become fidgety; their attention spans decrease.

Section E

Laughter and play are important in our human behavioral repertoire, a response both ancient and modern. When we laugh spontaneously, we use a capacity rooted in our most primitive biology. When we laugh at a subtle joke, we build on this primitive process, employing an advanced capacity of our brains. In both cases, our laughter has a surprisingly important role. Panksepp summarizes this with wisdom and beauty: Play and laughter not only fertilize the brain but they fertilize the human spirit. These are the types of systems that allow us to be joyous, sharing creatures that do the right things in the world — or usually do the right things. If other people are interacting with us in positive ways and we respect the way they feel and they respect the way we feel, if we read each other's minds correctly, then I think we have a better world. And play and laughter are a big part of that.

Questions 19–24

Do the following statements agree with information given in Reading Passage 2?

In boxes 19–24 on your answer sheet, write

TRUE	*if the statement agrees with the information*
FALSE	*if the statement contradicts the information*
NOT GIVEN	*if there is no information on this*

19. Children in hospital who watch funny shows feel less pain than those who do not.
20. Laughter can cause the blood in the body to circulate faster.
21. The psychological benefits of laughter outweigh the physical ones it brings to us.
22. Laughter is always associated with some stimulus.
23. People with brain damage usually have pathological laughter.
24. Restriction on play made some American children to do extreme things.

Questions 25–27

Complete the sentences below.

*Choose **NO MORE THAN TWO WORDS** from the passage above for each answer.*

Write your answer in boxes 25–27 on your answer sheet.

25. Play is important for developing children's personality and ______.
26. When we understand a joke and laugh, we are using a(an) ______ of our brains.
27. Play and laughter can enrich our brain as well as the ______.

READING PASSAGE 3

*You should spend about 20 minutes on **Questions 28–40**, which are based on Reading Passage 3 below.*

Tool use to crow about

Crows have an unspoken motto: Sticks and stones may break my bones, but they sure can come in handy. Two new studies unveil the ability of at least some crows to use tools in sophisticated ways, without training, to obtain food. Crows' problem-solving feats in these studies underscore a substantial intelligence that has attracted relatively little scientific attention, according to both research teams.

Scientists have previously noted tool use among members of the crow family, or corvids, including dropping stones on intruders or prey and using paper as a rake and sponge. But few birds display comparable behavior, and researchers have largely concentrated on the extensive, flexible tool practices of chimpanzees and other nonhuman primates. Evidence from apes and monkeys, as well as other large-brained, social animals such as dolphins, has debunked the traditional view that tool use is a defining human characteristic.

In one study, appearing online August 6 and in the August 25 Current Biology, zoologists Christopher Bird of the University of Cambridge in England, and Nathan Emery of Queen Mary, University of London report that captive rooks — members of the crow family — rapidly learn to use stones to obtain food on their own. The rooks dropped stones into a tube containing water in order to raise the water level and bring a floating worm within reach. This behavior recalls one of Aesop's fables, in which a thirsty crow plunked rocks into a pitcher to raise the water level high enough for a drink.

All four rooks tested used stones provided by the researchers to raise the water level. Two birds succeeded on their first try. The other two needed two tries. In all successful cases, birds put in only the number of stones needed to snatch the worm. Most of the time rooks did not begin by dropping the biggest stones into the water, but the birds quickly learned to do so. The four rooks also quickly learned not to drop stones into a tube containing sawdust with a worm on top. Although no evidence indicates that rooks use tools in the wild, the animals possess general mental abilities that they can apply to tool use, Bird and Emery propose. These include insights about physical rules, such as water in a container rising after a stone gets dropped in. In the team's view, such insight fostered the birds' success in the new study."Rooks do not use tools in the wild because they do not need to, not because they can't," Bird says. They get everything they need in their natural habitat without having to resort to devising tools.

In a comment slated to be published with Bird and Emery's study, zoologists Alex Taylor and Russell Gray, both of the University of Auckland in New Zealand, note that the birds don't have to have a plan in mind when they begin the task. The rooks in the study had already learned on their own to drop stones into a tube in order to collapse a platform inside and release food. Based on that experience, crows could have decided right away to try dropping a stone into the water-filled tube. After seeing the water rise and the worm move closer, birds would have added more stones. Other researchers reported in 2007 that, in similar fashion, orangutans collected water from a drinking container in their mouths and spat it into a tube to raise the water level so that they could snatch a peanut floating on the surface. It's unclear whether orangutans and rooks devise a mental plan before acting or simply have the capacity to notice when a random act causes food to move closer and then repeat the act, comments experimental psychologist Amanda Seed of the Max Planck Institute for Evolutionary Anthropology in Leipzig, Germany.

In a paper published online August 4 in PLoS ONE, zoologist Joanna Wimpenny of the University of Oxford in England and her colleagues report that captive New Caledonian crows can manipulate three wooden sticks, one at a time and in the correct sequence, to obtain food. Three-step tool use didn't require, but was enhanced by, earlier training with the sticks. New Caledonian crows have been shown to modify twigs and leaves to remove insects from crevices in the wild. In earlier work directed by Oxford's Alex Kacelnik, a New Caledonian crow bent or unbent strips of metal as needed to reach pieces of food. Five of seven crows in the new study managed on their own to grab an available, short stick with their beaks, use it to drag a longer stick from a transparent tube and then pull food out from another tube with the longer stick. Four crows succeeded on their first trial. Further testing showed that four crows, including one that had no prior experience with the experimental set-up, frequently used three sticks in correct sequence to obtain food. Birds used a short stick to drag a longer stick out of a tube, and used the longer stick to drag an even longer one from another tube. The birds could reach the food only with the longest stick.

Each crow committed its own pattern of errors in performing the three-tool task. Crows perceived food depth and tool length with varying degrees of accuracy, leading to a range of errors, the researchers hypothesize."Crows made errors that would not be expected if they had full knowledge of the requirements of the task and an ability to plan a complete sequence of novel actions, but critically, it was not possible to say which ability was lacking," remarks Seed.

Whatever the case, New Caledonian crows' brains can generate the mental firepower needed for tool use, Gray says. He and his colleagues have shown that New Caledonian crows have larger brains for their body size than most bird species, including other corvids. In an unpublished study, the researchers find that regions of the brain that integrate information have expanded in the New Caledonian crows. Brain evolution, and thus the emergence of a tool-using capacity, probably proceeded independently in corvids and nonhuman primates, Gray notes.

Questions 28–35

Do the following statements agree with information given in Reading Passage 3?

In boxes 28–35 on your answer sheet, write

TRUE	*if the statement agrees with the information*
FALSE	*if the statement contradicts the information*
NOT GIVEN	*if there is no information on this*

28. Crow's remarkable intelligence has been thoroughly studied in science.
29. No other birds can match the crow family in the skill of using tools.
30. Some crows displayed higher intelligence than some primates.
31. Not all the rooks succeeded in dropping the stones to catch the food.
32. The rooks could not distinguish between water and sawdust.
33. Rooks may rarely have the opportunity to use tools in the wild.
34. New Caledonian crows' brains are larger than those of other bird species.
35. Corvids and nonhuman primates might be born with the ability to use tools.

Questions 36–40

Look at the following comments and the list of researchers.

Match each comment with the correct researcher.

NB *You may use any letter more than once.*

36. Larger brain sizes may explain corvids' tool-using capacity.
37. It is not clear whether rooks had any plan in their mind before the task.
38. Rooks have the mental abilities required for tool use.
39. Crows can use wooden sticks in the correct sequence.
40. It is uncertain which factor causes crows made errors in the three-tool task.

List of Researchers

A	Bird and Emery
B	Alex Taylor
C	Russell Gray
D	Amanda Seed
E	Joanna Wimpenny
F	Alex Kacelnik

Keys:

1. H	2. F	3. A
4. E	5. B	6. G
7. D	8. T	9. NG
10. F	11. F	12. T
13. NG	14. viii	15. v
16. ii	17. vi	18. ix
19. T	20. T	21. NG
22. F	23. F	24. NG
25. social behavior	26. advanced capacity	27. human spirit
28. F	29. T	30. NG
31. F	32. F	33. T
34. NG	35. T	36. C
37. D	38. A	39. E
40. D		

4周攻克

雅思阅读周计划

第四周　雅思阅读模拟试题

星期一

模拟试题 1

READING PASSAGE 1

*You should spend about 20 minutes on **Questions 1–14**, which are based on Reading Passage 1 below.*

The Future of the Tablet Computer

The iPad, Apple's latest gadget, seems to have lived up to its maker's lofty expectations: 2m of them have been sold in two months, with more presumably to follow after the device's debut outside America on May 28th. But will the iPad's success trigger explosive growth for other sorts of "tablet" computers, a category that had previously been seen a sideshow, much as the iPhone did for smart-phones?

The answer appears to be yes, if the proliferation of tablets at Computex, a trade show held this week in Taiwan, is anything to judge by. The exhibition floor was teeming with prototypes, especially from Taiwanese firms such as Acer and Asustek. Dell, an American rival, had unveiled its offering, Streak, a few days earlier. Even Google and One Laptop per Child, a charity, have tablets in the works.

Yet the flurry of activity is deceptive. Not all the computer-makers rushing to produce tablets are convinced they will be a huge success; they are simply hedging their bets after their failure, in many cases, to predict the popularity of netbooks (no-frills laptops), which shot to success in 2008. Tellingly, most of the new devices will not hit the stores before the end of the year, if not later.

It is still unclear what people will use tablets for, says Jeff Orr of ABI Research. They are unlikely to edge out established devices such as televisions, personal computers, games consoles and smart-phones. Most buyers so far have been habitual early-adopters of new gadgets. But tablets may find a niche, he believes, as portable video players and magazine racks.

Much will depend on price. The cheapest iPad costs $499. For tablets to become a mass-market product like DVD players, analysts reckon, the price must fall to $100 at most. Some iPad clones are to be sold at this level, but they lack many of its most attractive features. Fancier tablets could become cheaper, however, if mobile-telecoms operators were to subsidise them, as they do with handsets.

This points to another barrier. To maximise their usefulness, tablets need a fast wireless-internet connection. But so far only a third of American households have Wi-Fi, reckons ABI Research. And mobile-data services are not getting cheaper, at least for heavy users. On June 2nd AT&T ditched its all-you-can-eat plan for iPads, which cost $30 a month, and replaced it with tiered rates.

What is more, tablets are less about hardware than about the software and services that run on them. Users of iPads can already download more than 5,000 applications from Apple's online store. Such variety is a distant prospect for owners of tablets powered by other operating systems, such as Google's Android. Yet the more competition there is among operating systems and devices, the more common tablets are likely to become.

Some of the most muscular players in the industry are still in the locker room. Hewlett-Packard is said to have killed the Slate, which was to be based on Microsoft's Windows, and is now reportedly working on a tablet using an operating system from Palm, the smart-phone maker that HP recently bought. Microsoft will certainly re-enter the fray, although none of its operating systems seems a good fit for tablets. Nokia, too, has yet to unveil its plans.

ABI Research thinks only 8m will be sold worldwide this year and that they will not become a mass-market device before the middle of the decade, by which time it foresees annual sales of 57m. Even this would be less than the number of netbooks expected to be sold this year. And it is not even a third of the global market for smart-phones in 2009.

But tablets may still have a big impact, argues Carolina Milanesi of Gartner, another research firm. Television-makers, for instance, may introduce more interactive features and computer-makers launch app stores in response. All very gratifying for tablet manufacturers, no doubt, but not exactly a money-spinner.

Questions 1–6

Do the following statements agree with the information given in Reading Passage 1?

In boxes 1–6 on your answer sheet, write

TRUE	*if the statement agrees with the information*
FALSE	*if the statement contradicts the information*
NOT GIVEN	*if there is no information on this*

1. The iPad has completely achieved the manufacturer's expect.
2. The iPad will be launched on May 28th in America.
3. The 'tablet' computers were regarded as the consumer's minor choice.
4. Most of the latest production will unwrap by the end of the year.
5. It's uncertain what consumer will use the new devices for.
6. It costs at least $499 to get one iPad.

Questions 7–11

Complete the summary below.

*Choose **NO MORE THAN THREE WORDS** from the passage for each answer.*

Write your answers in boxes 7–11 on your answer sheet.

For tablets to become popularity like DVD, the price must fall to $100 maximize. ___7___ copies at this level, however, they've got less features. Moreover, the tablets will lack of it's usefulness if there isn't a speedy ___8___ available. In addition, ___9___ is more important than ___10___ on use tablcts. The fans of iPad could get over ___11___ apps from the store online.

Questions 12–14

*Answer the questions below using **NO MORE THAN THREE WORDS** from the passage for each answer.*

Write your answers in boxes 12–14 on your answer sheet.

12. How many tablet will be sold all over world this year from ABI's research?
13. How much is the all-you-can-eat plan?
14. Which system is Hewlett-Packard relied on?

READING PASSAGE 2

*You should spend about 20 minutes on **Questions 15–28**, which are based on Reading Passage 2 below.*

Hard Yards

Europe's shipbuilders may break out of the doldrums before Asia's

A For those who regard the smashing of a champagne bottle as a tragic waste, the problems facing the world's shipbuilders are excellent news. It takes such a long time to construct huge ocean-going container ships, bulk carriers and oil tankers that the vast shipyards of South Korea, China and Japan will still be cracking bottles of bubbly over newly launched ships for a couple of years yet. But once these vessels, ordered in the boom before the financial crisis, are in the water, the course ahead looks rocky. Oddly, Europe's shipyards, although still storm-lashed after 30 years of low-cost competition from Asia, seem to face a slightly brighter horizon.

B Fresh orders for the world's shipyards are at a low ebb. Last year they were more than 80% lower than in 2007, when sky-high freight rates and cheery economic forecasts encouraged shipping companies to scramble for new vessels. The subsequent recession in the rich world sent shipping rates tumbling. A swift rebound is unlikely: despite more scrapping and some cancellations, hundreds of ships are poised to hit the oceans this year.

C Asia's shipyards, streamlined and efficient, concentrate on building large, standardised ships. These are the sort in greatest oversupply. South Korea's shipyards won over half of global orders for new ships in the first quarter of 2010, but they were worth just $2.2 billion. In 2008

Korean yards won orders worth $32 billion. Hyundai Heavy Industries, one of four big Korean shipbuilders, has not won a single order for a ship since late 2008.

D European shipbuilders are suffering from a dearth of new orders too. The Odense shipyard owned by A.P. Moller-Maersk, one of the world's biggest shippers, has an illustrious history: it produced the world's biggest container ship. But cheap Asian competition for this type of vessel has holed it below the waterline. It will close in 2012.

E Europe's shipmakers are turning to national governments and the European Union for help, claiming that their industry is close to collapse. In early April representatives from nine EU countries called for an emergency programme to support the industry. Shipyards want help in gaining access to credit lines and soft loans, as well as rules to promote greener ships. This would support them until shipping finance recovers and hesitant customers regain faith in the world economy.

F Yet the restructuring forced by low-cost Asian competitors has left Europe's shipyards with some advantages. Their revenues of €30 billion-40 billion ($40 billion-53 billion) a year come mainly from niche markets which are not suffering from as much overcapacity as the mainstream.

G Cruise ships are a particular speciality, and the market is growing. Four orders have been placed with European yards this year, compared with one in 2009. Ferries, another area of European dominance, are also in demand, and ageing ferry fleets in the Mediterranean are due for replacement soon. The offshore wind farms sprouting around the continent provide another opportunity. Europe's shipmakers are adept at designing cable-laying ships and other service vessels. And as oil firms are forced to drill in ever deeper waters, ships suited to the task of towing and maintaining new rigs will be needed.

H Pressure to make ships greener will also favour European shipyards. The International Maritime Organisation is discussing regulations that may force ships to belch out less carbon dioxide, and has introduced tighter limits on other pollutants. Europe leads in this type of technology, too. European shipmakers will also benefit from plans to encourage greater use of the continent's inland waterways to ship goods instead of hauling them by road. If they can weather the current storm, Europe's shipyards may yet resound again to the smashing of bottles.

Questions 15−20

Reading Passage 2 has eight paragraphs, **A−H**.

Which paragraph contains the following information?

*Write **A−H** in boxes 15−20 on your answer sheet.*

15. The dockyards' order form from all over the world is facing with crisis.
16. The rapidly recovery for this depression is improbable.
17. Asia's shipyards focus on the ships which have the call.
18. Shipyards ask for loan from governments and EU.
19. The ferries which cruise in the Mediterranean will be exchanged before long.
20. European shipyards would benefit not from water route but road transport.

Questions 21–25

Complete the table below.

*Choose **NO MORE THAN TWO WORDS** from Reading Passage 2 for each answer.*

Write your answers in boxes 21–25 on your answer sheet.

	2008	21	2010
South Korea's shipyards	$320 billion		22 of new ship's order which were worth 23
24 ship-makers		one	25

Questions 26–28

*Choose THREE letters from **A–E**.*

Which THREE of these tasks are mentioned by the writer of the text?

Write your answers in boxes 26–28 on your answer sheet.

A. European ship-makers are facing with a drawback of fresh orders.

B. European dockyards have already the support from governments.

C. European shipbuilders' income mainly depend on niche market.

D. The offshore wind farm sprouting is another chance for European dockyards.

E. Europe's shipbuilders used to design cable-lying ships and other service vessels.

READING PASSAGE 3

*You should spend about 20 minutes on **Questions 29–40**, which are based on Reading Passage 1 below.*

Last in Class

South Africa spends 6.1% of its GDP on education, a bigger chunk than most other countries, yet its results are among the worst. In the World Economic Forum's latest Global Competitive Index it ranks bottom (out of 133 countries) in both maths and science education. In the 2006 Progress in International Reading and Literacy Study it also came bottom (out of 40 countries), as it did in the 2003 Trends in International Maths and Science Study (out of 48 countries). Humiliated, it withdrew from the next TIMSS in 2007. The difficulty with such studies is that they reflect averages. At the top, South African students do as well as anyone, but the great majority are performing way below their capabilities.

Graeme Bloch of the Development Bank of Southern Africa describes South Africa's education system as a "national disaster". He reckons 80% of schools are "dysfunctional". Half of all pupils drop out before taking their final "matric" exams. Barely 11% get a good enough pass to qualify for university. Of those who do, most are found to be functionally illiterate and innumerate when they get there, requiring intensive first-year remedial classes to bring them up to scratch. A third of students drop out in their first year at university. After five years only one in three has obtained a (three-year) degree. Even then, employers say that many graduates emerge inarticulate, unable to think critically and barely able to read or write.

Black South Africans generally do much worse than whites. Almost 13% of black adults are functionally illiterate, compared with 0.4% of whites. Fewer than 2% of black adults have a degree, compared with 17% of whites (which is still low by international standards). Barely a third of black pupils pass their matric, whereas almost all whites do. And only around one in 20 black students ends up with a degree, compared with almost one in two whites. It is not that the blacks are any less bright; some perform brilliantly. They are just massively disadvantaged.

Under apartheid blacks were deliberately kept down, given a vastly inferior education and banned from most skilled jobs. Explaining the government's new Bantu (black) education policies to the Senate in 1954, Hendrik Verwoerd, then minister for native affairs, famously asked: "What is the use of teaching a Bantu child mathematics when it cannot use it in practice?" By the end of Verwoerd's decade as prime minister in 1968 the government was spending 16 times more on the education of a white child than a black one.

Spending per pupil is now the same for black and white, yet black children generally continue to fare worse than whites because most of them continue to attend vastly inferior schools. Although public education was desegregated in 1994, most former black schools remain overwhelmingly black because they are generally in deprived black areas, whereas the former white schools tend to have a good racial mix because middle-class blacks have moved into their catchment areas. Catering for just 10% of all pupils, the former white schools are usually much better endowed, better run and far more disciplined than former black schools.

Angie Motshekga, the schools minister, admits that black schools are "in crisis". Fewer than 10% have libraries or laboratories. Very few offer extracurricular activities. Most of their teachers are not properly qualified. Black schools tend to lack leadership and are often plagued by drugs, alcohol and sex abuse (by teachers as well as older boys). Their pupils generally come from poor, often broken homes. And, unlike white pupils, they are usually taught in a language (English) that is not their own, by teachers who themselves cannot speak it properly.

It often seems a miracle that black pupils make it to university at all. Most of those who do will probably have been either to one of the top 10% of black schools that do perform well, or to a former white school, or to one of the burgeoning private schools. Fees for day pupils range between 5,000 and 80,000 rand a year. But with class sizes generally half those in state schools and an average matric pass rate of 97%, compared with just 30% at state schools, even some relatively poor parents think they are worth paying for. Under apartheid few white parents bothered to send their children to private school because the state schools for whites were of such high standard. Now nearly 400,000 pupils (3% of the total) attend private schools, more than double the number in 1995. Six out of ten of them are black.

At university level black students have made similar strides. In 1994 half of South Africa's 528,000 university students were black; now two-thirds out of 800,000 are; a quarter are white. But university standards vary hugely. Jonathan Jansen, the first non-white vice-chancellor of the University of the Free State, says that at least three-quarters of South Africa's 23 higher-education establishments are "fraudulent and bad, not really universities at all". He cites exam standards being lowered to cut failure rates; students who "regularly trade their bodies" to pass their exams; others who blame their poor marks on "racist" teachers; and those who blatantly cheat and threaten to secure that piece of paper.

According to Mr Jansen, South Africa has no "great" universities, only six or seven "good" ones. One of them is the University of Cape Town, the only African university to be ranked among the world's top 200 by the Times Higher Education Supplement. Under the leadership of Max Price, UCT has introduced a controversial new entrance scheme that makes it easier for non-whites to get in. This can mean that white students have to get a matric mark some 20-30 percentage points higher than their black peers. Mr Price, who is white, admits that the system is not perfect, but at least it takes account of the huge handicap suffered by most black applicants.

Mr Zuma has vowed to make education his government's "priority number one". In speech after speech he insists that teachers and pupils must be "in school, in class, on time, learning and teaching for seven hours a day". It might seem obvious enough, but in South Africa it will require a small revolution to achieve. Mr Zuma also plans to bring back the apartheid-era's hated schools inspectors, but in future they will be called "assessors" and required to support teachers as well as criticise them. Independently monitored tests are being introduced for pupils aged nine, 12 and 15, doubtless as much to spot the incompetent teachers as the failing pupils.

Questions 29−34

Look at the following statements (Questions 29−34) and the list of people below.

*Match each statement with the correct person **A−E**.*

Write your answers in boxes 29−34 on your answer sheet.

***NB** You may use any letter more than once.*

29. He predicts that four fifth of school can't work in normal condition.
30. Mathematics should be used in daily life.
31. Acknowledges that black schools are in crunch.
32. South Africa has not a 'great' university.
33. The University of Cape Town is one of 'good' institute.
34. Recognizes that the entrance scheme is not a perfection solution.

A. Graeme Bloch
B. Hendrik Verwoerd
C. Angie Motshekga
D. Jonathan Jansen
E. Max Price

Questions 35–40

Do the following statements agree with the information given in Reading Passage 3?

In boxes 35–40 on your answer sheet, write

TRUE	*if the statement agrees with the information*
FALSE	*if the statement contradicts the information*
NOT GIVEN	*if there is no information on this*

35. The cost of education in South Africa is more than others.
36. The expression from most of the top ones is less than others.
37. Over one in tenth black schools own libraries and labs.
38. Most of black school teachers haven't got paper qualification from the respected institutes.
39. The teachers of black school can't speak English correctly themselves.
40. Three forth of South Africa's 23 higher-education are good at teaching.

Keys:

1. FALSE
2. TRUE
3. TRUE
4. TRUE
5. TRUE
6. TRUE
7. Some iPad
8. Wi-Fi / wireless-internet
9. software
10. hardware
11. 5,000
12. only 8m
13. $30 per month
14. Microsoft windows
15. B
16. B
17. C
18. E
19. G
20. G
21. 2009
22. 50% / half
23. $2.2 billion
24. Europe's
25. 4
26. A
27. C
28. D
29. B
30. D
31. F
32. I
33. I
34. I
35. TRUE
36. FALSE
37. TRUE
38. NOT GIVEN
39. TRUE
40. NOT GIVEN

星期二

模拟试题 2

READING PASSAGE 1

*You should spend about 20 minutes on **Questions 1–14**, which are based on Reading Passage 1 below.*

Questions 1–4

*Reading passage 1 has four sections, **A–D**.*
*Choose the correct heading for sections **A–D** from the list of headings below.*
*Write the correct number, **i-vi**, in boxes 1–4 on your answer sheet.*

List of Headings

i	Home of astonishing various creature
ii	Specific organisms in the deep sea
iii	Spectacular diversity of fishes
iv	Hydrothermal marvels
v	The start of deep sea exploration
vi	Seamounts and exploration

1. Section **A**
2. Section **B**
3. Section **C**
4. Section **D**

Mysteries of the Deep Sea

Section A

That makes the deep sea the largest of all habitats, but it is also one of the least hospitable. It is extremely cold, utterly dark, often low in oxygen and smothered by a pressure 1,000 times greater than at the surface—so immense it alters biochemistry.

Despite these obstacles to life — and the fact that even in the best-known regions, we have sampled less than 1% of the seafloor — we are now beginning to realise the deep is home to a spectacular diversity of organisms.

Section B

The bizarre inhabitants of the deep include: deep water sharks; devilish-looking dragonfish, that fire beams of red illumination from "lamps" under their eyes; many bioluminescent fish; ancient coelacanths; creeping sea lilies; blood-red squid; an octopus with glow-in-the-dark suckers; bell-shaped, metre-wide jellyfish, snails with armour-plated feet and a deadly jellyfish relative that uses fluorescent tentacles to lure prey.

Perhaps the most dramatic creature is the 13-metre-long giant squid, Architeuthis (recently captured live on film for the first time) and the even more fearsome 15-metre-long colossal squid, never seen alive. Sperm whales and Antarctic sleeper sharks are the only animals equipped to take on these deep-sea prey.

Life is also found in the form of bacteria, worms and crustaceans, which teem in the abyssal plains that cover vast stretches of the deep. They feed off organic "snow" that falls from above. Deep below the sea floor, life was not thought to be possible. But then in 2003 researchers found many unique bacteria in sediments 300m beneath the Pacific seafloor, feeding on sediments millions of years old.

More spectacular are the deep-sea corals, found at depths of up to 6,000m in waters as cold as 2℃. Despite this, they rival their tropical, shallow-water cousins in splendour. These slow-growing animals are now found from Ireland to New Zealand, and have even been discovered growing on the legs of oil rigs. But, it is only as destructive fishing practices, such as trawling, have started to destroy them that the realisation of how widespread they are has dawned. The largest known, near Norway, covers 100 square kilometres, yet was discovered only in 2002.

Section C

In some places, life is found in an extraordinary abundance. One of the most fascinating deep-sea ecosystems are found around hydrothermal vents, where superheated water, rich in chemicals, spews from volcanically active mid-ocean ridges. Here, bacteria feeding on methane and sulphides support large communities of animals including giant clams, bizarre fish, and massive tube worms up 2m in length, such as *Riftia pachyptila*.

Photosynthetic bacteria which harvest the vents' faint glow have even been discovered, while others can thrive in water hotter than 121℃. These vents are often isolated, and spinning plumes of water may break off like flying saucers, carrying bacteria to other vents.

These vents, known as "black smokers", were first discovered in 1977 using the US submersible ALVIN. The discovery of an entire ecosystem 2,000m down, that did not depend on photosynthesis, revolutionised our view of life. We now know these ecosystems are commonly found from Scandinavia to the Pacific Ocean. They occur along the mid-ocean ridge system, from relatively shallow water to as deep as several kilometres.

Some even believe that life on Earth may have begun at these vents, which can be up to 60m in height. Others think similar geological features could harbour life in frozen lakes on Earth and on other planets and moons, such as Mars or Europa.

Hydrothermal vents are not the only oases of life on the deep sea floor. In 1984, biologists discovered cold seeps. These are places where chemical-rich water oozes from the seafloor, supporting an abundance of life. They are usually found around the edges of continents.

Another rich community of organisms thrives on massive whale carcasses that settle on the sea floor and decay over many decades. "Whale falls", weighing up to 160 tonnes, can nourish over 400 species from hagfish and sharks to bone-eating zombie worms and sulphide loving bacteria.

Section D

Then there are seamounts, the peaks of undersea volcanic mountains. These are the submarine equivalent of islands, with as many as half the species on some seamounts seemingly unique to that location.

Although there is heavy fishing around many of the 100,000 large seamounts in the oceans, we have detailed knowledge of only a few, making them ripe for expeditions to discover new biological riches. The biggest underwater mountain range is formed from mid-ocean ridges and stretches for 70,000 kilometres around the planet.

Deep sea exploration began in the 1930s, when US oceanographers descended 1 000m down in a tethered steel ball. In the 1960s the Swiss Bathyscaphe descended 11 kilometres down into the Marianas trench off the Phillipines-the deepest place on the planet. Since then, no person has ventured so deep.

But a new generation of submersible technologies is helping uncover the mysteries of the deep. These include: Kaiko, the Japanese remotely operated vehicle (ROV) that made it to the bottom of Marianas Trench in 1995, but was later lost; a new replacement for ALVIN, due for release in 2009, which will be able to access 99% of the seafloor; several underwater vehicles that fly more like jet fighters than submarines; a network of robot subs and autonomous labs on the seabed and other subs that are streamlined and fin-less, built from concrete, or swim like a fish.

Questions 5－10

Complete the table below.

Choose ***NO MORE THAN TWO WORDS*** *from Reading Passage 1 for each answer.*

Write your answers in boxes 5－10 on your answer sheet.

	species	features
bizarre inhabitants	devilish-looking __5__	fire beams of red illumination from 'lamps' under their eyes
dramatic creature	13-meter-long __6__ squid, Architeuthis and 15-meter-long __7__	difficult to seen alive
life in the form of bacteria	__8__ and __9__	teem in the abyssal plains
deep-sea corals	deep-sea corals	spotted at depths of up to __10__ in waters

Questions 11–14

Answer the questions 11–14 below using ***NO MORE THAN TWO WORDS*** *from the passage for each answer.*

Write your answers in boxes 11–14 on your answer sheet.

11. What does bacteria feed on?
12. When did ALVIN find "black smokers"?
13. When did the search of deep sea undertake?
14. What did biologists find in 1984?

READING PASSAGE 2

You should spend about 20 minutes on ***Questions 15–27****, which are based on Reading Passage 2 below.*

Virtual Prisons

how e-maps are curtailing our freedom

A Electronic maps are arguably the quintessential innovation of 20th-century cartography. Although a few academic cartographers accord the map mystical powers, it is merely a tool, useful for good, evil or both, which citizens can resist or constrain-up to a point. The question is not whether e-maps will restrict where we go and what we do, but to what extent.

B What I call "restrictive cartography" is not in itself new. Property maps are at least as old as Roman times, and boundary maps no younger than kingdoms and nation states. What is new, however, is the substantial increase in both the number and diversity of restrictive maps. A comparison of mapping in 1900 and 2000 underscores my point.

C Since 1900, we have used maps to exclude industry from residential neighbourhoods, ban new construction on floodplains, help delineate "historic" districts that constrain a homeowner's choice of paint colour or replacement windows, put limits on where and with what weapons we can hunt game, restrict travel by foreign diplomats and journalists, prevent sex offenders from living near schools and playgrounds, and keep aircraft a nautical mile away from a vice-president's weekend retreat.

D The public tolerates these cartographic restrictions because many, if not most, are not only benign but essential. Environmental protection, for instance, relies on mapping as a regulatory instrument to safeguard water resources and wildlife habitat. Maps delineating rights of way for gas lines and other underground facilities guard against accidental breaches by a digger arm, at least by conscientious contractors. "Call before you dig" is a mantra of restrictive cartography. Property maps show rights of way that might thwart a buyer's plan to enlarge a home or re-configure an access road, and maps of quarantine areas aimed at farmers stem the spread of fruit-fly infestations. Government officials publish restrictive maps because they assume the boundaries will be heeded.

E In 2010, however, restrictive cartography is on the verge of more invasive applications as electronic technology replaces graphic lines requiring conscious interpretation with invisible fences, erected by proactive, self-enforcing geographical restrictions.

F The most impressive examples, and the most frightening, reflect the integration of geographical information systems (GIS), the Global Positioning System (GPS), and wireless telecommunications. A tracking device can instantly report its location to a GIS that determines whether the person, car or ship under surveillance has entered a prohibited area. Depending on circumstances and severity, a future system might be able to debit an offender's bank account, transmit a vocal warning or electronic pinch, notify the police or military, disable an engine, or even release a soporific drug into the violator's bloodstream.

G Electronic tagging and tracking on an unprecedented level is virtually certain, and could happen very soon. Motorists who appreciate the convenience of paying road tolls and parking fees automatically are unlikely to resist mandatory RFID tags—what's the use if electronic scanners can collect the same information from licence plates or bar-coded registration stickers? Electronic tracking makes it easy to limit access to congested areas and keep heavy trucks off residential streets, while adding a transponder that reports location enables automatic enforcement of traffic regulations. Smart algorithms are likely to be built into the software controlling the transponders, which could detect erratic driving characteristic of drunkenness or aggression, perhaps. Minimal resistance to cameras mounted above traffic lights attests to creeping acquiescence.

H Because the public is willing to trade control over their lives for convenience, the cellphone already doubles as a tracking device, and raises the possibility of "spatial micromanagement": of employees by employers, of children by parents, of elderly parents by grown children, and of suspected subversives by the authorities. Meanwhile, strategies for encouraging cooperation include GPS wristwatches, security badges, ankle bracelets and even subdermal chips.

I Threats to privacy and personal freedom are well known and obvious. In the spring 2003 issue of the *IEEE Technology and Society Magazine*, geographers Jerome Dobson and Peter Fisher warned of "geoslavery" by obsessive husbands or boyfriends, poised to punish perceived transgressions.

J The fact that geospatial tracking might be equally efficient for enforcing restraining orders on those who abuse their partners underscores an inherent ambiguity that impels acceptance, especially in the name of public safety or national defence. If the tracking of sex offenders, stalkers and people with Alzheimer's is acceptable, why not the tracking of thieves and drunk drivers?

K Once in place, a national geospatial surveillance administration can accommodate an ever-wider variety of electronic boundary lines, and offer disgruntled taxpayers an alternative to costly incarceration. For many crimes, an electronic map makes more sense than a prison, which may well only reinforce antisocial behaviour and allow criminals to exchange tricks of the trade.

L Efficient, but hardly fail-safe. Electronic cartography is vulnerable to incompetent technicians, malevolent hackers, cyber-terrorists and lobbyists for "special interests". Like traditional maps, e-cartography invites manipulation by government or corporations, often in the guise of national defence or free-market capitalism. While maps on the internet can advertise prohibitions and justify new delineations, this apparent openness is easily compromised. Particularly portentous is the way online mapping blurs details presumed useful to saboteurs but which are in fact easily viewable, after a little research, elsewhere on the internet.

M Boundaries developed for one purpose are too easily adopted for another, as when postal codes (designed merely to speed up mail delivery) are used to set rates for car insurance.

N More troubling are the incongruities that might arise from mixing maps compiled from different sources. For example, it's risky to transfer boundaries from a detailed property survey onto a generalised highway map on which curves have been smoothed out or symbols shifted to avoid clutter.

O And consider the electronic maritime navigation system that combines satellite positioning with a visual display derived from conventional, less geographically precise maps: quite likely the maps scanned into the system were made by hydrographers who had a less accurate sense of where they were than the 21st-century mariner's GPS. Although a skipper might snicker when a screen shows the ship on the beach when it's clearly offshore, only a fool would surrender all control to an electronic navigator.

P But it would be a mistake to portray this new brand of restrictive mapping as Orwellian: it is a natural part of social, political and cartographic evolution. In the end, then, we must hope that fear of litigation or other pragmatic issues may prove more influential than concerns over privacy in limiting the growth of restrictive cartography in an electronic age. We shall see.

Questions 15–20

Reading passage 2 has sixteen paragraphs, **A–P**.

Which paragraph contains the following information?

Write the correct letter, ***A–P****, in boxes 15–20 on your answer sheet.*

15. The electronic maritime navigation system consists of satellite positioning and traditional visual display.

16. An description of the discord which from mixing maps complied from distinct sources.
17. E-cartography was dominated by government as same as conventional maps.
18. It's not difficult to keep heavy trucks off residential streets for electronic tracking.
19. The location be reported by tracking device to GIS.
20. The new significant improve of "restrictive cartography" are number and diversity about restrictive maps.

Questions 21−27

Do the following statements agree with the information given in Reading Passage 2?

In boxes 21−27 on your answer sheet, write

TRUE	*if the statement agrees with the information*
FALSE	*if the statement contradicts the information*
NOT GIVEN	*if there is no information on this*

21. The typically invention of electronic maps was regarded as a dispute one.
22. Property maps are more necessary than boundary maps.
23. The public endure restrictions for begin and essential.
24. The heyday of electronic tagging and tracking is virtually certain.
25. The public is eager to management their lives for facility.
26. The tracking device threats to privacy.
27. Electronic cartography is insensitive to incompetent technicians.

READING PASSAGE 3

*You should spend about 20 minutes on **Questions 28−40**, which are based on Reading Passage 3 below.*

A Quantum Hop

Not a leap, perhaps, but two important steps on the way to making quantum computing practical

A Some technologies seem a long time coming. Their story has a familiar script: a breakthrough is hailed; overblown expectations are aroused; disappointment follows. Away from the public's impatient gaze, however, tinkering scientists turn out incremental improvements, furtively catching up with the revolutionary rhetoric of yore. This appears to have been the case with the sequencing of the human genome. It also illustrates the recent history of quantum computing.

B An ordinary computer stores and processes information using bits, which take the value of either one or zero (physically represented by different voltages of electric current). In the bizarre world of quantum mechanics, however, subatomic particles can exist in several states at once. Such "superposition" means, for instance, that the property of an electron known as its spin can be not only "up" (representing, say, one) or "down" (representing zero) but also some combination of the two. In quantum computing, such superposed values are named qubits.

C Additional qubits can be added by a process called entanglement. Each extra entangled qubit doubles the number of parallel operations that can be carried out. A three-qubit device could run eight operations, a four-qubit system 16, and so on. At least in theory. In practice the results so far have been disappointing. Experimental quantum computers require exotic materials and work only at a tad above absolute zero. But the latest incremental improvement may help lift the field out of the slough of despond. First, it does its computing in silicon—the workhorse of more familiar computers. Second, it does it at the balmy temperature of −269°C, or four degrees above absolute zero.

D The magicians who have pulled off this double trick are Thornton Greenland of University College, London, and his colleagues. As they describe in this week's *Nature*, they first doped the silicon with phosphorus atoms. They then used a short, high-intensity pulse from a fancy laser to jolt electrons orbiting those phosphorus atoms into what is known as a Rydberg state.

E In this state, each atom's quantum wave-function—its effective size—extends several billionths of a metre from its nucleus. That is huge in atomic terms, and permits the entanglement of atoms that would normally be too far apart to interact. This, in turn, means they can become collaborative qubits.

F Once their wave-functions had been expanded, the atoms were zapped again, inducing them to emit a controlled burst of light called a photon echo. This would be used to read out the result of any calculation the system had performed.

G The result is something that could, in principle, do calculations and spit out the answers—and which could be made industrially using the sort of equipment that turns out conventional chips. That it works at four degrees above absolute zero is a bonus. It might sound pretty chilly, but it is a temperature that can be maintained fairly easily using liquid helium, which boils at 4.22 degrees above absolute zero.

H Dr Greenland's discovery, then, brings practical quantum calculation closer. And a second paper in *Nature*, by Morgan Hedges, of the Australian National University in Canberra, and his colleagues, has advanced another aspect of the field by describing a type of quantum memory that uses light.

I Atoms and electrons are not the only particles that can get entangled. Photons, the particles of light, are also susceptible. If they could be integrated into the world of quantum computing, that would help with the transfer of qubits from place to place. The problem with light, though, is its speed. However handy its high velocity is for whizzing information over great distances through optical fibres, it is unhelpful if any calculating has to be done. For that to happen light needs to be pinned down.

J In 2008 Hugues de Riedmatten of the University of Geneva and his team managed to do that. They built what was, in essence, an echo chamber on a chip and held a single photon there for a microsecond (a period when that photon would normally have expected to cover about 300 metres).

K Dr Hedges's echo chamber did considerably better than that. By using such exotic materials as yttrium orthosilicate crystals and praseodymium ions it trapped photons in bunches of as many as 500 at a time. It was also good at preserving entanglement, increasing the amount of quantum information it could hold without being corrupted or destroyed to a level that might be practically useful.

L Sadly, the developments of Dr Greenland and Dr Hedges do not spell supermarket shelves stacked with quantum PCs any time soon. They do mean, though, that the tinkerers have more to tinker with—and that, ultimately, is how new technologies really develop.

Questions 28−33

Reading passage 3 has twelve paragraphs, **A−L**.

Which paragraph contains the following information?

*Write the correct letter, **A−L**, in boxes 28−33 on your answer sheet.*

***NB** You may use any letter more than once.*

28. Entanglement makes qubits increase.
29. Subatomic particles can exist in several states at the some time in quantum mechanics field.
30. We can use a photon echo to read out the result of any calculation the system had performed.
31. The echo chamber was introduced by Hugues de Riedmatten.
32. Speed of light is still a difficult problem.
33. The description of qubits.

Questions 34−40

Do the following statements agree with the claims of the writer in Reading Passage 3?

In boxes 34−40 on your answer sheet, write

YES	*if the statement agree with the claims of the writer*
NO	*if the statement contradicts the claims of the writer*
NOT GIVEN	*if it is impossible to say what the writer thinks about this*

34. Bits takes the value of either 1 or 0.
35. A 3-qubit device could work 16 operations.
36. Entanglement performed badly in practice.
37. Experimental quantum computer operates solely at a tab above absolute zero.
38. The photo echo principle has already turned out to be industrial product.
39. The echo chamber could trap photons as many as 500 at a time.
40. Dr Greenland and Dr Hedges will give another developments soon.

Keys:

1. i	2. ii
3. iv	4. vi
5. dragonfish	6. giant
7. colossal squid	8. worms
9. crustaceans	10. 2℃
11. sediments	12. 1977
13. 1930s	14. cold seeps
15. O	16. N
17. L	18. G
19. F	20. B
21. TRUE	22. NOT GIVEN
23. FALSE	24. TRUE
25. TRUE	26. TRUE
27. FALSE	28. C
29. B	30. F
31. J	32. D
33. B	34. YES
35. NO	36. YES
37. YES	38. NO
39. NO	40. NOT GIVEN

星期三

模拟试题 3

READING PASSAGE 1

You should spend about 20 minutes on ***Questions 1–12****, which are based on Reading Passage 1 below.*

Questions 1–5

Reading passage 1 has six paragraphs, ***A–F****.*
Choose the correct heading for sections ***A–F*** *from the list of headings below.*
Write the correct number, ***i-ix****, in boxes 1–5 on your answer sheet.*

List of Headings

i	Lasers could be used to zap mosquitoes.
ii	The military use.
iii	Photonic mosquito fence.
iv	Focus on Anopheles Gambiae.
v	Imagine of the search.
vi	A simpler approach.
vii	Detail of Dr Marka's study.
viii	Spent of Dr Marka's research.
ix	Malaria cancan kill a million children per year.

1. Paragraph **A**
2. Paragraph **B**
3. Paragraph **C**
4. Paragraph **D**
5. Paragraph **E**

Example	*Answer*
Paragraph **F**	**vii**

Illustration by Belle Mellor

Zap!

A Towards the end of the cold war Ronald Reagan announced plans to use powerful lasers to shoot down any incoming intercontinental ballistic missiles that the Soviet Union aimed at America. The lasers were real but the plan was fanciful. Scientists now propose a more modest system, aimed at insects rather than nuclear warheads. They think lasers could be used to zap the mosquitoes that carry malaria, a disease which kills more than a million people each year, most of them children, and debilitates hundreds of millions more.

B Researchers at Intellectual Ventures, an innovations company established by former Microsoft executives in Bellevue, Washington, have developed what they call a photonic mosquito fence. It has a series of posts, each of which is equipped with a cheap camera and a light bulb (which will be swapped for a light-emitting diode in future versions). The cameras are connected to a central computer. When a camera detects movement, the computer analyses it to see whether it is consistent with the behaviour of a mosquito. If it is, then the computer trains a laser onto the insect and blasts it into oblivion.

C Jordin Kare, an astrophysicist and a former scientist on the missile-defence programme, leads the effort. He says it is possible to detect different species of mosquito because their wings beat with a distinctive frequency. He is aiming for *Anopheles gambiae*, the species most effective at spreading plasmodium, the parasite that causes malaria, when it bites people to feed on their blood.

D Dr Kare imagines that the mosquito fence will be set up around a hospital or a village in a malarial area. His experiments with prototypes have shown that posts spaced 100 metres apart work best. The lasers would target only mosquitoes, although Dr Kare says some work still needs to be done to ensure that the laser is safe for people and animals. Although he will not give an exact figure, Dr Kare says he built his prototype from parts bought at surplus stores and on eBay, and has calculated that the cost will be comparable to that of supplying all the inhabitants of a medium-sized village with bed nets.

E Another, somewhat simpler, approach is being developed by Szabolcs Marka, an astrophysicist, and his colleagues at Columbia University in New York. Dr Marka has created a curtain of invisible light that mosquitoes cannot penetrate. He uses a common diode laser, a simple lens and a power supply to generate an infra-red barrier that can cover a door or window. Mosquitoes are very sensitive to heat and light (indeed, their sensitivity to infra-red radiation helps them sense the presence of food, in the form of people). The idea is that when a mosquito encounters the infra-red curtain, its senses are overwhelmed and it flies away. Tests have shown that the curtain kills some mosquitoes that fly into it.

F Even if a mosquito somehow managed to penetrate such a barrier, a second light curtain set up around a bed, for example, would provide further protection. Dr Marka envisages two or three light curtains in a home: one at the door, one around a sleeping person and one surrounding the area in which mosquitoes typically hide (under the thatched roof of a hut, for example). Dr Marka calculates that if there is a 6% chance that a mosquito will penetrate a light curtain, and a hut contains four curtains, then only one in 100,000 mosquitoes will be able to spread malaria. Dr Marka, whose research is funded by the Gates Foundation, says that a prototype of his machine costs a little over $100.

Questions 6–8

*Choose the correct letter, **A**, **B**, **C** or **D**.*

Write the correct letter in boxes 6–8 on your answer sheet.

6. Which following statement is not tune about photonic mosquito fence?
   a. It has a series of posts.
   b. Each post has a camera.
   c. It has a central computer.
   d. Each post has a light bulb.

7. Which description about Dr Kare is not mentioned?
   a. Astrophysicist.
   b. Former scientist.
   c. Has carried out the research.
   d. Studys on Anopheles gambiae.

8. Which one is not true about Dr. Marka?
   a. Astrophysicist.
   b. Experiments with prototypes.
   c. Invents a curtain of invisible light.
   d. Was funded by the Gates Foundation.

Questions 9–12

Do the following statements agree with the information given in Reading Passage 1?

In boxes 9–12 on your answer sheet, write

TRUE	*if the statement agrees with the information*
FALSE	*if the statement contradicts the information*
NOT GIVEN	*if there is no information on this*

9. The intercontinental ballistic missiles has been shot down by powerful lasers.
10. More than a million people were killed by the mosquitoes that carry malaria.

11. Anopheles gambiae is more likely causes malaria than other ones.
12. A prototype of Makra's machine costs a little over $100.

READING PASSAGE 2

*You should spend about 20 minutes on **Questions 13−26**, which are based on Reading Passage 2 below.*

True-bluefin

A During May and June, when the mighty bluefin tuna returns to the Mediterranean to spawn, fishermen arrive from all over the world to catch it. In days gone by, the fish were netted and killed on the spot. Now, in high-tech operations involving divers and video cameras, they are transferred from the nets into "farms"—arrays of cages anchored to the sea floor from Spain to Malta, to be fattened up. Then, come October, they are sold to Japanese boats, killed, frozen and shipped to Japan.

B It is a lucrative arrangement. Anthony Grupetta, the director general of agriculture and fisheries regulation in Malta, says that in those few months most farmers can increase the weight of a wild-caught bluefin by 27-30%. (He claims the Maltese farms do better than this, but does not say exactly how much better.) The cages do not cost much, and the fish fed to a tuna are worth a lot less than the added kilos of tuna-meat that result. What is more, Japanese buyers prefer fish raised this way. They say the quality of the meat from a bluefin killed straight after being caught is less tasty, as the fish has been stressed.

C Charlie Azzopardi, the managing director of Azzopardi Fisheries, which runs two of Malta's seven farms, brought the idea of raising caged bluefin to Malta ten years ago, after seeing it done in Spain and Australia. According to Mr. Azzopardi the bluefin industry now generates about 1.5% of Malta's GDP. Japanese freezer boats take 95% of his production. The other 5% is sold fresh, to order, at all times of year. It can be a precarious business, though. A collapse in demand meant the price of bluefin fell by 40% last year and Mr. Azzopardi chose to keep his fish on the farm until prices improved. On the supply side, fishermen complain that the size of the bluefin they are catching has plummeted in recent years. That reduction in individual size could be the result of a reduction in the tuna population that is causing fewer fish to reach maturity.

D Mr. Azzopardi says that despite the warnings from scientists, he does not believe the numbers of wild fish are falling. A number of green groups disagree, and believe that the quota allowed for fishing in these parts is far too high. One activist group, Greenpeace, has attempted to take matters into its own hands and has made several attacks on legal tuna-fishing operations over the past few weeks.

E Things might be better for the bluefin if it were possible to breed them in captivity, as well as raising them there. Though they call it farming, what Mr. Azzopardi and his competitors are engaged in is actually more like ranching. Real husbandry nurtures animals from birth to death rather than just fattening up wild-caught individuals. That could bring economic benefits. It would also, some people think, take the pressure off wild stocks.

F Clean Seas Tuna, an Australian company, has been working on the idea of farming bluefins for more than a decade, and seems to have made some progress. Last year it posted a video on YouTube showing baby southern bluefin that it had bred.

G But there is more to farming than just breeding. A recurring problem for tuna-rearers is "spooking and walling". Alex Mühlhölzl of Oceanic Tuna, a company based in Scotland which also claims to be able to breed bluefin, explains that the fish are easily frightened. In the sea, there are no walls and a frightened fish's best escape is to swim off very fast indeed in whatever direction takes its fancy. In tanks and cages, however, this is a bad—often fatal—strategy.

H Another argument against both ranching and farming is that the tuna still have to be fed, and that means with other fish caught from the wild. But this could change. In the case of salmon, a carnivorous species that is now farmed routinely, it has proved possible to mix veggies and other sources of protein into the fish's chow. The fish content of salmon food has been reduced from 70% in 1972 to around 20% today, says Kjell Bjordal, the head of Ewos, a Norwegian fish-food company.

I Feeding has also become more efficient. Mr. Bjordal says that for salmon the conversion rate—the number of kilos of food needed for a gain of one kilo of body weight—is now almost 1.1:1. For tuna it can be as bad as 6:1. But that is where salmon farming was 35 years ago, so there is plenty of scope for improvement.

J If bluefin could be farmed routinely, it might bring the price down, relieving pressure on wild stocks, as happened with salmon. That would be a boon to the hungry consumer. It would also be a boon to the species itself, though—again, as with salmon—the wild animal might become a premium product in its own right.

Questions 13–18

Reading passage 2 has ten paragraphs, **A–J**.

Which paragraph contains the following information?

*Write the correct letter, **A–J**, in boxes 13–18 on your answer sheet.*

***NB** You may use any letter more than once.*

13\. Cut the price of bluefin down will relief pressure on wild stocks, if it could be farmed routinely.

14\. The fish content of salmon food has been sharply decline these years.

15\. It has been proved possible to mix veggies and other sources of protein into fish's chow.

16\. Feeding in tanks and cages will cost Tuna's life.

17\. Clean seas Tuna has made distinct progress last ten years.

18\. Greenpeace has made several attacks on legal Tuna-fishing works.

Questions 19-26

Do the following statements agree with the information given in Reading Passage 2?

In boxes 19-26 on your answer sheet, write

TRUE	*if the statement agrees with the information*
FALSE	*if the statement contradicts the information*
NOT GIVEN	*if there is no information on this*

19. Fisherman from global gathered in Mediterranean to catch bluefin tuna.
20. Japanese boats ship bluefin tuna to Japan all the year.
21. Most fisherman can improve the weight of bluefin in 27-30% in few months.
22. Japanese buyers prefer fish which artificial feeding.
23. The price of bluefin fell by four tenth for a booming in demand.
24. Downsize bluefin link with reduction in population.
25. The bluefin industry now operates 1.5 percent of Malta's GDP.
26. Bluefin industry is a steady business.

READING PASSAGE 3

*You should spend about 20 minutes on **Questions 27-40**, which are based on Reading Passage 3 below.*

Medicine Goes Digital

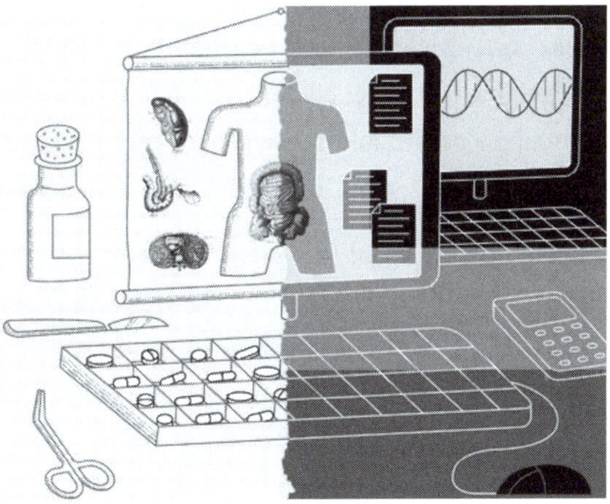

Innovation and medicine go together. The ancient Egyptians are thought to have performed surgery back in 2750BC, and the Romans developed medical tools such as forceps and surgical needles. In modern times medicine has been transformed by waves of discovery that have brought marvels like antibiotics, vaccines and heart stents.

Given its history of innovation, the health-care sector has been surprisingly reluctant to embrace information technology (IT). Whereas every other big industry has computerised with gusto since the 1980s, doctors in most parts of the world still work mainly with pen and paper.

But now, in fits and starts, medicine is at long last catching up. As this special report will explain, it is likely to be transformed by the introduction of electronic health records that can be turned into searchable medical databases, providing a "smart grid" for medicine that will not only improve clinical practice but also help to revive drugs research. Developing countries are already using mobile phones to put a doctor into patients' pockets. Devices and diagnostics are also going digital, advancing such long-heralded ideas as telemedicine, personal medical devices for the home and smart pills.

The first technological revolution in modern biology started when James Watson and Francis Crick described the structure of DNA half a century ago. That established the fields of molecular and cell biology, the basis of the biotechnology industry. The sequencing of the human genome nearly a decade ago set off a second revolution which has started to illuminate the origins of diseases.

The Great Convergence

Now the industry is convinced that a third revolution is under way: the convergence of biology and engineering. A recent report from the Massachusetts Institute of Technology (MIT) says that physical sciences have already been transformed by their adoption of information technology, advanced materials, imaging, nanotechnology and sophisticated modelling and simulation. Phillip Sharp, a Nobel prize-winner at that university, believes that those tools are about to be brought to bear on biology too.

Robert Langer, a biochemist at MIT who holds over 500 patents in biotechnology and medical technologies and has started or advised more than 100 new companies, thinks innovation in medical technologies is about to take off. Menno Prins of Philips, a Dutch multinational with a big medical-technology division, explains that, "like chemistry before it, biology is moving from a world of alchemy and ignorance to becoming a predictable, repeatable science." Ajay Royyuru of IBM, an IT giant, argues that "it's the transformation of biology into an information science from a discovery science."

This special report will ask how much of this grand vision is likely to become reality. Some of the industry's optimism appears to be well-founded. As the rich world gets older and sicker and the poor world gets wealthier and fatter, the market for medical innovations of all kinds is bound to grow. Clever technology can help solve two big problems in health care: overspending in the rich world and under-provisioning in the poor world.

But the chances are that this will take time, and turn out to be more of a reformation than a revolution. The hidebound health-care systems of the rich world may resist new technologies even as poor countries leapfrog ahead. There is already a backlash against genomics, which has been oversold to consumers as a deterministic science. And given soaring health-care costs, insurers and health systems may not want to adopt new technologies unless inventors can show conclusively that they will produce better outcomes and offer value for money.

If these obstacles can be overcome, then the biggest winner will be the patient. In the past medicine has taken a paternalistic stance, with the all-knowing physician dispensing wisdom from on high, but that is becoming increasingly untenable. Digitisation promises to connect doctors not only to everything they need to know about their patients but also to other doctors who have treated similar disorders.

The coming convergence of biology and engineering will be led by information technologies, which in medicine means the digitisation of medical records and the establishment of an intelligent network for sharing those records. That essential reform will enable many other big technological changes to be introduced.

Just as important, it can make that information available to the patients too, empowering them to play a bigger part in managing their own health affairs. This is controversial, and with good reason. Many doctors, and some patients, reckon they lack the knowledge to make informed decisions. But patients actually know a great deal about many diseases, especially chronic ones like diabetes and heart problems with which they often live for many years. The best way to deal with those is for individuals to take more responsibility for their own health and prevent problems before they require costly hospital visits. That means putting electronic health records directly into patients' hands.

Questions 27−32

From the information in the text, indicate who first invented or used the items in the list below.
Write the appropriate letter ***A, B*** *or* ***C*** *in boxes 27− 32 on your answer sheet.*
NB *You may use any letter more than once.*

A. Ancient Egypt
B. Roman
C. Modern times

27. Antibiotics
28. Heart stents
29. Surgery
30. Forceps
31. Surgical needles
32. Vaccines

Questions 33−39

Complete the summary below.
Choose ***NO MORE THAN THREE WORDS*** *from the passage for each answer.*
Write your answers in boxes 33− 39 on your answer sheet.

The first technological revolution in modern biology started with described the __33__ almost 50 years ago. Nearly ten years ago set out the __34__ which begin to light up the __35__. Till now, the __36__ is convinced that a third revolution that the __37__ and __38__, it will be led by __39__.

Questions 40

*Choose the correct letter, **A**, **B**, **C** or **D**.*

Write the correct letter in boxes 40 on your answer sheet.

40. Which of the following is the most suitable title for paragraph ?
    A. The great revolution.
    B. The great convergence.
    C. The great future.
    D. The great improvement.

Keys:

1. i
2. iii
3. iv
4. v
5. vi
6. C
7. C
8. B
9. FALSE
10. TRUE
11. NOT GIVEN
12. NOT GIVEN
13. I
14. H
15. H
16. G
17. F
18. D
19. TRUE
20. FALSE
21. NOT GIVEN
22. TRUE
23. FALSE
24. TRUE
25. NOT GIVEN
26. FALSE
27. C
28. C
29. A
30. B
31. B
32. C
33. structure of DNA
34. second revolution
35. origins of diseases
36. industry
37. convergence of biology
38. engineering
39. information technologies
40. B

星期四

模拟试题 4

READING PASSAGE 1

*You should spend about 20 minutes on **Questions 1-15**, which are based on Reading Passage 1 below.*

The Line of Beauty

A Who was the first modern artist? How about Giorgione? A far-fetched notion, perhaps, but this Renaissance Venetian revolutionised painting—and his work, focusing on secular subjects such as nudes, landscapes and female beauty, was dubbed "modern" by the leading art commentator of the day, Vasari.

B Giorgione was not alone, as illustrated by the excellent catalogue accompanying the exhibition "Bellini, Giorgione, Titian, and the Renaissance of Venetian Painting" now showing at the National Gallery of Art in Washington, DC. What made him, and the generation of artists he inspired, so special was his ability to absorb the new currents of culture then flowing through Venice. A catalyst was Leonardo da Vinci, who briefly visited Venice in 1500. In Leonardo's drawings, Giorgione, as well as the younger artist, Titian, and their master, Giovanni Bellini, glimpsed a new conception of the human form, based on observation and expressed in smoky contours and subtle shades of light and dark.

C Over the subsequent 30 years, one of the most exciting periods in the history of art unfolded. In readable, engaging essays, David Brown and Sylvia Ferino-Pagden, the exhibition's curators, together with a team of top scholars, tell its story. We learn how this triumvirate of Venetian painters devoured not only Leonardo's ideas, but also those of Albrecht Dürer, the German artist whose realistic rendering of nature was known in Venice through prints, even before his sojourn there in 1506-7. Dürer's work taught Venetian artists that landscape could be an independent element of a painting, rather than just a symbolic backdrop for religious subjects.

D The result was a new style full of natural movement, sensuality and poetic atmosphere. Venetian painting had long been characterised by its jewel-like colour—obtained by grinding coloured glass and minerals such as lapis lazuli into the pigments—but now it was applied in a way that gave art the kiss of life.

E Giorgione blazed the trail. A top student of Bellini, he later forged his own style, inspired by the current vogue for pastoral love poetry based on recently discovered ancient texts, then the bestsellers of Venice's flourishing printing industry. He excelled at what was known among the educated elite as the paragone: a competition between painting and poetry in which painters sought to prove that they could rival poets in conveying beauty by appealing to the eyes, as well as to the mind. This was revolutionary because it implied that painting originated in the imagination of the artist, rather than being a simple recording of the great and the good, history and religion. It proved painters were creators and not just craftsmen.

F His most enigmatic paintings, such as "The Tempest" and "The Three Philosophers", have no obvious subject. Instead they evoke a series of allegorical meanings that would have mystified all but his coterie of young, aristocratic patrons. Giorgione's work displays an unprecedented feeling for landscape as a poetic and erotic space, where mortals and muses play. Even in religious paintings, such as his famous "Adoration of the Shepherds", he emphasises the pastoral nature of the scene by placing the shepherds centre-stage and shifting the Christ Child to the side, something never before seen in art.

G Giorgione gained an almost cult status after his tragically early death of the plague in 1510, aged 33. Hot on his heels came the ambitious Titian, who had graduated from Bellini's workshop around 1506 and become a student of Giorgione's. He finished Giorgione's "Sleeping Venus", now in Dresden, by painting the pastoral landscape in which the recumbent nude rests. But Titian realised that he needed to diversify his market and combine elite patronage with a broad studio practice like that of Bellini, whose altarpieces catered to wealthy Venetians keen to secure their salvation by donating art to churches.

H The real prize for Titian, as for Michelangelo before him, was an aristocratic patron. So when Alfonso d'Este asked him to complete the camerino, the private exhibition hall in his palace in Ferrara, he jumped at the chance. Bellini had begun the job by painting "The Feast of the Gods" for the libertine duke, who wanted the best artists in Italy to paint canvases on themes of classical drunken revels. After Bellini's death in 1516, Titian painted three mythological scenes to complement his work, repainting the background of his teacher's painting so that it matched his own. The current exhibition, like the recent Titian show in London and Madrid, brings together paintings from this legendary, now destroyed, pleasure chamber.

I Even the aged Bellini, patriarch of Venetian painting, was not too old to learn from the new energy around him. A sense of reverie had always pervaded his painting, but his late art, such as the altarpiece for the church of San Zaccaria (1505), possessed what Mr Brown calls a "restraint and refinement" unmatched by any of his pupils. In 1515, when he was 85, he painted a piece of silent poetry that many consider his masterpiece: "Lady with a Mirror". This famous nude, at once erotic and chaste, is possibly a response to the work of his star pupils and their fashion for portraying female beauties and poetical landscapes.

J "Lady with a Mirror" was called "an apotheosis of seeing" by the late art historian, Otto Pacht. The phrase could also describe Venetian art of the first decades of the 16th century. It was as though artists' eyes had been opened to the myriad possibilities of seeing and creating beauty.

K The past five years have seen a flowering of scholarship on this period and the current catalogue builds on this. Anyone within travelling distance of Washington or Vienna should rush to see the new exhibition. But if you can't, don't despair. As the next best thing, the exhibition's scholarly catalogue opens minds and eyes to the poetry and passion of Venetian art, just as its creators would have wished.

Questions 1-6

Reading passage 1 has eleven paragraphs, **A-K**.
Which paragraph contains the following information?
Write the correct letter, ***A-K****, in boxes 1-6 on your answer sheet.*
NB *You may use any letter more than once.*

1. "Lady with Mirror" was regarded as Venetian art of the first decades of the 16th century.
2. Both Michelargelo and Titian were given money by an noble patron.
3. Titian accepted to complete the camerino.
4. "The feast of the Gods" was painted by Bellini and Titian.
5. Venetian artists learnt from Durer that landscape could be an independent element of a work.
6. Three great Venetian painters devoured not only Leonardo's idea, but Durer as well.

Questions 7-11

From the information in the text, indicate who painted the picture in the list below.
Write the appropriate letter ***A-E*** *on your answer sheet.*
NB *You may use any letter more than once.*

7. The Tempest
8. Adoration of the Shepherds
9. sleeping Venus
10. Lady with Mirror
11. The three philosophers

A. Titian
B. Michelargelo
C. Giorgione
D. Bellini
E. Leonardo

Questions 12–15

Do the following statements agree with the information given in Reading Passage 1?

In boxes 12– 15 on your answer sheet, write

TRUE	*if the statement agrees with the information*
FALSE	*if the statement contradicts the information*
NOT GIVEN	*if there is no information on this*

12. The painting of Giorgione was called “modern” by critic.
13. Durer’s work have already spread widely before his arrival.
14. Venetian painting was famous for Lazuli.
15. Giorgione was the best student of Bellini.

READING PASSAGE 2

*You should spend about 20 minutes on **Questions 16–27**, which are based on Reading Passage 2 below.*

A Global Love Affair

There has rarely been a tougher time to be a carmaker. Squeezed by the credit crunch, rocked by the seesawing price of oil and now faced with a nasty recession as the banking crisis infects the real economy, the traditional markets of North America, western Europe and Japan, already sluggish for several years, have all but packed up. In America car sales are running at about 16% below last year’s level. Detroit’s struggling big three—General Motors, Ford and Chrysler—are in dire straits. They have wrung a $25 billion bail-out from Congress and are now looking for much more. In Europe the market is also collapsing. Sales in Japan this year are expected to be the lowest since 1974.

However, not all is doom and gloom. Mature vehicle markets may be close to saturation, but there is huge unsatisfied demand in the big emerging car markets of Brazil, Russia, India and China (the so-called BRICs). Although not immune from the rich countries’ troubles, they are likely to suffer much less. For one thing, levels of personal debt are far lower and a smaller proportion of cars are bought on credit. For another, the BRIC economies have been expanding so fast that even a slowdown should still leave them with growth rates that look respectable to Western eyes.

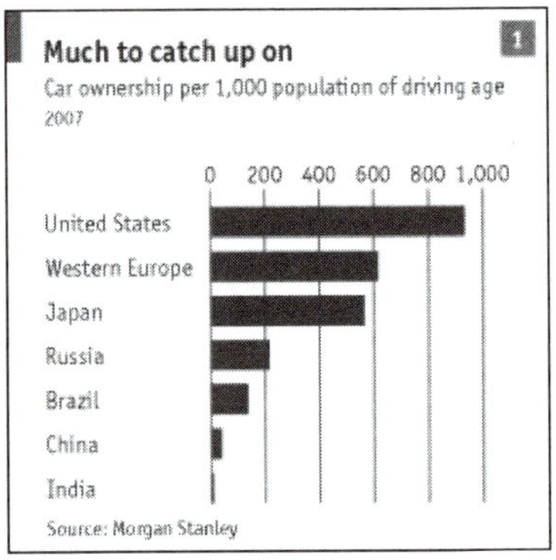

One measure of the BRIC countries’ new importance to the car industry is that, recession or not, global car sales in 2008 may still hit an all-time record of about 59m. For the first time passenger-vehicle sales in the BRICs, at around 14m, are likely to overtake those in America, which are expected to be the worst since 1992. As recently as 2005 America outsold them by over 10m. By the end of this decade China, already the world’s second-biggest market, will probably overtake America's sales of 16m-17m in a "normal" year. In Brazil sales have increased by nearly 30% in each of the past two years. Russia is likely to overtake Germany as Europe's biggest market within the next two years, with sales of around 3.5m. Meanwhile, Tata's $2,500 Nano, due to be launched in early 2009, is designed to do for India what the Model T Ford did for America 90 years ago.

It is the irresistible combination of rapid economic growth, favourable demographics and social change in the BRICs that is coming to the carmakers' rescue and that is likely to account for nearly all their growth for the foreseeable future. America has more than 900 cars (including light trucks) for every 1,000 people of driving age. In the big western European countries and Japan, where public transport is better and population is denser, the figure is a little over 600. But in Russia it is below 200, in Brazil about 130, in China around 30 and in India less than ten.

When times are hard, an American family that already has two or three cars will simply postpone buying a new one. But a potential customer in an emerging market who has been saving for years to buy his first car will still want to go ahead. As Carlos Ghosn, the boss of the Renault-Nissan alliance, put it at this year's Beijing motor show: "Nothing can stop the car being the most coveted product that comes with development."

The New Champions

No wonder that all the big carmakers are fighting like rats in a sack to win the largest piece of the action. Already, emerging markets have made the difference between life and death for some of the most famous names in the industry. GM's survival would be in even greater doubt without the meteoric growth it is seeing in China. Thanks in large part to the BRICs, a record 65% of GM's sales in the first quarter were outside America.

When Italy's Fiat was in danger of going out of business a few years ago, its Brazilian operation came to the rescue. Adam Jonas of Morgan Stanley, a bank, estimates that 65% of its net income last year came from emerging markets, mostly from Brazil. Volkswagen, the market leader in China, believes it will soon be able to challenge Toyota as the world's biggest carmaker. In Russia Renault has taken a 25% stake in the country's biggest local carmaker, AvtoVAZ, and its Logan is the first of a new wave of global low-cost cars.

Makes such as Mercedes, BMW and even Bentley and Ferrari are now common sights on the streets of Moscow and Shanghai. As Mr. Jonas points out, emerging markets account for more than a third of the world's rich but only about 15% of luxury-car sales.

These markets have much in common, but each is also remarkably different. In China buyers turn up their noses at small cars. The market is still dominated by joint ventures with foreign firms, but the strongest local manufacturers are rapidly expanding production.

Russia still has a sizeable indigenous industry, but many of its products hark back to the old

Soviet Union. Like the Chinese, Russians like high and wide SUVs. By contrast Brazilians prefer their cars small. India has established itself as an exponent of what car-industry executives call "frugal engineering" —innovation in the cause of ultra-low cost. Diesel engines are almost unknown in emerging markets other than India because poor-quality diesel fuel is associated with trucks. In Brazil nearly all new cars are able to run on ethanol.

Despite the social and economic benefits that widespread car ownership brings, its spread in developing countries has raised fears about its environmental consequences, especially carbon emissions that have climate-changing effects. Given a rapidly growing world car population and dwindling oil supplies, fuel prices are bound to rise in the long term.

Infrastructure is another big worry. In China new highways are being built on much-needed agricultural land. In India nearly half the traffic runs on just 2% of the country's roads. In the megacities of the developing world, from São Paulo in Brazil to Mumbai in India, cars often move at less than walking speed, stuck in traffic jams.

According to Mr Ghosn, the only way to give people the cars they want without wrecking the planet is to move quickly to producing zero-emission vehicles, probably powered by batteries. "Nothing else will prevent the world from exploding," he says. Others in the industry may quietly agree, but they are less confident that the technology to power them will arrive in time and at an acceptable price. And only governments can build the roads that will accommodate so many more cars. For the world's carmakers the road ahead is full of opportunities, but also many risks.

Questions 16–19

Complete the summary below.

Choose ***NO MORE THAN THREE WORDS*** *from the passage for each answer.*

Write your answers in boxes 16–19 on your answer sheet.

It's a rough time for carmaker. It's __16__ lower than last year's level in U.S. car-sales. However, there is large __17__ in the so called BRICs, one of BRICs, China, already the __18__. It will be likely to __19__ America's sales of 16m-17m in a "normal" year.

Questions 20–23

Write the appropriate letter ***A****,* ***B*** *or* ***C*** *on your answer sheet.*

A. United States

B. Japan

C. China

D. India

E. Brazil

F. Western Europe

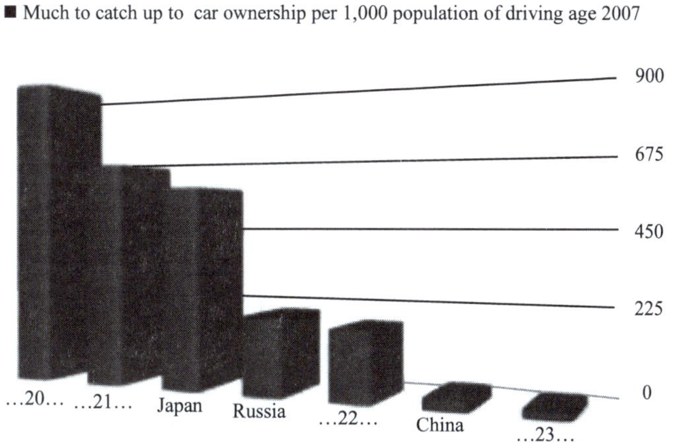

Questions 24–27

Complete the sentences below.

*Choose **NO MORE THAN TWO WORDS** from the passage for each answer.*

Write your answer in boxes 24–27 on your answer sheet.

24. Russians are fascinated with ______, just the same as Chinese.
25. In Brazil almost all new cars can drive with ______.
26. Considering about swiftly growing and dwindling oil supplies, ______ must be rise in the long run.
27. Nearly half the traffic run on ______ of the country's roads.

READING PASSAGE 3

*You should spend about 20 minutes on **Questions 28–40**, which are based on Reading Passage 3 below.*

Questions 28–32

Reading passage 3 has nine paragraphs, **A–I**.

*Choose the correct heading for sections **A–E** from the list of headings below.*

*Write the correct number, **i-vii**, in boxes 28–32 on your answer sheet.*

List of Headings

i	A person's face reflects his own character
ii	The importance of exterior
iii	The importance of facial language
iv	Peer-to-peer lending site
v	The requirements for borrowers
vi	Web site for Dr. Duarte's study
vii	Mechanical Turk

28. Paragraph **A**
29. Paragraph **B**
30. Paragraph **C**
31. Paragraph **D**
32. Paragraph **E**

About Face

A Science proceeds by trial and error. The successes are trumpeted. The errors are often regarded with embarrassment by subsequent generations, and locked away in attic rooms of the subject's mansion like mad relatives in a Victorian novel. Usually, they stay there. Craniology, phrenology and eugenics, once-respectable fields of endeavour that are now regarded with a shudder, may shriek from time to time, but few sane people pay attention to them. One, however, has escaped recently, and is trying to rehabilitate itself. For years physiognomy—the idea that a person's face is a reflection of his character—was sneered at. Now, it is making a come back.

B Appearances certainly count. Women, for instance, judge men by their faces. Testosterone levels are reflected in the face, and who is seen as a one-night stand and who as a potential husband depends in part on this physical feature. Similarly, a male face betrays the owner's underlying aggressiveness and even his business acumen. Facial beauty in either sex is also associated with higher incomes. The latest research, though, cuts to the moral quick. For Jefferson Duarte of Rice University in Houston, Texas, and his colleagues are suggesting that one of a person's most telling moral features, his creditworthiness, can also be seen in his face.

C Dr Duarte's research was enabled by the internet. Once, if you wanted to borrow money, you had either to visit a bank or to tap a rich friend or relative. Now it is possible to do business directly with a stranger, using a peer-to-peer lending site. The needy advertise themselves, and how much they want. Those flush with cash assess potential borrowers and decide who to lend to, and at what rate of interest.

D The borrowers themselves have to disclose their financial positions, credit histories, jobs and education. Often, though this is not required, they also post photographs of themselves. That means it might be possible to assess the effects of appearance on the outcome. And the process is an open auction, which means that all offers, acceptances and rejections are in the public domain.

E For his research, Dr Duarte chose a site called Prosper.com. His intention was twofold: to see if physiognomy-based prejudices about creditworthiness existed and, if they did, whether they were justified. To do so he used another peer-to-peer website to subcontract the job of assessing creditworthiness to a number of ordinary people. The site in question (which is run by Amazon) is called Mechanical Turk. In this case the people it matches are those who have a task that needs doing, and those willing to perform it.

F The team recruited 25 Mechanical Turk workers and asked them to assess pictures of potential borrowers that had been posted on Prosper.com. In particular, they were asked to rate, on a scale of one to five, how trustworthy these people looked, and to estimate the percentage probability that each individual would repay a $100 loan. They were also asked to make several other assessments, such as the individual's sex, race, age, attractiveness and obesity. The 25 results for each photograph were then averaged and analysed.

G The researchers looked at 6,821 loan applications, 733 of which were successful. Their first finding was that the assessments of trustworthiness, and of likelihood to repay a loan, that were made by Mechanical Turk workers did indeed correlate with potential borrowers' credit ratings based on their credit history. That continued to be so when the other variables, from beauty to race to obesity, were controlled for statistically. Shifty physiognomy, it seems, is independent of these things.

H That shiftiness was also recognised by those whose money was actually at stake. People flagged as untrustworthy by the Mechanical Turks were less likely than others to be offered a loan at all. To have the same chance of getting one as those deemed most trustworthy they were required to pay an interest rate that was, on average, 1.82 percentage points higher, even when the effects of historical creditworthiness were statistically eliminated.

I For trustworthiness, then, physiognomy works. Unfortunately, Dr Duarte's method was not designed to find out which features label someone as trustworthy. But credit-rating agencies are no doubt working on that question even now.

Questions 33–40

Do the following statements agree with the claims of the writer in Reading Passage 3?

In boxes 33–40 on your answer sheet, write

YES	*if the statement agree with the claims of the writer*
NO	*if the statement contradicts the claims of the writer*
NOT GIVEN	*if it is impossible to say what the writer thinks about this*

33. The study team employed twenty-five workers.
34. Mechanical Turk workers only estimate pictures of possible mortgagor.
35. The 25 results for each picture were averaged and estimated.
36. 6,068 loan applications are fail to be approved.
37. People regarded as untrustworthy were more likely than others to be approved a loan.
38. Physiognomy really works on trustworthiness.
39. The borrowers needn't show their personal information to lombard.

40. Dr. Duarte sets up the third website for his research.

Keys:

1. J
2. H
3. H
4. H
5. C
6. C
7. C
8. C
9. A
10. D
11. C
12. TRUE
13. TRUE
14. NOT GIVEN
15. TRUE
16. 16%
17. unsatisfied demand
18. world's second-biggest market
19. overtake
20. A
21. F
22. E
23. D
24. SUVs
25. ethanol
26. fuel prices
27. 2%
28. i
29. ii
30. iv
31. v
32. vi
33. YES
34. NOT GIVEN
35. YES
36. YES
37. NO
38. YES
39. NO
40. NOT GIVEN

星期五

模拟试题 5

READING PASSAGE 1

*You should spend about 20 minutes on **Questions 1–16**, which are based on Reading Passage 1 below.*

Questions 1–6

Reading passage 1 has eight paragraphs, **A–H.**

*Choose the correct heading for sections **B – G** from the list of headings below.*

*Write the correct number, **ii -viii**, in boxes 1 – 6 on your answer sheet.*

List of Headings

i	The nap is good for learning
ii	Sleep links with memory
iii	The experiment rules
iv	The result of research
v	Hippocampus and memories
vi	The ideal nap
vii	Effect of nap
viii	Hippocampus and non-sleep

Example	*Answer*
Paragraph **A**	**i**

1. Paragraph **B**
2. Paragraph **C**
3. Paragraph **D**
4. Paragraph **E**
5. Paragraph **F**
6. Paragraph **G**

Sleepy Heads

Researchers say an afternoon nap prepares the brain to learn

A Mad dogs and Englishmen, so the song has it, go out in the midday sun. And the business practices of England's lineal descendant, America, will have you in the office from nine in the morning to five in the evening, if not longer. Much of the world, though, prefers to take a siesta. And research presented to the AAAS meeting in San Diego suggests it may be right to do so. It has already been established that those who siesta are less likely to die of heart disease. Now, Matthew Walker and his colleagues at the University of California, Berkeley, have found that they probably have better memory, too. A post-prandial snooze, Dr Walker has discovered, sets the brain up for learning.

B The role of sleep in consolidating memories that have already been created has been understood for some time. Dr Walker has been trying to extend this understanding by looking at sleep's role in preparing the brain for the formation of memories in the first place. He was particularly interested in a type of memory called episodic memory, which relates to specific events, places and times. This contrasts with procedural memory, of the skills required to perform some sort of mechanical task, such as driving. The theory he and his team wanted to test was that the ability to form new episodic memories deteriorates with accrued wakefulness, and that sleep thus restores the brain's capacity for efficient learning.

C They asked a group of 39 people to take part in two learning sessions, one at noon and one at 6p.m.. On each occasion the participants tried to memorise and recall 100 combinations of pictures and names. After the first session they were assigned randomly to either a control group, which remained awake, or a nap group, which had 100 minutes of monitored sleep.

D Those who remained awake throughout the day became worse at learning. Those who napped, by contrast, actually improved their capacity to learn, doing better in the evening than they had at noon. These findings suggest that sleep is clearing the brain's short-term memory and making way for new information.

E It is already well known that fact-based memories are stored temporarily in an area called the hippocampus, a structure in the centre of the brain. But they do not stay there long. Instead, they are sent to the prefrontal cortex for longer-term storage. Electroencephalograms, which measure electrical activity in the brain, have shown that this memory-refreshing capacity is related to a specific type of sleep called Stage 2 non-REM sleep.

F The ideal nap, then, follows a cycle of between 90 and 100 minutes. The first 30 minutes is a light sleep that helps improve motor performance. Then comes 30 minutes of stage 2 sleep, which refreshes the hippocampus. After this, between 60 and 90 minutes into the nap, comes rapid-eye-movement, or REM, sleep, during which dreaming happens. This, research suggests, is the time when the brain makes connections between the new memories that have just been "downloaded" from the hippocampus and those that already exist—thus making new experiences relevant in a wider context.

G The benefits to memory of a nap, says Dr Walker, are so great that they can equal an entire night's sleep. He warns, however, that napping must not be done too late in the day or it will interfere with night-time sleep. Moreover, not everyone awakens refreshed from a siesta.

H The grogginess that results from an unrefreshing siesta is termed "sleep inertia". This happens when the brain is woken from a deep sleep with its cells still firing at a slow rhythm and its temperature and blood flow decreased. Sara Mednick, from the University of California, San Diego, suggests that non-habitual nappers suffer from this more often than those who siesta regularly. It may be that those who have a tendency to wake up groggy are choosing not to siesta in the first place. Perhaps, though, as in so many things, it is practice that makes perfect.

Questions 7–13

Complete the summary below.
*Choose **NO MORE THAN THREE WORDS** from the passage for each answer.*
Write your answers in boxes 7–13 on your answer sheet.

Matthew and his colleagues collected a team of 39 subjects to enter for __7__, one at noon and __8__. One should remained __9__, another get a __10__ which had one hundred minutes. Those who remained awake the whole day getting worse performance at __11__, those who napped in contrast, actually improved their __12__ to learn. These findings suggest that sleep is cleaning the __13__ and making way for new information.

Questions 14–16

*Answer the questions below using **NO MORE THAN THREE WORDS** from the passage for each answer.*
Write your answers in boxes 14–16 on your answer sheet.

14. What is the first thirty minutes called?
15. Which area in brain is associated with memories store?
16. What's name of grogginess that due to unrefreshing siesta?

READING PASSAGE 2

*You should spend about 20 minutes on **Questions 17–27**, which are based on Reading Passage 2 below.*

Junk Bond

A For seasoned shoppers, "buyer's remorse" is a familiar feeling. "Seller's remorse" may also become common soon, as ever more governments order manufacturers to assume the cost of disposing of their products after consumers are done with them. Until recently, most laws on "extended producer responsibility" (EPR) or "product stewardship" applied only to specific types of goods, such as car tyres or electronics. But in late March Maine, following the lead of several Canadian provinces, became the first American state to enact a blanket EPR law, which could in principle cover any product.

B Governments are eager to unload some responsibility for waste management onto manufacturers, especially for products that are hard to recycle or may be toxic, such as electronics, batteries, paint, car parts and pesticide containers. It helps them cut costs, for one thing—handy for local authorities short of cash in the recession. In Maine, which has had an EPR law for electronic waste since 2004, municipalities save \$1.5m-3m annually because manufacturers have picked up the cost of collection, according to the Natural Resources Council of Maine. Governments also hope that EPR laws will encourage firms to rethink the way they make products, designing them for longevity and recyclability rather than for the landfill.

C Thirty-one of America's 50 states have product-specific EPR laws. The European Union requires manufacturers to dispose of packaging, electronics and vehicles. Canada and Japan also have EPR laws. Other countries, such as Australia, have flirted with the idea.

D Maine's new "framework" law makes it much easier to expand the scope of EPR schemes, by establishing a process for adding products to the list of those covered without requiring a new law each time. The state government, which already enforces five product-specific EPR laws, is now said to have carpet-makers and drugs firms in its sights.

E This worries businesses, few of which are eager to pick up the bill for waste disposal. Some business associations, such as the California Chamber of Commerce, have denounced EPR bills as "job killers". They point out that the increased costs are ultimately borne by consumers. But that does not worry supporters of EPR, who argue that the price of a product should reflect its full "life-cycle" costs, including disposal, rather than simply leaving taxpayers to make up the difference. Moreover, unless manufacturers are forced to bear the costs, they will have no incentive to make their wares easy to dispose of.

F Scott Cassel, executive director of the Product Stewardship Institute, a non-profit organisation, says he has noticed different "stages of grief for companies" coping with the reality of EPR, starting with denial and moving to begrudging acceptance. Not all companies are mourning, however. Some manufacturers and retailers have voluntarily rolled out collection programmes in states that do not require them. Hewlett-Packard, a technology firm, claims to design its products with ease of recycling in mind—cradle-to-cradle, as the jargon has it. Staples, which sells office supplies, and Home Depot, a home-improvement retailer, both offer national take-back programmes in their stores for such items as computer monitors, compact fluorescent light bulbs and batteries. Such programmes may enhance customer loyalty, particularly among environmentally conscious consumers.

G Some companies may also be hoping that starting their own collection programmes could help them pre-empt legislation. "We thought we could get out in front of this and set up a system to collect our products, and the exact opposite happened," says Doug Smith of Sony, an electronics giant. He does not believe EPR laws have much impact on product design.

H Companies' biggest gripe about EPR laws is not their cost but their inconsistency. Few states have the same requirements, making compliance complicated for manufacturers. Many businesses would favour a national policy rather than a patchwork of local laws. EPR laws, it seems, are set to win extended responsibility themselves.

Questions 17–22

Reading passage 2 has eight paragraphs, **A–H**.
Which paragraph contains the following information?
Write the correct letter, ***A–H****, in boxes 17–22 on your answer sheet.*
NB *You may use any letter more than once.*

17. Companies complain about EPR laws.
18. Doug Smith's statement about collection programmes.
19. Hweleh-packard's slogan which claims that cradle-to-cradle.
20. Staples and Home Depot introduced take-back programmes in their stores.
21. Governments are willing to pass the buck to manufactures.
22. An EPR law for electronic waste was actualized since 2004 in Maine.

Questions 23–27

Write the correct letter in boxes 23–27 on your answer sheet.

Which Five are mentioned that hard to recycle?

A. Electronics
B. Reyboard
C. Batteries

D. Car parts
E. Furniture
F. Pesticide containers
G. Computer monitors
H. Paper

READING PASSAGE 3

*You should spend about 20 minutes on **Questions 28−40**, which are based on Reading Passage 3 below.*

Shooting Down Cancer

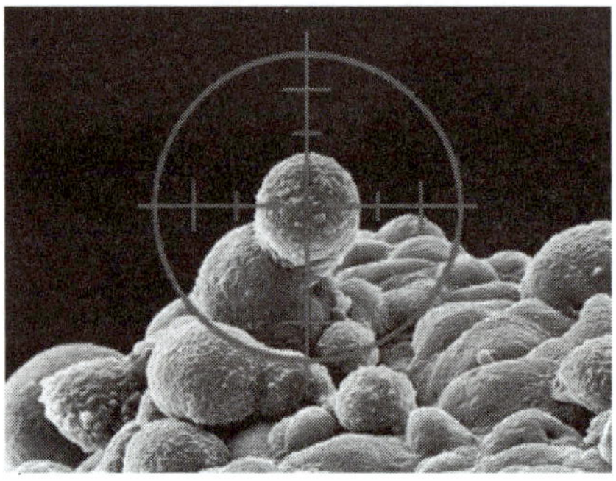

Every age is afraid of plagues. For the most part, such plagues have been infections. The rich world, though, has brought infectious disease under control and, AIDS aside, the memory dims with every generation. Instead, the fear of disease has transferred itself to cancer. How to prevent it, and how to treat it if prevention has failed, fills the health pages of the newspapers. How this or that celebrity won or lost his or her battle with it seems to fill much of the rest.

The military metaphor is not confined to newspapers. It is 37 years since Richard Nixon, then America's president, declared war on the disease. During that time, the prognosis for cancer patients has got a lot better. Scientists have refined old therapies and found new ones. Moreover, governments have waged a relentless public-health campaign against the biggest cause of cancer—the smoking of tobacco. The war, however, has never looked close to being won. Scan the horizon and there is no sign of a cure.

Nor is there likely to be until the enemy is properly understood. Though luck plays its part in medicine, as it does in warfare, the big breakthroughs usually come from dramatic shifts in understanding. It was not, for example, until Louis Pasteur and Robert Koch proved the connection between germs and infection that doctors realised that to cure such diseases you had to kill the germs. The germ theory of disease made sense of a collection of illnesses that obviously had things in common (a tendency to appear in waves, for example, or to pass from person to person) but were maddeningly different in their details. It took a while, but proof of that theory led to antibiotics that can destroy a whole range of infections.

For cancer, a similar moment of enlightenment may now have arrived. Like infections, cancers have prominent features in common, yet they are bafflingly different in their details. But, borrowing an idea from another part of biology, oncologists are coming to believe that most—possibly all—cancers involve stem cells, or something very like them. They are, in other words, caused and sustained by a small number of cells whose daughters grow into the tissue of a tumour rather as the daughters of healthy stem cells grow into the normal tissues that make up a body.

This opens new ways of thinking about and treating the cancers. If its stem cells are eradicated, the rest of a tumour may die off. And if the secondary tumours—the truly feared killers in many forms of cancer—are the result of stem cells escaping from a primary tumour, as looks likely, then this knowledge may make them yield more easily to treatment.

This discovery is not a cure. But it does point the way towards one—or, at the least, towards better therapies. Some might be in action soon. For example, it seems that cancer stem cells are less vulnerable to radiation than other cancer cells, because their DNA-repair mechanisms are better. Radiotherapy might thus be made more effective against them by dosing them with existing drugs that inhibit DNA repair. Some existing drugs which are known to interfere with stem cells' biochemical pathways could be used to attack them selectively.

Other treatments will take far longer—the time needed for clinical trials would see to that and, in any case, a lot more research is in order. And there is the problem of designing drugs that can distinguish between cancer stem cells and those that spin off healthy tissues. But it all looks promising.

The other interesting aspect of the stem-cell link is that it was inspired by work outside the mainstream of the huge cancer-research industry: stem-cell research is now a huge field in its own right. In science you never know where the answer is going to come from. Pasteur found it in a piece of practical science: he was trying to prevent food going off. Charles Darwin, by contrast, found a lead for his theory of natural selection in the whimsical hobby of pigeon fancying, where the birds showed an enormous variety of form and behaviour. And some discoveries happen by accident. Radioactivity came to light a century after the discovery of uranium when Henri Becquerel used uranium salts and photographic plates in the same experiment and found that one fogged the other.

In the 19th century it was commonplace to do an experiment simply to see what would happen. That was, in part, because experimenters were often amateurs who were spending private money. In these days of taxpayer-financed science, most experiments are executed with a pretty clear idea of what the outcome ought to be, especially when they are part of wars and campaigns against this or that. The paradox is that, although such efforts do not eliminate Becquerel-like discoveries, they risk limiting the chances of making them.

This accent on targeted research is understandable. Plenty of the work now done on cancer will be of the targeted sort. The Large Hadron Collider, the huge particle accelerator in Switzerland which was switched on this week, is a grand project that could yield all sorts of discoveries. Yet the easiest way to sell it to politicians was to frame it as a search for a single particle, the Higgs boson.

Like natural selection and germs, the discovery of cancer stem cells illustrates how the most fruitful scientific findings are often not those of individual experiments, however intriguing, but those that organise knowledge into theory. The chemical industry took off within a decade or so of Dmitri Mendeleev's arrangement of the chemical elements into the periodic table, just as radio communications followed James Clerk Maxwell's mathematical unification of electricity and magnetism, and antibiotics came after Pasteur and Koch.

With luck, something similar will soon happen in biology in the wake of such things as the Human Genome Project. In retrospect, the discovery of stem cells—cancer stem cells included—may come to be seen as a step in a comprehensive theory of how organisms work. That understanding would be a formidable, if unforeseen, part of the legacy of the war on cancer and an essential part of its mission to save lives.

Questions 28–30

Look at the following researchers (Questions 28–30) and the list of findings below.
Match each researcher with the correct finding.
*Write the correct letter **A–E** in boxes 28–30 on your answer sheet.*

28. Dmitri Mendeleev
29. James Clerk Maxwell
30. Pasteur and Koch

LIST OF FINDINGS

A	Periodic table of chemical elements
B	Antibiotics theory
C	Radio communications
D	Human Genome project
E	Cancer stem cells

Questions 31–36

Do the following statements agree with the claims of the writer in Reading Passage 3?
In boxes 31–36 on your answer sheet, write

YES	*if the statement agree with the claims of the writer*
NO	*if the statement contradicts the claims of the writer*
NOT GIVEN	*if it is impossible to say what the writer thinks about this*

31. We are afraid of plagues all the time.

32. The developed countries are more controllable than developing countries on infectious disease.
33. Richard Nixon has fought back the cancer for 37 years.
34. It's impossible to cure the cancer.
35. The biggest cause of cancer is plagues.
36. Medicine is more important than other facts in this field.

Questions 37–40

Complete the sentences below.

Choose ***NO MORE THAN TWO WORDS*** *from the passage for each answer.*

Write your answer in boxes 37–40 on your answer sheet.

37. The rest of a tumour will be killed if eradicate the ______.
38. Some drugs can be used as anti-cancer. Since they interfere with biochemical pathways of ______.
39. Pasteur found his theory while trying to stop food ______.
40. Henri Becquerel made the discovery of ______.

Keys:

1. ii
2. iii
3. iv
4. v
5. vi
6. vii
7. two learning sessions
8. one at 6p.m.
9. awake
10. monitored sleep
11. learning
12. capacity
13. brain's short-term memory
14. a light sleep
15. hippocampus
16. sleep inertia
17. H
18. G
19. F
20. F
21. B
22. B
23. A
24. C
25. D
26. F
27. G
28. A
29. C
30. B
31. YES
32. NOT GIVEN
33. YES
34. YES
35. NO
36. NOT GIVEN
37. stem cells
38. stem cells
39. going off
40. uranium

星期六

模拟试题 6

READING PASSAGE 1

*You should spend about 20 minutes on **Questions 1-15**, which are based on Reading Passage 1 below.*

Signs of Life

A Half a century ago a radio astronomer called Frank Drake thought of a way to calculate the likelihood of establishing contact with aliens. He suggested the following figures should be multiplied: how many stars are formed in the galaxy in a year; what fraction of these have planets and thus form solar systems; the average number of planets per solar system that have the potential to support life; on what percentage of those where it is possible do such biospheres actually form; what percentage of such biospheres give rise to intelligent species; what percentage of intelligent life is able to transmit signals into space; and for how long could such intelligence keeps sending signals.

B This calculation became celebrated as the Drake equation—perhaps the best attempt so far to tame a wild guess. Most of the terms remain hard to tie down, although there is a consensus that about ten stars are formed per year in the galaxy. Also, recent searches for extrasolar planets have concluded that planets are not rare.

C At the AAAS, Dr Drake reflected on his search for alien signals. One reason this is hard is that radio telescopes must chop the spectrum into fine portions to study it, like tuning into a signal on a car radio. Another is the trade off between a telescope's field of view and its magnification. Small telescopes see a lot of sky but can detect only strong signals. Large ones, which can detect weak signals, have a narrow focus. Astronomers therefore have difficulty looking both carefully and comprehensively.

D Dr Drake said there may be another difficulty. Researchers tend to look for signals similar to those now made by humanity. The Earth, though, is getting quieter because the rise of spread-spectrum communication makes stray emissions less likely than in the past.

E Spread-spectrum works by smearing a message across a wide range of frequencies. That has the advantages of combating noise and allowing many signals to be sent at once. But it also makes those signals hard for eavesdroppers to hear (which is why spread-spectrum is beloved by military men). If technologically sophisticated aliens came to the same conclusions, and thus used spread-spectrum technology, humans would have a hard time hearing them. Dr Drake suggests, therefore, that there might be only a narrow window of time in the development of civilisations, analogous to the past 50 years on Earth, during which noisy electromagnetic signals are generated in large amounts.

F It is, however, also possible that someone is actively trying to send signals to the Earth. If that were the case, the best way to do this, reckons Paul Horowitz, a physicist at Harvard, is with a laser.

G Although radio power has changed little over the decades, the power of lasers has grown exponentially. Today's most powerful versions can shine ten thousand times brighter than the sun, though only for a billionth of a second. If aliens have made similar progress, and point a laser towards the Earth's solar system, such brief flashes would be detectable at a distance of many light-years. Dr Horowitz has already set up one suitable detector and this, because no huge magnification is involved, is capable of looking at broad swathes of sky.

H There is also potential for improvement on the radio side. For many years, the Arecibo telescope in Puerto Rico, which is 300 metres across, has led the search for alien life. (Sadly, its founder, William Gordon, died on February 16th.) Now the Chinese are building a 500-metre telescope, known as FAST, in Guizhou province, and an international collaboration called the Square Kilometre Array is trying, as its name suggests, to build a grid of radio-telescopes over a square kilometre of land in either South Africa or Australia. Both may be helpful. As indeed may a large new telescope in northern California built by Paul Allen, a co-founder of Microsoft.

I Many of the terms in the Drake equation are likely to remain elusive, so it is still impossible to predict how likely such efforts are to succeed. But even after 50 fruitless years—if the eagerness in the eyes of Dr Drake and his colleagues is any guide—it still is fun looking.

Questions 1−6

Reading passage 1 has nine paragraphs, **A−I**.

Which paragraph contains the following information?

*Write the correct letter, **A−I**, in boxes 1−6 on your answer sheet.*

***NB** You may use any letter more than once.*

1. The telescope contributes to universal discovery.
2. The power of laser has increased exponentially.
3. The detector which set up by Dr. Horowitz.

4. Spread-Spectrum which is popularity in military use.
5. It's hard looking both carefully and comprehensively for Astronomers.
6. Frank Drake invented a way to calculate the possibility of contract between a liens and human-beings.

Questions 7–9

*Choose three letters from **A–F**.*
Write the correct letter in boxes 7–9 on your answer sheet.
Which three were excluded Frank's method?

A. The figures should be multiplied.
B. Sending signal with radio.
C. New formed stars in the galaxy.
D. New formed stars in the universal.
E. The duration of keeping contract.
F. The ratio of biospheres evolved intelligent species.

Questions 10–15

Do the following statements agree with the information given in Reading Passage 1?
In boxes 10–15 on your answer sheet, write

TRUE	*if the statement agrees with the information*
FALSE	*if the statement contradicts the information*
NOT GIVEN	*if there is no information on this*

10. It's a common view that nearly 10 stars are formed in the galaxy each year.
11. The focus of small telescope is narrower than larges ones.
12. The signal detection of small telescope is stronger than large ones.
13. The Earth is getting quieter as less stray emissions.
14. The probable that alien is trying to contact with us.
15. There's no modify on radio power during last 10 years.

READING PASSAGE 2

*You should spend about 20 minutes on **Questions 16–26**, which are based on Reading Passage 2 below.*

International Roaming

For a business that has done so much to make people feel closer together some phone operators have been wary about extending the hand of friendship across borders. But as a new round of consolidation kicks off in Europe, America and elsewhere it seems that the world is getting smaller for the phone giants.

France Telecom admitted on Thursday June 5th that it had begun discussion with TeliaSonera about a long-anticipated takeover offer for the Swedish firm, in a deal worth some SKr252 billion ($42 billion). The same day on the other side of the Atlantic, Verizon Wireless agreed to acquire Alltel, a regional operator, in a $27 billion deal that would create America's largest mobile company.

This deal and potential tie-up are the latest of a flurry of activity among the world's big phone operators. In developed markets the prospects for growth are poor—in many countries there are more mobile phones than people. So bulking up makes sense: with greater size comes the opportunity to cut costs and reap other rewards that come with economies of scale. And opportunities abound. In Europe mobile-telecoms markets are highly fragmented and ripe for more consolidation. Deutsche Telekom made its own move across borders last month with the acquisition of a 25% stake and control of the management of OTE, a Greek operator.

France Telecom cannot yet celebrate its foray abroad, which, if successful, would create Europe's biggest mobile-phone company by revenue, and boast 237m customers in 30 countries. The firm is particularly enticing because along with its more mature mobile and fixed-line operations in the Nordic region come faster growing businesses in Eastern Europe and Central Asia. The board of its Swedish target has rejected the informal offer of cash and shares as too low, despite the bid representing a big premium on the company's share price before the French firm's interest became apparent in April.

Even if that deal falls through there are plenty of other possible tie-ups in the offing. Spain's Telefonica and Britain's Vodafone are both thought by some analysts to be on the hunt for acquisitions and smaller firms in Belgium, the Netherlands, Portugal, Switzerland. Vodafone may bid to extend its stake in Vodacom, a South African operator. A handful of other countries could make tempting targets.

More deals are in the works elsewhere. Late last month India's Reliance Communications said that it was in talks with South Africa's MTN about a deal that would forge a firm valued at over $60 billion with a presence in India, Africa and the Middle East and with over 114m subscribers. Reliance's move came shortly after MTN broke off talks with Bharti Airtel, an Indian rival to Reliance, when structuring a deal between the two proved too complicated.

The current clamour to do deals is driven by the belief that bigger is better. And cross border tie-ups are also becoming more acceptable to regulators. Previously cross-border collaboration between operators was accepted, but that was usually as far as it went.

As with other businesses such as airlines that are reckoned to be strategic by governments, alliances were tolerated by regulators while full mergers were blocked. But as is happening in other businesses such as energy, governments in Europe and elsewhere are becoming less inclined to use the security concerns they used to cite to prevent certain types businesses from coming together across borders. It has become apparent that preventing foreign energy companies from gaining access to national markets has little bearing on energy security. By the same token allowing phone operators to fall to foreign predators is unlikely to compromise national security. So even if some the current set of proposed deals fail to come to fruition, it still looks likcly that a round of consolidation is on the way.

Questions 16–20

Complete the summary below.

Choose ***NO MORE THAN THREE WORDS*** *from the passage for each answer.*

Write your answers in boxes 16–20 on your answer sheet.

The discussion between __16__ and __17__ set off on 5th June. It's worth $420 billion. There's a __18__ deal that would bring up the top __19__ in America. It's the latest of a __20__ among the global giant mobile operators.

Questions 21–26

Do the following statements agree with the claims of the writer in Reading Passage 2?

In boxes 21-26 on your answer sheet, write

YES	*if the statement agree with the claims of the writer*
NO	*if the statement contradicts the claims of the writer*
NOT GIVEN	*if it is impossible to say what the writer thinks about this*

21. France Telecom boast 237 million customers in 30 countries.
22. Regulators are used to accept cross-border business.
23. Previously cross-border collaboration between operators was limited.
24. Governments regard airlines as strategic business.
25. Stopping foreign energy business from entering for global markets has few bearing on energy security.
26. The following tie-up will coming soon.

READING PASSAGE 3

You should spend about 20 minutes on ***Questions 27–40****, which are based on Reading Passage 3 below.*

Questions 27–31

Reading passage 3 has ten sections, ***A–J****.*

*Choose the correct heading for sections **A–E** from the list of headings below.*
*Write the correct number, i-viii, in boxes **27–31** on your answer sheet.*

List of Headings

i	Not water crisis but food crisis
ii	Farmer waste more water than others
iii	More crop one drop
iv	Make water go further
v	The method of saving
vi	The method of repairing
vii	The problem in poor countries
viii	Wasteful when water in scarce

27. Paragraph **A**
28. Paragraph **B**
29. Paragraph **C**
30. Paragraph **D**
31. Paragraph **E**

Running Dry

The world has a water shortage, not a food shortage

A Most people may drink only two litres of water a day, but they consume about 3,000 if the water that goes into their food is taken into account. The rich gulp down far more, since they tend to eat more meat, which takes far more water to produce than grains. So as the world's population grows and incomes rise, farmers will—if they use today's methods—need a great deal more water to keep everyone fed: 2,000 more cubic kilometres a year by 2030, according to the International Water Management Institute (IWMI), a research centre, or over a quarter more than they use today. Yet in many farming regions, water is scarce and likely to get scarcer as global warming worsens. The world is facing not so much a food crisis as a water crisis, argues Colin Chartres, IWMI's director-general.

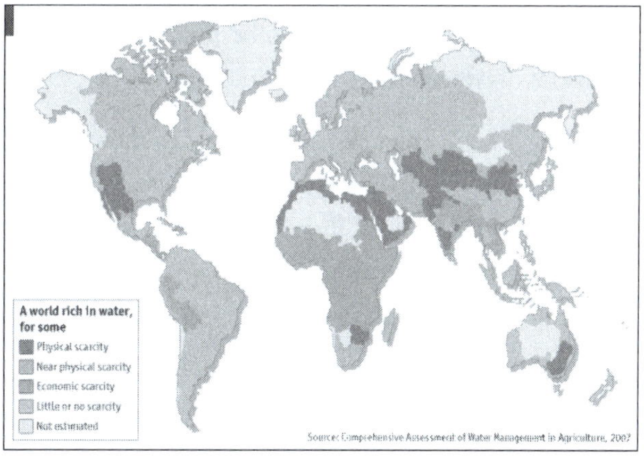

B The solution, Mr Chartres and others contend, is more efficient use of water or, as the sloganeers put it, "more crop per drop". Some 1.2 billion people, about a fifth of the world's population, live in places that are short of water (see map). Farming accounts for roughly 70% of human water consumption. So when water starts to run out, as is happening in northern China, southern Spain and the western United States, among other places, farming tends to offer the best potential for thrift. But governments, whether to win votes or to protect the poor, rarely charge farmers a market price for water. So they are usually more wasteful than other consumers—even though the value they create from the water is often less than households or industry would be willing to pay for it.

C The pressing need is to make water go further. Antoine Frérot, the head of the water division of Veolia Environnement, a French firm, promotes recycling, whereby city wastewater is treated until it can be used in industry or agriculture. This costs about a third less than desalination, and cuts pollution. He expects his recycling business to quadruple in the next decade.

D Yet as Mr Frérot himself concedes, there are many even cheaper ways to save water. As much as 70% of water used by farmers never gets to crops, perhaps lost through leaky irrigation channels or by draining into rivers or groundwater. Investment in drip irrigation, or simply repairing the worst leaks, could bring huge savings.

E Farmers in poor countries can usually afford such things only if they are growing cash crops, says David Molden of IWMI. Even basic kit such as small rainwater tanks can be lacking. Ethiopia, for example, has only 38 cubic metres of storage capacity per inhabitant, compared to almost 5,000 in Australia. Yet modest water storage can hugely improve yields in rain-fed agriculture, by smoothing over short dry spells. Likewise, pumping water into natural aquifers for seasonal storage tends to be much cheaper than building a big dam, and prevents the great waste of water through evaporation.

F Even when water is scarce, it is often squandered. Mr. Molden cites the example of cotton-farmers in Uzbekistan, who used to receive a fixed allocation of water for irrigation whether they needed it or not, in a holdover from the days of Soviet central planning. Simply putting farmers in control of the irrigation network, and allowing them to decide how much water they needed, cut consumption by 30%.

G Similarly, rice farmers can sharply cut water consumption by flooding paddy fields only some of the time. Wheat growers in hot places such as India and Australia can conserve water by minimising tilling, leaving a layer of mulch on the fields' surface to absorb rainwater and limit evaporation. In arid regions like the Middle East, Mark Zeitoun of the London School of Economics suggests substituting thirsty crops such as oranges with more abstemious olives and dates. Ideally, countries that are short of water would concentrate on growing the most valuable cash crops, and use the proceeds to import staples.

H Agronomists are beginning to devise tools to help monitor the efficiency of water use. Some have designed algorithms that use satellite data on surface temperatures to calculate the rate at which plants are absorbing and transpiring water. That allows governments and development agencies to concentrate their efforts on the most prodigal areas.

I But efficient use of water, cautions Pasquale Steduto of the United Nations' Food and Agriculture Organisation, is just one step to better agricultural yields. Even if farmers use the right amount of water they also need decent seeds and enough fertiliser. In Africa in particular, these and other factors such as pest control, storage and distribution are a bigger drag on yields than a shortage of water.

J Raising yields does not always involve greater water consumption, especially when farms are inefficient. It would take little extra water to double cereal output in many parts of Africa, Mr. Molden argues. IWMI reckons that some three-quarters of the extra food the world needs could be provided simply by bringing yields in poor countries closer to those of rich ones. That is more palatable than the puritanical alternative: giving up meat and other thirsty products altogether.

Questions 32–34

Complete the sentences below.

Choose ***NO MORE THAN THREE WORDS*** *from the passage for each answer.*

Write your answer in boxes 32–34 on your answer sheet.

32. Antoine Frerot promotes recycling, depurative wastewater can be used in ______.
33. This costs nearly 33% less than ______ and decreases contamination.
34. Antoine predicts that recycling approach will be fourfold in ______.

Questions 35–40

Complete the summary below.

Choose ***NO MORE THAN THREE WORDS*** *from the passage for each answer.*

Write your answers in boxes 35–40 on your answer sheet.

There are many even __35__ to save water. Almost __36__ used by farmers never gets to crops. David Molden said that farming __37__ can usually afford investment in __38__ and simply repairing the __39__. Similarly, rice farmers can decrease water consumption by a large margin by __40__ just from time to time.

Keys:

1. H
2. G
3. G
4. E
5. C
6. A
7. B
8. D
9. E
10. TRUE

11. FALSE
12. NOT GIVEN
13. TRUE
14. TRUE
15. FALSE
16. France Telecom
17. Teliasonera
18. $ 27 billion
19. mobile company
20. flurry of activity
21. NO
22. NO
23. YES
24. YES
25. YES
26. NOT GIVEN
27. i
28. ii
29. iv
30. v
31. vii
32. industry or agriculture
33. desalination
34. the next decade
35. cheaper ways
36. 70% of water
37. cash crops
38. drip irrigation
39. worst leaks
40. flooding paddy fields

星期日

模拟试题 7

READING PASSAGE 1

*You should spend about 20 minutes on **Questions 1-12**, which are based on Reading Passage 1 below.*

Climate Wars

As the planet warms, floods, storms, rising seas and drought will uproot millions of people, and with dire wider consequences. Barack Obama, collecting his Nobel peace prize, said that climate change "will fuel more conflict for decades". He took the analysis not from environmental scaremongers but from a group of American generals.

The forecast is close to becoming received wisdom. A flurry of new books with titles such as "Global Warring" and "Climate Conflict" offer near-apocalyptic visions. Cleo Paskal, at the Royal Institute of International Affairs in London, predicts that floods, storms, the failure of the Indian monsoon and agricultural collapse will bring "enormous, and specific, geopolitical, economic, and security consequences for all of us…the world of tomorrow looks chaotic and violent". Jeffrey Mazo of the International Institute for Strategic Studies, also in London, calls climate change an "existential threat" and fears it could usher in "state failure and internal conflict" in exposed places, notably Africa.

Yet surprisingly few facts support these alarming assertions. Widely touted forecasts such as for 200m climate refugees in the next few decades seem to have been plucked from the air. Little or no academic research has looked at questions such as whether Bangladeshis displaced by a rising sea would move a series of short distances over a long period, or (more disruptively) a greater distance immediately.

So scientists preparing the fifth report of the Intergovernmental Panel on Climate Change, due in 2013, are for the first time including a chapter on threats to human security. An early effort came at a conference last month in Norway, under the auspices of the Peace Research Institute in Oslo.

One idea is to find previous occasions when big environmental changes came alongside social, political and military shifts. Droughts in the Central Asian steppe, for example, led to mass westward migration and the "barbarian" invasions that helped topple the Roman Empire (pictured above). Hunger and drought led to the collapse of Mayan civilisation a millennium ago. Sudden cooling wiped out an early European settlement on Greenland. The Dust Bowl of the 1930s forced over 2m people to migrate within the United States.

Those examples may be relevant in Africa, where in many countries around three-quarters of the population survive by cultivating a few varieties of crops watered directly by rain, the form of farming most vulnerable to climate change. Africa has warmed by 0.5℃ on average in the past half century, and may heat by 1.5-4℃ more this century. Heat hits cereal yields (especially maize), perhaps by 10-20% for a 1℃ rise. Rainfall patterns will also shift.

The hardest evidence for a link so far comes from a team led by Marshall Burke of the University of California, which studied African wars from 1980 to 2002 and found that rising temperatures are indeed associated with crop failure, economic decline and a sharp rise in the likelihood of war. It predicted a "50% increase" in the chance of civil war in Africa by 2030.

But that claim is now heavily revised, since researchers redid their sums to take account of the more peaceful period of 2002-08. Others say that political and other factors such as ethnic conflict and outside intervention are far better indicators of the likelihood of fighting.

Take the widely cited case of the war in Darfur, the western region of Sudan. Ban Ki-moon, the UN secretary-general, described it as "an ecological crisis, arising at least in part from climate change". Environmental problems have probably worsened the Darfuris' dreadful plight, offering grist to those who call climate change a "threat multiplier". Average rainfall in the region fell abruptly (by a third or more) in the early 1970s and Darfur repeatedly suffered droughts. Clashes over grazing and then displacement of villagers were followed, from 2003, by horrific war.

Yet the connection is elusive. Roughly three decades elapsed between the rain stopping and war starting. Many other factors—political, ethnic, demographic and economic—conspired to stoke violence. Those were specific to Darfur, whereas the sharp drop in rainfall hit the whole Sahel, without intensifying conflict elsewhere.

Another commonly cited example is violent competition for scarce grazing between nomadic herdsmen in the Horn of Africa. Yet a study of fighting among pastoralists on the border between Kenya and Somalia in the past 60 years (presented at the conference) showed instead that conflict worsened when grazing was abundant and fell during droughts. Hungry people were too busy staying alive, or too exhausted, to fight. By contrast, when rains made herdsmen's lives easier, they could release surplus young labour for the violent sport of raiding other groups.

Other researchers look at the political or military consequences of phenomena unrelated to weather, such as rapid urbanisation, migration or earthquakes. Yet the evidence here too is mixed at best. Where natural disasters do show predictable political outcomes, they are very slight. A study of the short-term impact of hurricanes on Haiti and the Dominican Republic from 1850-2007, for example, suggests that the storms have grown more intense (if not more frequent), but their arrival is not associated with more political violence. Another study showed that natural disasters usually produced short-term economic pain but no sign of increased political violence.

Earthquakes, too, tend to produce mixed outcomes. A Mexican quake in 1985 may have stoked an insurgency. But the tsunami of 2005 offered a moment for secessionists in Aceh and the central Indonesian government to co-operate. Climate change could indeed cause woes aplenty. That is all the more reason to be precise about them.

Questions 1−5

Do the following statements agree with the information given in Reading Passage 1?

In boxes 1−5 on your answer sheet, write

TRUE	*if the statement agrees with the information*
FALSE	*if the statement contradicts the information*
NOT GIVEN	*if there is no information on this*

1. Climate change will fuel more conflict for decades.
2. Barack Obama takes the analysis from a group of American generals.
3. Threats to human security has been introduced for years.
4. The way of farming largely depend on climate condition in Africa.
5. Elevated temperature makes yields cut down.

Questions 6−8

From the information in the text, match 6−8 to ***A−D***.

Write the appropriate letter ***A−D*** *in boxes 6−8 on your answer sheet.*

6. Cleo Paskal
7. Barack Obama

8. Jeffrey Mazo

A. Global warring and climate conflict
B. The future looks like unsteady
C. State failure and internal conflict
D. Floods, storms and earthquake

Questions 9–12

*From the information in the text, match 9–12 to **A–F**.*
*Write the appropriate letter **A–F** in boxes 9–12 on your answer sheet.*
***NB** You may use any letter more than once.*

9. Sandstorm of the 1930's
10. Hunger and drought
11. The cold air descend
12. The central Asian steppe

A. Environmental changes
B. The Roman Empire dies out
C. Social and political
D. Collapse Mayan civilization
E. Early European settlement disappear
F. American migrate to other places

READING PASSAGE 2

*You should spend about 20 minutes on **Questions 13–26**, which are based on Reading Passage 2 below.*

How to Save a Billion Lives

A Even more than tempting liquors like tequila, tobacco is a pleasure that the Old World wishes it had never taken from the New. In 1492, when Christopher Columbus was met by tribesmen with "fruit, wooden spears and certain dried leaves which gave off a distinct fragrance", he threw the last gift away. But his shipmates brought home the custom of sucking in the smoke, and the taste spread so rapidly that in 1604 King James I of England was prompted to issue a denunciation of the "manifold abuses of this vile custome".

B Vile indeed, but habit-forming and therefore lethally dangerous: it cuts short the lives of between a third and half of its practitioners. According to the World Health Organisation (WHO), perhaps 100m people died prematurely during the 20th century as a result of tobacco, making it the leading preventable cause of death and one of the top killers overall. Another 1 billion more may die from it in this century if current trends continue unchecked.

C In recent years smoking has been sharply restricted in some unlikely places. In 2004 Ireland amazed the world by successfully imposing a tobacco ban on all workplaces; and at the start of this year, France's café culture suddenly went smoke-free. The draconian curbs introduced by California in 1998 have been followed, at least in part, by well over half America's states. But the number of smokers in China, India and other developing countries is continuing to grow, as addiction spreads faster than information.

D Hence the determination of almost everybody involved in global public health to escalate the war on smoking. Over 150 countries have already ratified the Framework Convention on Tobacco Control, which requires countries to take a range of anti-smoking measures. Last July negotiators agreed on international norms for banning smoking in public places. Next week they meet in Geneva to discuss a protocol on tobacco smuggling.

E In addition to new international rules, the WHO is pushing for aggressive policies at the national and local levels. On February 7th Margaret Chan, the WHO's director-general, and Michael Bloomberg, New York's zealously anti-smoking mayor, were due to unveil the most comprehensive survey of tobacco use ever carried out. The venue was fitting. Tom Frieden, the city's health commissioner, notes that the mayor's efforts have reduced smoking among the adults in New York by 20% and among teenagers in public schools by 50%. Mr. Bloomberg's private charity, which supports many anti-smoking efforts worldwide, also funded the global survey, known as MPOWER.

F The study is "a call to action to avoid a public-health catastrophe", says Douglas Bettcher, head of the Tobacco Free Initiative at the WHO. The report lists the anti-smoking efforts of countries worldwide, offering benchmarks for aspiring reformers. What the survey shows, says Dr Bettcher, is that most countries have yet to implement even those policies that are proven to work.

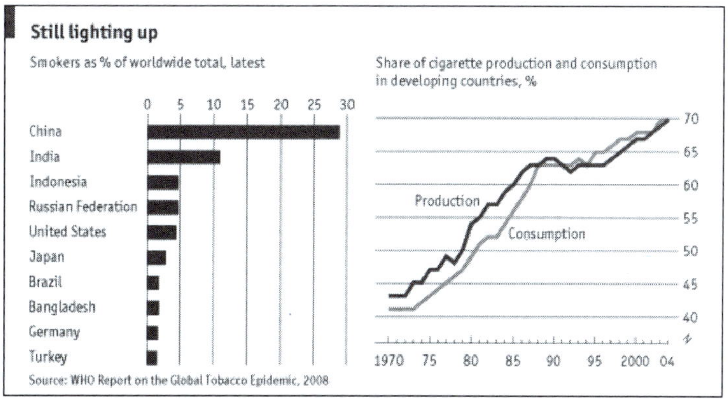

G The WHO says countries must do six related things. The first is to improve the quality of data on tobacco use. The second is to impose sweeping Irish-style smoking bans; only 5% of the global population is now covered by such curbs. The third is to intensify efforts to induce and assist smokers to drop the habit. Only nine countries offer the kind of well-funded, accessible programmes of which the WHO approves.

H Those ideas concern the existing users of tobacco; another three are aimed at persuading people not to light up in the first place. It may be hard to believe, but the WHO insists that most smokers still do not understand the full extent of the health risks. It wants all countries to mandate large, grotesque pictorial warnings on cigarette packets. Another policy proven to work (in the handful of countries, representing 5% of the world's population, to have tried it) is a complete ban on marketing. The agency is adamant that "partial bans on tobacco advertising, promotion and sponsorship do not work."

I The final prescription offered by the WHO is also the most powerful one: higher taxes. Studies show that raising tobacco taxes by a tenth may cause a 4% drop in consumption in rich countries and an 8% drop in poor ones, with tax revenue rising despite lower sales. The agency wants a 70% increase in the retail price of tobacco, which it says could prevent up to a quarter of all tobacco-related deaths worldwide. The claim is that higher taxes not only bring in revenue to fund anti-smoking efforts; they actually benefit the poor.

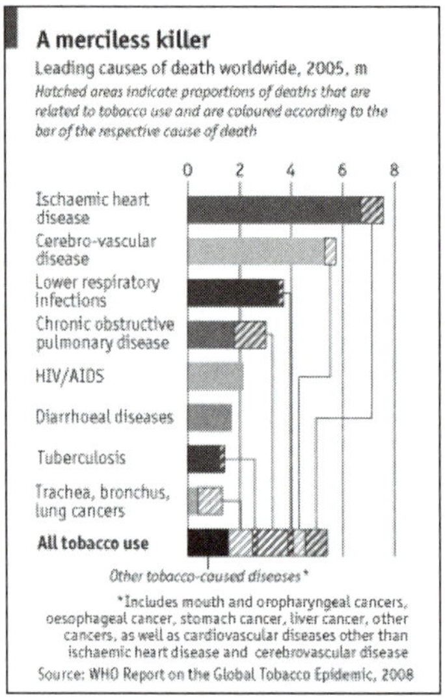

J How come? A forthcoming paper by two scholars (Jonathan Gruber of the Massachusetts Institute of Technology and Botond Koszegi of the University of California) notes that smokers face a familiar choice between short-term pleasure and a long-term desire to quit. Tobacco taxes are an incentive to make the right choice, and because the poor are price-sensitive, they benefit the most. Indeed, the authors calculate that in the United States, "the monetary value of the health damage from a pack of cigarettes is over $35 for the average smoker, implying both that optimal taxes should be very large and that cigarette taxes are likely progressive."

K The practical argument for action is simpler: the tobacco industry is getting the world's poor hooked before governments can respond. In recent years, as rich countries have clamped down on smoking, tobacco firms have shifted their focus to poorer places. A study by Britain's Bath University found that by using aggressive tactics, such as targeting women, international tobacco firms had helped to double smoking rates in Russia since 1991.

L The tobacco industry is regrouping in order to focus on "promising" markets and escape the pesky lawsuits it is likely to face in rich, litigious countries. For example, Altria, a global tobacco concern based in the United States, plans to spin off Philip Morris International as a stand-alone foreign entity in late March. China is now home to more than a quarter of the world's smokers; it will soon be manufacturing Marlboro cigarettes for Philip Morris, and the firm will be exporting Chinese tobacco to other countries.

M At times, the strategy used by public-health campaigners may seem heavy-handed; they retort that nothing else can work against a rich adversary. Indeed, Dr Bettcher argues that just as mosquitoes convey malaria, Big Tobacco is the "vector spreading this epidemic". And eradicating tobacco may prove every bit as hard as fighting insect-borne disease.

Questions 13−18

Reading passage 2 has thirteen paragraphs, A−M.

Which paragraph contains the following information?

Write the correct letter, A−M, in boxes 13−18 on your answer sheet.

***NB** You may use any letter more than once.*

13. Tobacco companies have changed their target to developing countries.
14. There are more smokers than it were in Russia.
15. China own one fourth of word's smokers.
16. The higher taxes on tobacco.
17. Framework convention on Tobacco control.
18. Non-smoke zone.

Questions19−22

Look at the following statements issued by the article.

Which four of the following statements, **A−G**, refer to the resolutions that were issued?

Match the statements with the appropriate resolutions.

*Write the correct letter, **A−G**, in boxes 19−22 on your answer sheet*

19. Resolution 1
20. Resolution 2
21. Resolution 3
22. Resolution 4-6

A. Persuade smokers give up the habit.

B. Set up the foundation.

C. Issue bans on smoking.

D. Improve the quality of data.

E. Keep it away from the beginning

F. Bans on advertising

G. Warning slogan

Questions 23–26

Complete the sentences below.

Choose ***NO MORE THAN ONE WORD*** *from the passage for each answer.*

Write your answer in boxes 23–26 on your answer sheet.

After Christopher Columbus landing, his shipmates brought home the smoking habit. It's dangerous: smoking decreases the __23__ currently. It has been rigorously __24__ in some unexpectable areas. However, the number of __25__ in the developing countries is ceaselessly __26__.

READING PASSAGE 3

You should spend about 20 minutes on ***Questions 27–40****, which are based on Reading Passage 3 below.*

Questions 27–32

Reading passage 3 has twelve paragraphs, ***A–L****.*

Choose the correct heading for paragraph ***B–G*** *from the list of headings below.*

Write the correct number, ***i-ix****, in boxes* ***27–32*** *on your answer sheet.*

List of Headings

i	Conservative perform of luxury companies
ii	Online business growing fast
iii	One second of luxury-goods firms
iv	Advantage about online-purchases
v	European firms situation
vi	Misunderstand about internet
vii	Eager to purchase on line
viii	Taker Nat-a poster
ix	Conflict between online and retailers

27. paragraph **B**

28. paragraph **C**

29. paragraph **D**

30. paragraph **E**

31. paragraph **F**
32. paragraph **G**

The Chic Learn to Click

A When Oscar de la Renta, an American fashion house, launched a transactional website some years ago, it expected people to buy mostly smaller items such as belts and perfume. The firm was stunned when it received an online order last spring for an $80,000 sable coat from a new customer in New Hampshire. He couldn't get to New York, apparently. Online customers have been snapping up the firm's core product: $4,000 cocktail dresses. "We could not have been more wrong in our expectations of the internet," says Alex Bolen, the firm's chief executive. Online purchases are still a small proportion of total sales, but growing rapidly.

B Most luxury-goods firms are less open-minded. Many scorn the internet as a plaything for plebs. A product sold online, wrote Jean-Noël Kapferer, a French branding guru, in "The Luxury Strategy", published last year, ceases to be a luxury item. In early 2008, of 178 luxury firms around the world surveyed by Forrester Research, only a third sold their products on the internet. That figure has risen, but still about half of firms don't sell online at all, estimates Federico Marchetti, the founder of Yoox Group, owner of Yoox.com, a luxury-goods website.

C Prada, an Italian design house, had no website until 2007. It did not start selling products online until last year. Several American companies, such as Tiffany & Co, have thriving web businesses, but European firms, especially the old French houses, such as Chanel and Hermès, are still afraid of mice.

D Luxury executives explain that the internet is too impersonal for their products, which need the human touch. Allowing anyone to buy online can mean a loss of cachet. Luxury firms like to dazzle customers with plush stores and sleek ads, so that they think only about beauty and not at all about price. The web, by contrast, shines a clear light on price. "That's the last thing I want people to think about," wails an executive from the watch industry.

E It is largely the industry's own fault that the internet is associated with lower prices for its products. For years, firms discreetly disposed of end-of-season stock at deep discounts via websites such as Yoox.com. Some fashion houses make clothing exclusively for Yoox.com as a way to use up left-over fabric. Also, by shunning the internet in its early days, legitimate firms helped to create a vacuum that counterfeiters were happy to fill, says Uché Okonkwo, the author of "Luxury Online".

F There is every sign, however, that buyers of full-price luxury goods crave the convenience of online shopping, so companies are being forced to adapt. In April Richemont, a Swiss luxury-goods giant, bought Net-a-Porter, a specialist fashion online retailer founded in 2000, in a deal valuing it at £350m ($535m).

G Net-a-Porter's appeal is not price, says Danny Rimer of Index Ventures, a venture-capital fund which backed the firm, but the convenience of getting items delivered to your door before they sell out. Executives are now watching to see whether Richemont will allow Net-a-Porter to sell its many other brands, including Cartier watches. Most luxury-watch firms, such as Hublot, do not sell online. This seems perverse: watches fit easily and buyers are usually collectors who know the models well. The main problem, explains Jean-Claude Biver, chief executive of Hublot, is that watch firms have long-standing agreements with independent retailers, and selling online would disrupt the system.

H Another sign of change is a new venture by a former Richemont executive, Mark Dunhill, to revive Fabergé, a jewellery-maker (one of whose baubles is pictured above), using the internet as its chief global distribution channel. Fabergé, owned by Pallinghurst Resources, a mining firm, launched last September with a single shop in Geneva and a sophisticated, interactive website. The industry is watching the experiment closely. If a luxury brand can thrive without a vast investment in retail space, says Luca Solca of Bernstein Research, barriers to entry will fall.

I A person close to Fabergé says it has reached its nine-month target of hooking 50 new clients, each spending on average $100,000. Even Prada now says that within five years, some 40% of its revenues in America will come from the internet. Observers, however, doubt that such an aggressive target is realistic, noting that Prada currently sells only bags, wallets and other accessories online, not its main clothing and footwear collections.

J Luxury firms may at last be waking up to the internet, but they have a long way to catch up. Carmakers have been innovating online for nearly a decade, observes Ms. Okonkwo. With exceptions, luxury websites tend to be showy but unoriginal, since firms often use the same web designers. Few are properly interactive: customers usually cannot view products from different angles, or try on clothes virtually.

K The most innovative online luxury firms are typically small start-ups, such as Net-a-Porter, Yoox (which went public late last year) or Gilt Groupe, a website which runs exclusive sales for members. All these companies have built successful new business models. The industry's ageing giants have been caught with their elegant trousers down.

L Louis Vuitton, a maker of leather goods and clothes, is one of the few luxury brands to have prospered online. Unlike many of its peers, it offers nearly all its products on the web. The internet brings in as much money as one of its biggest bricks-and-mortar shops, says Antoine Arnault, the firm's communications director. But Louis Vuitton's parent, LVMH, was last year forced to shut down eLuxury, a website founded in 2000 which sold a wide variety of luxury brands, because it lost money by the suitcasefull. According to insiders, it failed mainly because it lacked focus: it sold expensive products alongside relatively cheap ones. It is odd that an industry that would not be seen dead in last season's colour is wedded to the last century's technology.

Questions 33–37

Do the following statements agree with the claims of the writer in Reading Passage 3?

In boxes 33–37 on your answer sheet, write

YES	*if the statement agree with the claims of the writer*
NO	*if the statement contradicts the claims of the writer*
NOT GIVEN	*if it is impossible to say what the writer thinks about this*

33. Oscar de la Renta expected customer to buy luxury on their online-shop.
34. We could not have been more mistake in our fantasy of the internet.
35. Most luxury companies consider the on-line shop as a popularity consumption.
36. Prada set off its internet business in 2007.
37. It's cost £350m to buy Net-a-Porter.

Questions 38–40

Answer the questions below using ***NOT MORE THAN TWO WORDS OR A NUMBER*** *from the passage for each answer.*

Write your answers in boxes 38–40 on your answer sheet.

38. How many customer does Faberge attract?
39. What's ratio the online-shop of Prada will occupy in the following five years?
40. How many years has carmakers been making change on their on-line business?

Keys:

1. NOT GIVEN
2. TRUE
3. FALSE
4. TRUE
5. TRUE
6. B
7. A
8. C
9. F
10. D
11. E
12. B
13. K
14. K
15. L
16. I
17. D
18. C

19. D
20. C
21. A
22. E
23. life
24. restricted
25. smokers
26. grow
27. i
28. v
29. iv
30. vi
31. viii
32. ix
33. NO
34. NOT GIVEN
35. YES
36. NO
37. YES
38. 50
39. 40%
40. 10 / a decade